POWER IN THE BLOOD?

The Bishop Henry McNeal Turner/Sojourner Truth Series in Black Religion

Editor: Dwight N. Hopkins
  The University of Chicago, The Divinity School

Associate Editors:
  James H. Cone, Union Theological Seminary, New York
  Katie G. Cannon, Temple University
  Cain Hope Felder, Howard University, School of Divinity
  Jacquelyn Grant, The Interdenominational Theological Center
  Delores S. Williams, Union Theological Seminary, New York

The purpose of this series is to encourage the development of biblical, historical, theological, ethical, and pastoral works that analyze the role of the churches and other religious movements in the liberation struggles of black women and men in the United States, particularly the poor, and their relationship to struggles in the Third World.

Named after Bishop Henry McNeal Turner (1843-1915) and Sojourner Truth (1797?-1883), the series reflects the spirit of these two visionaries and witnesses for the black struggle for liberation. Bishop Turner was a churchman, a political figure, a missionary, and a pan-Africanist. Sojourner Truth was an illiterate former slave who championed black emancipation, women's rights, and the liberating spirit of the gospel.

Previously published in the Turner Series:

1. *For My People* by James H. Cone
2. *Black and African Theologies* by Josiah U. Young
3. *Troubling Biblical Waters* by Cain Hope Felder
4. *Black Theology USA and South Africa* by Dwight N. Hopkins
5. *Empower the People* by Theodore Walker, Jr.
6. *A Common Journey* by George C.L. Cummings
7. *Dark Symbols, Obscure Signs* by Riggins R. Earl, Jr.
8. *A Troubling in My Soul* by Emilie Townes
9. *The Black Christ* by Kelly Brown Douglas

In the Turner/Truth Series:

10. *Christianity on Trial* by Mark L. Chapman
11. *Were You There?* by David Emmanuel Goatley
12. *My Sister, My Brother* by Karen Baker-Fletcher and Garth (Kasimu) Baker-Fletcher
13. *Embracing the Spirit: Womanist Perspectives on Hope, Salvation, and Transformation* by Emilie M. Townes, editor
14. *Exorcizing Evil: A Womanist Perspective on the Spirituals* by Cheryl A. Kirk-Duggan

The Bishop Henry McNeal Turner/Sojourner Truth Series
in Black Religion, Volume XV

POWER IN THE BLOOD?

The Cross in the African American Experience

JoAnne Marie Terrell

Maryknoll, New York 10545

The Catholic Foreign Mission Society of America (Maryknoll) recruits and trains people for overseas missionary service. Through Orbis Books, Maryknoll aims to foster the international dialogue that is essential to mission. The books published, however, reflect the opinions of their authors and are not meant to represent the official position of the society.

Published by Orbis Books, Maryknoll, NY 10545-0308
Manufactured in the United States of America
Manuscript editing and typesetting by Joan Weber Laflamme

Unless otherwise indicated, scripture quotations are from the Revised Standard Version, copyright © 1962 by The World Publishing Company.

Library of Congress Cataloging-in-Publication Data

Terrell, JoAnne Marie.
    Power in the blood : the cross in the African American experience
/ JoAnne Marie Terrell.
      p. cm. — (The Bishop Henry McNeal Turner/Sojourner Truth
series in Black religion : v. 15)
    Includes bibliographical references.
    ISBN 1-57075-216-8 (pbk.)
    1. Afro-Americans–Religious life.   2. Holy cross–History of
doctrines.   3. Womanist theology.   4. Black theology.   I. Title.
II. Series.
BR563.N4T39   1998
232'.4'08996073–dc21   98-27278
                                              CIP

To My Mothers:
Altermeze Francina Henry Coles Coleman Terrell Bowers ("Dot")
(1930-1973)
Geraldine Henry Green ("Geri")
(1934-1992)

and my sister and friend:
Saundra Lee Harden
(1948-1996)

Contents

Acknowledgments

This book discusses matters that have long occupied my religious and theological imagination, which was activated in early childhood and heightened by years of study with some very fine teachers and classmates at Union Theological Seminary. More than this, it attests to my pursuit of freedom and wholeness and the assistance that I have been given to achieve them, divine and human, through the Christian message of redemption and release. Although putatively an academic project, this work is in fact an outpouring of gratitude from the heart of a devotee, a protégé and a friend.

My mentor, Dr. James H. Cone, taught me some "hard" lessons. Among the hardest were developing discipline as a scholar and learning to be ever more honest with myself as a human being. Dr. Cone has certainly been a demanding academic advisor; he has been an equally gracious friend. Dr. Delores S. Williams inspired me to write with "holy boldness" through her own marvelous art. Her ability to ask the right questions taught me to ponder the implications of the things I think, say and do with and for other black women. I have also tried to emulate worthily the faithful "gospelling" of Dr. Christopher L. Morse. His love for the church, method of rigorous inquiry and solidarity with struggling others endlessly challenge, inspire and delight me. I am also grateful to Dr. Kelly Brown Douglas for her assistance. Drs. James M. Washington, Vincent L. Wimbush, Beverly W. Harrison, and Robin Scroggs pointed out sources that helped me develop the heuristic framework of my thesis. They offered criticism at the beginning stages of the work and urged me to be grounded, thoughtful and clear.

Dr. Arnold Wettstein of Rollins College gave me a wide cosmological perspective to which I feel especially accountable. Dr. Hoyt Edge, also of Rollins, persuaded me to arrive at the truth of my own experience skillfully, with good humor and patience. I still have occasion to draw upon the academic and spiritual guidance of these philosopher-friends.

My friends and colleagues at Union Seminary were staunch supporters of this project. Dr. Augustine Musopole, now a theologian residing and teaching in his native Malawi, demonstrated great faith in me at the very beginning of my graduate career, as did Dr. Mark L. Chapman

(Fordham University), the Revs. Anne R. Elliott and Edward Turner, and Robin Lytle Turner. By the time I commenced writing, faithful friends Raphael Warnock and Leslie Callahan were my first recourse, whether I needed encouragement or help untangling my thoughts. In love and solidarity my fellow sojourners raised pertinent issues, made commentary or gave editorial assistance at various stages. Caroline "Betty" Bolden, Eun Ja Lee, Drew Kadel and Seth Kasten of Union's Burke Library helped me acquire nearly every text I needed for my research; likewise Abdelilah Enassef, Henry Morren and Jack Saviano (formerly) of the Book Store. Their congeniality and professionalism attest to the power of *communitas* at the Seminary.

President Kenneth Smith, Academic Dean Bill Myers, Drs. Lee Butler, W. Dow Edgerton, Julia Speller, George Cairns, Theodore Jennings, Andre LaCoque, Robert Moore, Ken Stone and Susan Brooks Thistlethwaite of the Chicago Theological Seminary (CTS) supported me through the completion of my project. At a low point, visiting professor Sipho Mtetwa of the University of Natal (Pietermaritzburg, South Africa) brought my muses back! Dr. Neil Gerdes, Joan Blocher and the staff of the Seminary's Hammond Library went to great lengths to acquire what remaining texts I needed. Tom Cutting, our pastor-in-residence, counseled me as needed *and* gave a bit of editorial assistance.

I must also express my appreciation to my office assistant, Elaine Everett, and to graduate students Michael Sykes, Jacki Belile, Wil Brant, Sammie Dortch, Terrell Goddard, and Phil Hobson of CTS, and Joel Albers of the Lutheran School of Theology, for assisting me with research during the final phases of my project.

Over the years, three church homes, the United Church of God by Faith (Winter Park, Florida), Convent Avenue Baptist Church (New York City) and Mount Hope AME Zion Church (White Plains, New York) gave me many opportunities for service and learning. Bishop Willie W. Matthews, the Right Reverends George W. Walker Sr., George E. Battle Jr. and the late William M. Smith; Elder Charles A. McKnight, the Reverends Clarence P. Grant, Daniel Dupree, the late Ralph W. Gullette, Gregory Robeson Smith Sr. and Odinga Lawrence Maddox Sr. helped shape my ministry as a theologian for the church. My godmother, Mrs. Nora Marshall and my spiritual father, the Rev. Dr. C. Guita McKinney, gave me material support and many valuable lessons in the exercise of agency.

I appreciate the intercession of my ancestors. The history and lore about the many great souls in my family give me a sense of accountability to something other than myself or my ideas alone, especially that concerning my great-grandparents, Ellis and Nancy Wilborn Henry; great-great uncle Demps Wilborn; great-great aunt Delia Wilborn

Scippio; my grandparents, Elder Donison and Agnes Haile Henry; and great-aunts Queen, Ethel and Lucretia Henry. I am proud of my heritage of piety and "faith plus nothing." My fathers' prayers, those of Willie B. "Pete" Woods, Elder Herbert Green Jr. and George Lee Terrell, helped to sustain me. My stepfather, James Wilson Bowers, provided me with a wealth of information on plantation farming out of his experience both as a farm worker and as a supervisor of a juice-processing plant for a major corporation. Along with my brothers and sisters Harry, Lynda, Althea, Joseph, Cheryl and Kenneth, and my cousins, the Rev. Michael Sherwood Henry, Derrick Henry and Paula Green Marshall, he helped me set the record straight concerning "the cross" in our family's experience. And furry friends Shoes and Hannah gave me love and company.

In various and sundry ways, all of my friends disclose my strengths and expose my vulnerabilities, reflecting withal my deepest commitments, rather like my manuscript itself. I am grateful for the gift of their friendship, for their generous affirmation of my gifts and for their magnanimous tolerance of my weaknesses.

Introduction

Were you there when they crucified my Lord?
Were you there when they crucified my Lord?
Oh! sometimes it causes me to
tremble, tremble, tremble . . .

—Negro Spiritual

Myriad images of the cross, the blood, and other accoutrements of
the doctrine of the Atonement[1] are pegged to my memory and cause
me, at times, to lumber ungainly through the various stations of my life.
The earliest image is of a religious icon that graced the walls of my first
home of recollection and that followed me for many years thereafter. It
was a brass, latticework whatnot, a mandala[2] with four outer shelves. At
its center was an 8″ x 10″, three-dimensional depiction of the crucifixion. Looking directly at the picture, one could see Jesus' suffering in all
its gory aspects. His seminude body was stretched to breaking; his head
lolled to the left side. Through the genius of 3-D technology, his long,
matted hair glistened with "sweat," and "blood" streamed from his
wounds. A malefactor hung on either side of him; an impotent crowd
lingered at his feet; a blackened sky could be heard grumbling by any
active imagination.

Looking askance and slightly above the Crucified One, one could
see the glorified Christ ascending into the now-opened, sun-washed
heavens. This entity, apparently *spirit*,[3] loomed large on the transmuted
palette. He was fully robed in white; his brunette hair now coiffured
and flowing. Blond, curly haired cherubs played harps to the left and
right of him. Below him, the crowd fawned, their formerly defeated
faces upturned and aglow as they hailed him.

As a very young child growing up in the rural South, I spent hours
gazing at this artifact, pondering the implications of both its head-on
and sidelong views for my native spirituality and nascent Christianity.
Although without much theological data from which to draw any
articulable conclusions, I had a clear preference for the second, skewed
representation—less because I was attracted to it, and more because I
strongly rejected the first. The triumphalist, incorporeal Christ was only
mildly frightening, if somewhat recognizable as an imperious-looking

1

white man! Minus the beard, he was startlingly similar to the way Celie, the protagonist in Alice Walker's *The Color Purple*, describes her first image of God: "He big and old and graybearded and white. He wear white robes and go barefooted."[4] The Christ of the second representation appeared to me to be *ageless* rather than aged. Indeed, he was my first image of God, before I acquired a working knowledge of the doctrine of the Trinity. I was impressed by this God and his projected qualities of ubiquity and benignity, not to mention the fact that he was *clean*. On the other hand, the bloody, anguished man on the cross frightened and repulsed me. His obvious pain was magnified by the very real sense of melodrama[5] that the artist was able to capture.

A second image of the cross burnished in my memory is a figurative one. Although I was only a preschooler, I recognized it as such through the revulsion I experienced upon seeing it and relating it to the disdain I possessed for the suffering man in my mandala; the sight of black bodies, en masse, picking cotton on white-owned plantations was to my imaginative and already theologically oriented mind a facsimile of Jesus' crucifixion. African American children, women and men–young, middle-aged and elderly alike–stooped and dragged burlap bags, "croker sacks" and other makeshift receptacles that ranged from five to five hundred pounds capacity for the white, lightweight stuff.[6] Exposed to a fierce southern sun, whole families sweated, ached and damaged their hands, backs and knees for life, trying to survive and to improve the material conditions of their lives.

My rather large family picked cotton and other crops regularly to supplement my stepfather's Air Force income or support ourselves during those early years of his and my mother's volatile relationship. Perhaps among other workers we were a bit elitist, owing to the grandeur we attached to his station. Yet we understood that because we were black and had few other options in the labor force, ours was an imposed lot that neither matched our social and political ambitions nor allowed us to address fully our spiritual and intellectual needs. Economic stress also highlighted the inability of my stepfather to fulfill the patriarchal expectations placed upon him by society. Thus, race and class oppression, concretized in the experience of plantation labor, reduplicated itself in the often violent interrelations of my family. Once more, I was frightened and repulsed by "the cross"–this time, of plantation labor– because I was sure that this kind of sweat, pain and toil would be my destiny, portending little agency in a world that held out so many prospects for fun, as well as for purposeful living. The mean conditions seemed *prescribed* for black people, and I internalized this as an affront to my personal dignity and human potential. Even though I could not name these realities as a child, I understood them. As it was with me then, so it is with me now: the overwhelming sentiment in my heart and mind is that of resentment toward black delimitation and the devastating effects it has had and continues to have on black families' lives.

My resentment has foundations in the African American collective experience of slavery. Beginning in the seventeenth century, European colonists effected the rise of agrarian capitalism on the backs of children, women and men of African descent through the imposition of chattel slavery and the gradual elimination of indentured servitude. Three, nearly four centuries later, this unpacked, encoded memory of my collective experience, adumbrated in the cotton fields of North Carolina, disclosed bales of resentment in my precocious, even "proto-womanist"[7] soul and stimulated my desire to examine the history and the burden of "the cross" of slavery. I have sought to understand both the black collective experience and my family history as they impinge on my spiritual and intellectual life by linking them to the story of Jesus. Just as the image of a cross recalls for nearly all Christians the physical and psychic injury Jesus sustained for us, the image of a croker sack recalls for me the physical and psychic injury my own and other black families sustained for the benefit of white families and southern agrarian economies, from slavery to the present.

Following the social, political and cultural upheavals occasioned by the Civil Rights and Black Power movements of the late 1950s and early 1960s (the years when this part of my narrative takes place), black theology arose to challenge the racist anthropological assumptions still used to justify and maintain white privilege. As an emergent theology of liberation, black theology affirmed the right of black people to live empowered lives in which their dignity, freedom, moral agency and ability to survive and thrive are upheld by all the social, political and economic structures of society. This was to be reflected in the value society placed on black people and that the circumscribed blacks needed to learn to place on their physical attributes, as well as on their religious insight and spirituality. Basing their claims on the biblical paradigm of the Exodus and the proclamation of Jesus that "the Spirit of the Lord is upon me . . . to proclaim release to the captives . . . to set at liberty those who are oppressed . . . to proclaim the acceptable year of the Lord" (Lk 4:18ff.), these African American male theologians espoused liberative hermeneutical principles which affirm that God is on the side of the oppressed, and they argued that the experience of oppressed people is the norm by which opposing truth claims are to be adjudicated.[8]

Critical inquiry by some black theologians broached the theme of unjust suffering and queried the adequacy of Christian theological anthropologies[9] for understanding black peoples' plight. Broadly, they addressed Christian sacrificial tradition with this question: How is the gospel message of the Atonement, or reconciliation of sinners with God through Jesus Christ's death on the cross, to be construed by black people, who are similarly persecuted and simultaneously indicted as sinners?[10] Although they did not hold monolithic christological views, black theologians identified their communities' seeming fascination with the cross as *theodicy*,[11] attempts by black Christians to understand the evil they encountered in white power structures and white people, who also claimed to be Christians. One task of this study is to survey the works of black theologians and discuss the liberative import they found in the gospel that enabled them to remain both black and Christian.

Another goal of this study is to discern theological dimensions of theodicy found in the interplay between gender and race. Riding the wave of social and political victories garnered by the Civil Rights movement, white women agitated for passage of the Equal Rights Amendment, again gaining moral impetus from the black struggle for equality, as they had in the nineteenth and early twentieth centuries during the struggle for abolition and suffrage. Their activism effected an opening, a "window of opportunity," for both groups' fuller participation in American society. The push for women's rights saw significant increases in the number of women willing to challenge that great bastion of white male supremacy, the church. As black men began to integrate white seminaries as students and as teachers, white women began attending in increasing numbers, as well. Enjoying privilege and wealth relative to black people, they began, in the 1960s, to question Christian anthropological emphases on (1) sin as pride (self-deification), for which it is presumed men have a peculiar proclivity; and (2) its derivative, sin as sensuality (other-deification), for which it is presumed women have a peculiar proclivity. They asked of Christian Atonement tradition: How are women to understand the churches' appeals to an ethic of sacrifice (found in scripture and social custom), when they are thereby encouraged to deify others?[12] In the late 1960s and early 1970s, other feminist theologians raised the issue of Jesus' maleness and its role in the entrenchment of patriarchy in orthodox, liberal and liberationist discourse and praxis.[13]

Yet the active collusion of some white, middle-class women in African American oppression caused some black male activists in both the Civil Rights and Black Power movements to equate feminist struggle with white women's issues, without allowing that the issues they raised in arenas such as employment and education—not to mention those related to sexism in its most rapacious forms—were also issues for the black community. Sexism retooled as paternalism among African American men, who downplayed the presence of black women in the struggle and proscribed the critical voices they raised against them. The focus on "manhood first" effectively subsumed the insights, experiences and contributions of black women such as Fannie Lou Hamer, Ella Baker,

Septima Clark, Gloria Richardson and Angela Davis to the African American struggle against racism[14] and obfuscated the reality of intracommunal gender struggle. In that context, Stokely Carmichael of the Student Nonviolent Coordinating Committee (SNCC) made the now-famous indecent proposal that a woman's place in the movement was "prone." The sense of *betrayal* in his comment and in white women's historical investiture in white supremacy is indicative of black women's lived experiences of the crosses of racism and sexism they still bear in the society, the church and the academy.

It is true that the challenges black and feminist theologians posed to white male hegemony allowed black women greater access to the church and the academy by widening the parameters of discourse. Yet, just as black theologians did not adequately express the concerns of all black people because of sexism, white feminist theologians did not adequately reflect the concerns of black women (who more often labor under the additional burden of poverty) because they were blind to their racism. Black women began to challenge the male-centered views of black theologians and the eurocentric views of white feminists, who also subsumed black women's insights, experiences and contributions to the struggle for freedom for women. Jacquelyn Grant's "Becoming Subjects in the Christological Debate"[15] is perhaps the first proto-womanist essay employing a critique of black and feminist theologies' assumptions and methodologies. Before Grant, Frances Beale was one of the first black feminists to identify the impact of multiple oppressions, terming the socioeconomic and political situation of black women "double jeopardy."[16] Theressa Hoover critiqued the intersection of racism, sexism and classism in black women's experience, dubbing their oppression "triple jeopardy," especially as it is experienced in black churches.[17]

In a March 1985 article in *Christianity and Crisis*, premier white feminist Rosemary Radford Ruether attempted to curtail this rising critique of white feminism, asserting that the common theme among feminists of diverse origins is "the legitimacy of encountering the divine as goddess."[18] In a later issue, emerging womanist Delores Williams charged Ruether with white supremacy because Ruether seemed to posit the divine as a *white* goddess.[19] Ruether dismissed Williams's criticism of her article as "irrelevant" because the magazine misparagraphed her words and because she had stated at the outset of the article that she was speaking from a white, Western context.[20] But in the process she missed an opportunity to address more crucial points of divergence between her thought and that of Williams on the exclusionary nature of feminist theology. Feminist theologians criticized sexism within the discourse without similarly criticizing the evils of racism and classism—black women's experience—not only as part of women's experience but also as part of black women's experience of white women. In response to this shortfall in feminist theology, Susan Brooks Thistlethwaite is, to date, one of few white feminists to deal extensively with the issue of racism among feminists. She attempts a corrective by focusing on racism in the history of the women's movement.[21] There is still resistance on the part of some white and black feminists to admit the necessity of the womanist enterprise, as they fear it potentially detracts from feminist unity and power.

Appropriating Alice Walker's use of the African American folk-term "womanish," black female scholars of religion named their emergent discipline womanist theology. Today the academic enterprise is being articulated as a means to address the spiritual, ecclesial, social, political and economic implications of the "tridimensional phenomenon of race, class and gender oppression"[22] in the experience of African American women. Building on the early contributions of Beale and Hoover, recent scholarship has identified the impact of multiple oppressions together, which womanist ethicist Marcia Riggs has termed the "logic of interstructured oppression."[23] Womanists' focus on the particularities of black women reflects the fact that black women encounter oppression on all these fronts at once; they can no more separate the analysis and remediation of the several sociopolitical conditions that circumscribe them than they can prioritize the ontological categories that describe them. Their holistic approach to their multidimensional experience of oppression raised questions that also challenged black theologians and revolutionized the way they must now consider the totality of the African American experience.

As in feminist theology, womanist God-talk disavows Jesus' maleness as significant for Christian faith, emphasizing instead his life and work. Thus, womanists are formulating a Christology "from below" that focuses more on the empowering, ennobling deeds of Jesus attested in scripture and less on the triumphalist Christ, who is also attested in scripture and appropriated for imperial ends in Western traditions. Womanist thought highlights the biblical themes of *communal survival* and *liberation*[24] of the marginalized, thereby modeling intellectual, social and political activism on behalf of black women and the entire African American community, a community in crisis. Such alternative views of Jesus, moreover, enable black women to see the divine working in and on behalf of themselves.

With feminist theologians, womanist theologians have recently identified the motif of Christ's *surrogacy* (on which hinge traditional theories of the Atonement) as problematic in the confession of faith not only because of its utility in sanctioning women's oppression[25] but also because of its similarity to the historical circumscription of black women in surrogate roles in relationship to white men, white women and their children.[26] Moreover, black women have historically been obliged to be surrogates for black men: in slavery, working in the fields, doing what was considered "man's work"; in the post-slavery labor force, assuming the traditional role of "provider" through whatever employment whites made available. In postmodernity,[27] perhaps singularly owing to the targeting, censuring and scapegoating of young, black men through the criminal justice system, black women continue in surrogate roles as providers for their families, as "mothers and fathers" for their children. Black women, too, have begun to question Christian sacrificial tradition: Does the image of Jesus as a surrogate figure have salvific power for black women, or does it reinforce the exploitation that accompanies their experiences of surrogacy? Are there ways for black women to be of service in the churches and in the communities that are non-proscriptive and non-exploitative? In other words, is the profession of faith in the cross inimical to black women's self-interests? Or, is there power in the blood?

In this book I explore the ways black theology and womanist theology have been informed by and contribute to African Americans' understanding of the central cultic symbol of Christianity, the cross. Consistent with the intellectual tradition of "faith in search of understanding," I seek to integrate the insights of both academic disciplines in my way of thinking about the significance of Jesus' crucifixion in light of Christian history and in light of the circumscription of black people in slavery, the post-slavery work force and postmodernity. I wish to determine, as far as possible, whether and how the African American Christian community's apprehension of the doctrine of the Atonement has empowered and/or disempowered us in our historic and ongoing attempts to negotiate the demands of survival, liberation and creative *self-expression*.

Womanist theological methodology is committed "both to reason and to the validity of female imagery and metaphorical language in the construction of theological statements," and is informed by a multi-dialogical, liturgical and didactic intent.[28] Since womanist methodology recognizes the need for insight from a variety of places in order to address the variegated experiences of the African American community, it is multidisciplinary of necessity. The current emphasis on multidisciplinary approaches in black theology, which "second wave" theologians Dwight Hopkins and George Cummings now advocate comports with this womanist focus. With respect to the Bible and other texts, I use the tools of historical criticism as employed by black and womanist biblical scholars, including Vincent Wimbush, Renita Weems, Clarice Martin, William Myers, Allen Callahan and Cain Hope Felder. I also rely on the insights of economic historians (also called *cliometricians*), especially the work of British Marxist historian G.E.M. de Ste. Croix, as well as the analyses of cultural critic and Marxist philosopher Cornel West.

Womanist epistemology also affirms the use of personal narrative in order to relate black women's history and religious experience. Since so much of what I "know" is experientially referenced, I utilize womanist methodology and epistemology as I survey the contributions both black and womanist theologians have made to African Americans' understanding of Atonement doctrine.

In chapter 1, through historical analysis, I discern the ideation of the cross as the central motif in black Christian thought, achieved through the imposition of chattel slavery and the hermeneutics of sacrifice, the key to understanding the early church's *melodramatic* response to its experience of state persecution. Drawing parallels between the actual, bodily experiences of the martyrs and the Christianized slaves, I locate the African American community's response in its emphasis on an ethic of love, which is both a corollary for the cross, and a *theodicy,* which, as ever, informs the Christian response to inimical sociopolitical environments.

The themes of survival and resistance are also found in the liturgical expressions and social activism of African Americans. In chapter 2 I discuss slave religion and black radicalism as they relate to the love ethic and the theme of theodicy. In an ostensibly *Christian* context of oppression, the congregation of the African American faithful has sought to bear *sacrificial* and/or *sacramental* witness to the character and creativity of God. Banking on the evangelical heritage of American civil religion, the Black Church continues to evolve liturgical practices, hymnody and confessional utterances that are socially liberating and ontologically affirming to its circumscribed communities. So I closely examine these important sources in the development of black and womanist theology.

In chapter 3 I delineate the divergent christological perspectives of three black theologians, Martin Luther King Jr., Albert B. Cleage and James H. Cone, on the themes of reconciliation, nationhood and liberation in their respective approaches, as these relate to a *sacrificial* or *sacramental* perspective on Atonement doctrine. Since scripture is foundational for reflection on the career and significance of Jesus, a comparison and contrast of their hermeneutical methods is instructive and I also address this task.

Womanist theologians' focus on Christology comports with the central place of Jesus in the lives of black church people. Womanist theologians have only recently begun to ask questions of the Christian doctrine of the Atonement, since it provides a deep pool for reflection on black women's suffering on the "underside of the underside" of human experience. In chapter 4 I make a first attempt to reckon the implications of womanist revisionings of Jesus/God in the writings of Jacquelyn Grant, Kelly Brown Douglas and Delores Williams for the hermeneutics of sacrifice and an adequate theology of the cross.

In chapter 5 I offer reflections on what it means to be a womanist *and* a theologian, with reference to each of the four instances of the definition of "womanist" enumerated in the prose of Alice Walker, one of the discrete sources of womanist theology. I also wrestle with questions she raises concerning theistic images of God in *The Color Purple*, putting Walker in conversation with the surrogacy experiences of black women in and since slavery and the religious experiences of black women in their quest for empowerment in the Black Church.

Jesus' experience of betrayal, imprisonment, torture and death prefigures the experience of black humanity in the legal constructs of the antebellum slavocracy, postbellum socioeconomic and political conditions and in postmodernity. In postmodern America this is nowhere more clearly seen than in the burgeoning of inmate populations with black men (and increasingly, black women) and of the prison industry itself. The recent revival of the death penalty in several states also evinces the politicization of imprisonment as a most insidious instrument of social control. Throughout, I examine the role of these hard sociopolitical realities in exacerbating the suffering of the black community, which is moreover beset by disease (specifically AIDS) and self-directed violence, or black nihilism. Finally, since language creates and reinforces the reality of domination, I discuss the ways African Americans use the language of sacrifice and address the mythological moorings of Atonement doctrine, testing their sufficiency for black Christians in postmodernity.

Chapter 1

The Refiners' Fire

African Slavery and Christian Martyrdom

For he is like a refiner's fire, and like fuller's soap . . . and he shall purify the sons of Levi, and purge them as gold and silver, that they may offer unto the LORD an offering in righteousness.
—Malachi 3:2b-3 (KJV)

'Twas mercy brought me from my Pagan land
Taught my benighted soul to understand
That there's a God, that there's a Saviour too:
Once I redemption neither sought nor knew.
Some view our sable race with scornful eye
"Their colour is a diabolic die."
Remember, Christians, Negros, black as Cain,
May be refin'd, and join th' angelic train.
—Phillis Wheatley
18th c. African American Poet

The ideation of the cross as the central motif in past and current African American religious expressions is traceable to enslavement and the process of Christianization. In and since slavery, black Christians realized that their experiences of discrimination, abuse, torture and death were analogous to the sufferings of Jesus, other biblical characters and the incipient church, which had similarly undergone state-sanctioned persecution and martyrdom. The experiences of the first Christian communities significantly informed the early church's understanding of Jesus' death as an act of unconditional, sacrificial love for his people. Although he was crucified for sedition, to his first interpreters Jesus' death involved his own agency and contributed to their development of a *hermeneutics of sacrifice,* which is ensconced in the Bible and Christian tradition and which has a historical corollary in an ethic of love—seen as the very heart of Christian morality—in the African American community. The early Christians provided African Americans historical precedents for interpreting theologically the meaning of their particular experiences of suffering, fully engaging intellect and emotion in the service of the community of faith in the activity of *apologetics.* Through apologetics, both groups of Christians developed comprehensive reckonings of the meaning of their suffering, thereby demonstrating their human, moral and artistic agency in contexts that denied them social, economic and political freedom and sought even to proscribe their religious freedom.

THROUGH THE FIRE: SLAVERY AND CHRISTIANIZATION

Through the lens of slavery, African Americans—bond and free—fixed their gaze on the cross of Jesus, deriving from it a way to understand and cope with their own painful experiences of proscribed existence. Jesus' presumed innocence, his betrayal by his friends, and his arrest, torture and execution in occupied Palestine mirrored the brutal conditions the slaves experienced in antebellum America. Just as Judas "handed over" Jesus to his detractors in exchange for thirty pieces of silver (Mt 26:15), likewise sub-Saharan Africans and Arabs from the north bartered away the lives of their black-skinned sisters and brothers to Portuguese, English, French, Dutch and Spanish merchants in exchange for a variety of inducements—among them, similarly shiny and deadly "trinkets" (weapons)—that held a bogus promise of industrialization and the supposedly civilizing influence of monotheistic faith.[1] Not all the slaves were subjects of barter; as the severity of slavery under European domination became known, outraged tribal leaders began to resist actively the merchants and missionaries who foraged the continent for free labor and lost souls for Christendom's sake. Among the African abolitionists Queen Ann Nzinga (c.1580-1663) of the area now known as Angola was the dreaded nemesis of the Portuguese, who, among the Europeans, exhibited the most missionary zeal toward the Africans, performing wholesale baptisms of slaves as they made their perilous journey to other lands.[2]

The European settlers of the New World sought survival and a quality of life that preserved or created social, political and economic privilege for themselves. Some were parties seeking to escape religious intolerance and/or poverty in their former homelands; others were commissioned to expropriate the land and mineral wealth of New World natives. Harnessing the considerable resources of North America required a labor pool of sufficient size and experience in agricultural methods superior to that of the indigenous populace, which the (mostly English) settlers decimated and effectively vilified. Construing skin color as a stratifying device, the colonists systematically extracted the "bound, controlled labor"[3] of black-skinned peoples through the imposition of chattel slavery. The white-skinned traders and raiders of the Gold Coast[4] assumed full, lifelong control of the individual and collective destinies of the captives they brought to America: breeding, buying and selling them and their progeny according to caprice and capital needs; committing acts of personal violence against the slaves—raping, beating and lynching them—in order to bolster their seized authority. Gradually eliminating indentured servitude, a temporary albeit brutal contractual arrangement under which white-skinned people, male or female, could be obligated, the settlers created a racial caste system that defined slavery and that still shapes the American socioeconomic and political context. There, the imported Africans were made to experience the cross of Jesus. Like the biblical African conscript Simon of Cyrene (Mt 27:32; Mk 15:21; Lk 23:26), they not only bore the cross, but they also quite literally *wore* the designated emblem of suffering and shame on their backs and arms and legs and faces, for Christ's sake.

Undoubtedly, religion and law were the most significant factors in the reification and expansion of slavery in North America, and they buttress the racial caste system to this day. Styling themselves as the ancient Israelites and the sprawling territory as "Canaan" (Ex 3:8) and the "new Jerusalem" (Rv 21:2) of scriptural promise, many of those who had left their homelands for religious freedom and economic gain regarded themselves "elected" to enjoy the bounty of America and to exercise dominion over the native inhabitants and the imported slaves. Over time, and with the southward and westward expansion of the nation, the settlers legally defined both groups as ontologically inferior,[5] keeping the social and civic prerogatives of "life, liberty and the pursuit of happiness" for whites only—white men, in particular.[6]

Different social and theological dynamics predominated in the North and South. New England Puritans possessed a strong sense of social cohesion formed in the crucible of persecution in their former homeland. Congregational polity and structures in the North evinced a covenantal theology premised upon the idea of their communal election. Evangelicalism,[7] pervasive everywhere, but institutionalized in the denominational structures of the South, emphasized religious conversion and stressed a more privatistic religious consciousness, although it brought poorer whites of diverse national origins together in their search for a common social identity. Church historian Donald Mathews attests to the idea that Evangelicalism started out as a social class movement:

> As social process, Evangelicalism enveloped the South in the following fashion: it first broke into the South as an extension of

revivals throughout the British world, a volatile social movement providing a value system to raise converts in their own esteem, give them confidence in themselves and their comrades and create the moral courage to reject as authoritative for themselves the lifestyle and values of traditional elites.[8]

Covenant theology socially leveled whites, and evangelical piety morally leveled every person (including those slaves admitted to communion), regarding each as a sinner "saved by grace" (Eph 2:5). But in the formative years of American agrarian capitalism, driven by slave labor and characterized by economic and social stratification, Christianity so defined made economic prosperity part of one's expectation of blessedness, obfuscating class differences among whites and thereby mitigating class struggle among them.

By the eighteenth century the agrarian economy was the major source of white prosperity in the southern colonies.[9] Although U.S. law outlawed the international slave trade in 1807, by the mid-nineteenth century the national traffic in black humanity was itself a principal source of income for whites, who equated social status with the number of slaves held in possession, and for whom a rise in social status was occasioned by the purchase of at least one slave. James Oakes reports:

> Slaveholding was the symbol of success in the market culture of the Old South. It was an ambition, an achievement, a reward for diligence, hard work, and tenacity. As one Louisiana master wrote, "A man's merit in this country is estimated according to the number of Negroes he works in the field." And as widespread as slaveholding was, it was no mean goal.[10]

Cliometricians[11] Robert William Fogel and Stanley L. Engerman argue that, although slavery and the Civil War constituted the nation's "time on the cross," evoking a sense of national shame, economic analysis shows that on a quantitative basis slave economy was a rational, adaptable and efficient system of production and the southern slavocracy a model of labor relations (if not of *social* relations) because of high regional growth rates and the increased market value for slaves during the late antebellum period.[12] They assert that the rise of the southern secessionist movement coincided with a wave of optimism or "sanguinity" on the part of slaveholders concerning their economic prospects prior to the war. The sanguinity of the planters and the efficiency of the slave-labor system redounded to the material well-being of the slaves, relative to that of free industrial workers. According to Fogel and Engerman, this is evinced in "typical" clothing and food allotments, housing and medical care (as reported by slaveholding planters) in comparison with that for free laborers in and beyond slavery.[13] These were putatively of nearly the same or superior quality to that of free laborers, as the planters would have wanted to provide for and protect their costly investment.

Fogel and Engerman's assertions belie reports of the brutality of American chattel slavery. Although the testimony of former slaves is ambiguous in some instances, most often it severely indicts the system of slavery.[14] Some of the ambiguity stems from the fact that brutality– namely, whipping, branding, mutilation, other forms of corporal punishment and rape–was an integral feature in the day-to-day lives of the slaves. Former slave Delia Garlic testified: "Folks a mile away could her dem awful whippings. Dey wuz a terrible part of livin'."[15] Another source of some slaves' hesitancy to define their experiences as brutal was the paternalistic ethos in which the slavocracy was shrouded, and the ways it sacralized the slaveholders. Alex Woods attests to the thinly veiled idolatry of the slaveholders in the exercise of their authority:

> Dey wouldn't allow 'em to call on de Lord when dey were whippin' 'em, but dey let 'em say, "Oh, pray! Oh, pray, Marster!" Dey would say, "Are you goin' to work? Are you goin' visitin' widout a pass? Are you goin' to run away?" Dese is de things dey would ax him, when dey wus whippin' him.[16]

Black people under the laws of slavery had no rights that any white person was obligated to respect. Privileged whites historically have had and presently have no obligation to redress this state of relations. Through the social power it grants to white people and to those non-whites who identify themselves with whites, the racial caste system facilitates the concealment of the true nature of economic power, which is the domain of very few in a capitalistic economy. As a result, to this day even the poorest whites can cut non-whites to the ontological core with very little fear of censure, through random and systemic discrimination, directed violence and unsavory epithets.

Moreover, according to G.E.M. de Ste. Croix, a historian of class struggle, "The fact that mid-nineteenth century American slaves were relatively many times as costly to buy as fifth/fourth century Athenian ones was due primarily to a large and expanding foreign market for cotton."[17] From 1820 to 1860 the forced, unpaid labor of black Africans in cotton fields signally accounted for the prosperity of southern, white Americans. As per my childhood insight, the white, lightweight stuff in croker sacks was a supreme symbol of black oppression. Gavin Wright likewise argues that there was only

> one fundamental dynamic force in the southern economy: expansion of cotton demand. From the time of the cotton gin until World

War II, the only periods of prosperity and progress for the South were periods of acceleration in world demand for this basic export crop. The greatest of these episodes happens to coincide with the late antebellum slave period . . . High regional growth rates, the apparent efficiency of slave labor and the sanguinity of slaveowners all rested on an inherently impermanent foundation—the extraordinary growth of world demand for cotton between 1820 and 1860. As the demand for cotton stagnated between 1860 and 1895, slave prices would have declined, and the growth rate of regional incomes would have been drastically reduced.[18]

Slavery benefited not only fledgling, southern America. Profits from the trade also financed the industrial revolutions of England, France and the United States. All these nations depended heavily upon the natural resources of Africa and the innovations of Africans to build up maritime trade and create technological advances in their social and cultural milieux. After the northern states prohibited the traffic in their territories, they still benefited from southern slaveholding (as did Europe) in that profits made from slavery went first to commercial ports and industrial cities such as New York, Boston and Portland (and Liverpool, etc.).[19] African Caribbean historian Walter Rodney states:

> Slavery [was] useful for early accumulation of capital, but it [was] too rigid for industrial development. Slaves had to be given crude, non-breakable tools which held back the capitalist development of agriculture and industry. This explains the fact that the northern portions of the U.S.A. gained far more industrial benefits from slavery than the South, which actually had slave institutions on its soil; and ultimately the stage was reached during the American Civil War when the Northern capitalists fought to end slavery within the boundaries of the U.S.A. so that the country as a whole could advance to a higher level of capitalism.[20]

Despite becoming later the locus of abolitionist activity, the North was no paragon of either moral or civic virtue. In most of the northern colonies that had previously permitted slaveholding, the "peculiar institution" lasted upward of a hundred years. Although slavery in the colonies actually began in 1629, statutory recognition of the institution began in Massachusetts and lasted from 1641 to 1780; in Connecticut, from 1650 to 1784; in New York, from 1664 to 1799; in New Jersey, from 1664 to 1804; in Rhode Island, from 1700 to 1784; in Pennsylvania, from 1700 to 1780. With the exception of Massachusetts, all of these northern colonies passed *gradual* emancipation laws.[21] After the passing of the Fugitive Slave Act (1850), white northerners "handed over" both free persons and former slaves to almost any white person making a claim on them. Its rabid enforcement indicated the extent and rigor with which the law provided for mutual respect among whites and for cooperation in the protection of white property. By contrast, toward the end of the Civil War, significantly, *after* federal emancipation, northern ambivalence toward slavery in general and African Americans in particular turned to outright hostility in the New York Draft Riots (1863), during which largely Irish mobs murdered scores of black folks and hanged their bodies on lamp posts.[22]

As proprietors of the church and as lawmakers in the process of nation-building, white northerners and southerners alike assaulted the humanity of African Americans with the duplicitous use of the Bible. The distinctly religious character of both groups of settlers generated intense debate concerning their chattels' spiritual status. Slave catechists employed the Bible in a literalist manner that sacralized black suffering and justified white privilege. Some whites reasoned that they were the "providential guardians"[23] as well as the temporal owners of the slaves, sanctioning black bondage with the so-called Hamitic curse (Gn 9:20ff.) and white dominance with the injunction, "Slaves, obey your masters" (Eph 6:5). Others posited the subhumanity of the Africans, constitutionally defining them as "hewers of wood" (Dt 29:11) and "drawers of water" (Jos 9:21), rendering moot any consideration of their spiritual status. In questioning the humanity of black people, the churchmen-cum-statesmen in America long and legally perpetuated the cross of slavery through the establishment of whites-only institutions and the enactment of laws prohibiting social intercourse between the races in a bid to keep the slaves and their descendants ignorant and materially impoverished, forever enslaved.

Despite the universal justice claims in America's sacred documents, which are themselves belied at every turn in the nation's juridical history by the experiences of African Americans, the legal, social, economic and ecclesial constructs derived from the covenantal theology of the settlers and the pietistic fervor of the evangelicals are essential elements in African American religious thought. Both election theology and Evangelicalism gave shape to American civil religion and impetus to the Protestant work ethic, another key element in the sacralization of America's violent history relative to the native inhabitants, poor whites and the slaves. They provided the foundling nation with a fundamentally Christian character, a template, to which black people are also heir and onto which they interpolated the story of their cross, that is, of the spiritual, psychological and physical burdens associated with their unjustly wrested labor. Like white Americans, African Americans freely used the motif of the Exodus to articulate their experiences of siege, sojourn and settlement, giving voice to comprehensive theological reckonings of their collective suffering. Former slave Isabella Baumfree changed her name to Sojourner Truth after her release from bondage (1827) because, as she stated, she wanted to keep "nothin' o' Egypt on me."[24] Harriet Tubman, "the Moses of Her People," brought over three hundred bondsmen and bondswomen out of the slaveholding South and into the free North on the Underground Railroad.

In and beyond slavery African Americans found themselves in the Bible among those for whom, with whom and *as one of whom* Jesus lived and died: the poor, the alienated, the tortured, the condemned. Humbled, they did not assume that their collective story was more important than his story; merely the inference that the crucifixion of Jesus was a mirror of their own suffering did—and, often, still does—cause many people within the black Christian community to "tremble, tremble," their trepidation perhaps also a mirror of their sometime hesitation to engage the opposing powers more proactively. But, despite their compassionate embrace of one who so identified with them, both cross and croker sack were thrust upon these latter-day "black Simons" through a hermeneutics of sacrifice ensconced in the Bible and Christian tradition. Having etiological roots in the Exodus experience of Passover (Ex 12:12-14) and Israelite/Jewish sacrificial tradition, it exhorts the followers of Jesus, the "Lamb of God . . . slain from the foundation of the world" (Rv 13:8) to imitate substantively his life of service, down to his final sacrificial act. A biblical outline and history of the Christian hermeneutics of sacrifice are instructive in order to illustrate its ideological utility in supporting the institution of slavery and the structures of domination that yet delimit black people and perpetuate their suffering.

THE HERMENEUTICS OF SACRIFICE IN BIBLICAL AND HISTORICAL PERSPECTIVE

In Israelite religion animal sacrifice was the instrument of reconciliation with Yahweh, which the Priestly writers regarded as Yahweh's own gracious provision to the people. The agent accomplishing this "at-one-ment" was believed to be the very blood of the sacrificial victim, by reason of the life, or vitality, that blood proffers (Lv 17:11). The nature of a sacrificial transaction is alternately described as an *expiation* or a *propitiation.* In the Hebrew Bible the word signifying atonement is *kaphar,* in the Greek New Testament the word is *hilasterion.* The clear meaning of the Hebrew term is "to smear" or "to wipe" with blood, and thus oblige God to "cover" sins and "pass over" those who are covered. The institution of the Passover in Exodus 12:1-28 gives a context for understanding the expiatory nature of sacrifice in the Israelite system. The meaning of the Greek term is "mercy seat" or "place of propitiation." Propitiation implies more forcefully that a penalty for sin is paid in the act of sacrifice, such that God is objectively changed by the sacrifice performed. At issue is whether the sacrificial system was intended to appease or assuage Yahweh. According to Frances Young, in early Israel,

> sacrifices were not simply gifts to turn away God's wrath, since only part was given to Jahweh. The purpose of the offerings is described as *lekhapper*, a term whose origin is disputed, but which has come to mean technically "to make atonement for." In the Old Testament it is construed with *the priests or Jahweh as the subject, and the Temple, altar or iniquity as the object. The object is never God, though the action is performed in God's presence.* The only possible conclusion is that the rites were not propitiatory, but were expiatory, *a means given by God to wipe away sin* and cope with the problem of failure to fulfill the Law. God acted through these cultic instruments to keep Israel from sin and calamity, making her ritually clean so that she could offer [him] fitting worship.[25]

The understanding that the system of sacrifice was given by Yahweh is instructive. Sin was a breach in covenantal relations between Yahweh and the people, and it always involved human choices; hence, ideally, there should never be a reason to sacrifice at all. In light of Yahweh's reverence for blood/life, the impetus for the practice of animal sacrifice among the Israelites was so that the people could indicate the seriousness of their intent to live in right relations with God and neighbor. Thus, in attributing the sacrificial system to the providence of Yahweh, the Levitical priesthood signified Yahweh's will to trivialize neither bloodloss—animal or human—nor the effects of sin. Nevertheless, the sacrificial system and the indisputably violent history of Israel relative to the Canaanites[26] expose the system of sacred violence that undergirded life in the ancient and developing Near East. Yet many prophetic writings support the claim that Yahweh *reveres* rather than *requires* blood and confirm the expiatory nature of sacrifice in the Priestly understanding (Hos 6:6; Am 5:23-24; Mi 6:6-8).

The New Testament authors also reasoned that the Christian plan of reconciliation was provided by God, emphatically stating that "the Father has sent his Son" (1 Jn 4:14) and that "through Christ [God] reconciled us to himself" (2 Cor 5:18ff.).[27] Appropriating the Levitical priesthood's cultic symbols, they construed Jesus' death as a blood sacrifice offered "*once for all*" and "*for our sins*" (or "*for our sake*").[28] These rhetorical flourishes served to bolster the early Christian community's messianic claims about Jesus and thus helped the community to surmount the ignominy of Jesus' death, that is, the *skandalon* ("scandal") of the cross.[29] The exclusivist saying "once for all" asserted the eternal efficacy of Jesus' human blood and bloodloss as opposed to the limited efficacy of the blood/bloodloss of animal sacrifices, which had to be repeated. Along with the saying "for our sins"—and not for ours only but for the sins of the *whole* world!—"once for all" affirmed the universal significance of his death, touting even "retrospective"[30] efficacy and subjecting all other religions' salvific claims regarding sacrifice to the Christian one.

The sacrificial theology of the New Testament also includes Jesus' priestly mediation of his own sacrifice. The letter to the Hebrews portrays him as sacrificial victim and high priest in a cacophony of roles that conformed to the symbols and elements in the Jewish rites. It asserts that the Levitical priesthood was limited in its efficacy because of the potential for sin within its ranks. To distinguish Jesus' priesthood from that of the Levitical priests, the author ascribes to him the office of "High Priest forever, after the order of Melchizedek" (6:20). This confession simultaneously accounts for Jesus' Jewish (rather than Levitical) lineage and supports the argument that Jesus' offering of himself was *once for all*, as the legendary Melchizedek had neither a known origin nor a known destiny, an idea which suggests his eternal nature (and so, Jesus'). Since the name *Melchizedek* means "king of righteousness" and "king of peace," the ascription also serves to illustrate Jesus' personal purity.

Consonant with their Jewish heritage, the early Christians were concerned with the ritual purity of the high priest as well as that of the sacrificial victim, typically a lamb or a goat. The declaration that in Jesus, Christians have a high priest "touched with the feelings of our infirmities . . . *yet without sin*" (4:15) highlights his innocence and personal worthiness. Although the gospel of Matthew likewise stresses Jesus' innocence, all of the synoptic gospels cite the institution of the Eucharist, supporting the notion that Jesus' surrogacy is at the heart of New Testament theology.[31] Evincing a more intrinsically developed eucharistic theology, the gospel of John describes Jesus as the "lamb of God who takes away the sin of the world" in language that purposefully recalls the scapegoat symbolically laden with the sins of the people and driven into the wilderness on the Day of Atonement (*Yom Kippur*). In the evolution of the Christian appropriation of the Jewish rites, the exclusivism evinced in Christian rhetoric and the themes of Jesus' innocence and surrogacy synergize in the concept of *substitutionary atonement*, in which the saying "for us" takes on additional meaning—"instead of us" or "in our place"—and confirms the *penal* and *propitiatory* nature of Jesus' atoning sacrifice in the Christian understanding.

In asserting that Yahweh requires mercy and not sacrifice, Jewish prophetic tradition had provided an incipient critique of the scapegoating phenomenon in sacrificial ritual. However, undergirded by structures of violence that from antiquity informed Near Eastern religious sensibilities and that characterized the Roman occupation of Palestine, the sacrificial system remained intact until the destruction of the Temple in 70 C.E.[32]

The first Christians were compelled to construct a counter-doctrine of Atonement by the impact of Jesus' witness on their lives and the cultural currency of animal sacrifice. They averred that the crucifixion was a repudiation of sacred violence because in its efficacy the need for sacrifice was eliminated, *once for all.* Moreover, this Atonement was an act of love involving Christ's own agency; thus it was a rejection of the themes of "generative scapegoating" and victimization in religious life and discourse "because God through Christ reconciled us to himself and gave us the ministry of reconciliation." This constant in the self-understanding of the church throughout its history remains as one impetus for the enduring emphasis on love in Christian moral thought. Robert G. Hamerton-Kelly states:

> That is why the rite of entry into the community is a rite of identification with the crucified. Co-crucifixion is part of an exposition of baptismal theology in terms of which baptism is an identification with Christ's death, burial and resurrection. The passage from the world to the church mimes the passage from the present age of sacred violence to the eschatological future of non-acquisitive love.[33]

Although the early church repudiated sacred violence by reinterpreting Jewish cultic symbols, the fact of persecution and martyrdom early in its history made a decisive impact on subsequent renderings of Jesus' mission and the implications of his life and death for authentic witness. Fledgling Christian communities embraced again the themes of victimization and scapegoating by signifying for themselves the theological meaning of their oppression. In much the same way the victimized, scapegoated and Christianized Africans understood their oppression and projected their own intellectual and spiritual agency onto their proscribed existence.

Suspected of being seditious and even cannibalistic and incestuous (based on the eucharistic language—for example, the "body and blood" of Christ—and the close-knit nature of relations among them), the first Christians became targets of persecution by Roman authorities and zealous Jews (for example, Saul of Tarsus).[34] They pointed to their Jewish heritage in order to allay suspicions that their religion was new but the apotheosis of Jesus was to the Jews a scandal that subverted the monotheistic doctrine that principally defined their national identity. The active suppression of Christianity combined with the adventism of the early church led to a cult of martyrdom that, like slavery in America, lasted for nearly three centuries. W.H.C. Frend states:

> It needed the sacrifice and death of Jesus Christ to give the doctrine of martyrdom a permanent validity. The Christian accepted Jesus as Lord, and as "the one faithful and true martyr" whose death he should imitate. He believed that by bearing witness of his faith until death, he would also witness his glory . . . Indeed, so long as the Second Coming was believed to be at hand, martyrdom and persecution at whomsoever's hands was bound to play a disproportionate part in the life of the church. It is quite natural that at the end of the first century martyrdom had come to be accepted as the goal of a Christian life.[35]

A cursory examination of the historical development of the doctrine of martyrdom reveals social class struggle in its Greco-Roman-North African context, in which slavery was sanctioned. The paterfamilias (an all-pervading cultural phenomenon in which the male head of the household had full social, legal and economic responsibility for all other males, women, children and slaves of the household) was the linchpin of Roman civil order. But the challenges that Christianity posed to traditional understandings of the family and property ownership had far-reaching spiritual, social and economic consequences for the imperial state and were contributing factors in the persecution of the church.[36] Yet, notwithstanding these laudable implications of the gospel message for the poor and the enslaved, the Bible never explicitly challenges the institution of slavery but presupposes it as an aspect of the culture.

In early America the ambiguity of the Bible regarding slavery was a vital link in the chain of justification for black oppression. This is an issue with which black exegetes are still attempting to reckon. Based on a critical exegesis of 1 Corinthians 7:17-24 and later patristic testimony, African American biblical scholar Allen Callahan claims that there was a policy regarding the manumission of slaves in the Corinthian church that reflected rising social class consciousness in the Christian movement, however muted it was by the immediate concerns of its persecuted members.[37] In verse 20 of that pericope Paul advises the Corinthians, "Remain in whichever worldly condition you find yourself, since worldly conditions or status cannot commend or separate from God." Vincent Wimbush avers: "'Remain' was not intended to support the status quo; it was designed only to *relativize* the importance of all worldly conditions and relationships,"[38] in light of the imminent return of Christ. Thoroughgoing *adventism* informed the church's witness to the social, political, economic and spiritual significance of Jesus' life and work and was a potent enabling factor in the martyrs' sacrifice of lives and limbs.

Thus, the early church's own cross had a profound impact on its development of Atonement doctrine. The interplay of persecution and adventism in its collective psyche was codified in scripture, generating a hermeneutics of sacrifice, that is, the understanding that personal sacrifice in the imitation of Christ is the sine qua non of Christian character.

In the construction of the American religious consciousness, advocates of both covenantal theology and Evangelicalism subscribed to the hermeneutics of sacrifice and benefited from its imposition on black and native peoples' theological understanding and sociopolitical reality. The first white settlers regarded their sufferings in their former homelands and their imperial mission in the New World as divine mandates, all of which made tenable the notion that America's bounty was their reward. In many ways Evangelicalism reproduced the ascetical impulse of historical Christianity: it stressed personal relationships with God in Christ through the direct action of the Holy Spirit, encouraged emotional conversion experiences and emphasized a life of holiness characterized by religious devotion, moral discipline and missionary zeal.[39] Yet the justification of chattel slavery enabled by the imposition of the hermeneutics of sacrifice exacerbated the problem of injustice for the oppressed blacks who confessed Christianity. During the first centuries C.E., in the inimical context of state persecution of the church, the confessional stance counseled in the hermeneutics of sacrifice was, in effect, an invitation to martyrdom. In *Uncle Tom's Cabin* Harriet Beecher Stowe acknowledged the replication of Christian martyrdom in the very character of slavery.[40]

SLAVE EXPERIENCE:
CHRISTIAN MARTYRDOM REVISITED, REINVENTED

The parallels between the suffering of the early Christian martyrs and that of the African American slave community seem obvious to me: the political circumstances in which each group developed were much the same. There are disparities in the rationales for their marginalization, in the related economic issues and in the cultural forces impinging on their lives. Rome willed to extirpate Christianity which, because of its missionary zeal and religious exclusivism, posed a pernicious social, political and economic threat to its central authority. The scapegoating of Christians also provided a focal point in the morally dissolute Empire's attempt to salvage itself spiritually. Moreover, Romans despised Christians as much for the melodramatic character of their commitment as for their intransigence toward state authority. Trajan

(53?-117) sent Pliny the Younger (62?-c.113) to the province of Bithynia to reorganize its affairs and deal with the Christians. Pliny reported the following:

> Meantime this is the course I have taken with those who were accused before me as Christians. I asked them whether they were Christians, and if they confessed, I asked them a second and third time with threats of punishment. If they kept to it, I ordered them for execution; for I held no question that whatever it was that they admitted, in any case obstinacy and unbending perversity deserve to be punished.[41]

Yet, although brutal, the Christians' suffering was intermittent; while tranquility prevailed in the provinces, persecution was stayed; and the act of martyrdom, glorified among them, was often thwarted.

American slavery was a lucrative enterprise. The slaveholders augmented their fortunes by trafficking in black bodies and hoped to exploit black labor in perpetuity. The system of slavery was an assertion of state authority by white imperialists, who arrogated unto themselves the divine right to control, command and determine the destinies of the African peoples, expressing ontological contempt for their humanity and agency.[42] In the slavocracy respect for the property and person of white people was the linchpin of the civil order, with priority given to the authority and person of white males. But in any conflict with the slaves, the authority of any white person—man, woman or child—was absolute and carried with it the power of life and death. Thus the Christian and the slave community emerged in an ethos of repression, subjugation, idolatry and death imposed by the state apparatus. Some of their actual experiences are remarkably similar. According to the Roman historian Tacitus (c.55–c.120), during Nero's reign (54-68) Christians were "sewed up in skins of wild beasts, and then worried by dogs until they expired; and others dressed in shirts made stiff with wax, fixed to axletrees and set on fire in his gardens, in order to illuminate them."[43] Likewise runaway slaves were "worried by dogs" and black bodies were fastened to magnolia trees; lynching was a favored mode of torture during slavery and beyond.[44] Rhais and her mother, Marcella were martyred during the reign of Severus (193-211). First, boiled pitch was poured over their heads; then they were burned to death. Slaves and hapless blacks outside of slavery were sometimes tarred and feathered as they were lynched; burning often accompanied a lynching.

Among the early Christians and among the slaves, women suffered the same and different depredations that men did. Rape was a form of terrorism with which both groups had to contend; the emphasis on chastity in the Christian movement led many of the women dissidents to choose death over rape, although they sometimes endured both.[45] Chastity was not a privilege afforded black women in slavery; they were legally compelled to gratify the lusts of the slaveholders and to breed with black men.[46] At the time of their martyrdoms (203 C.E.), Perpetua was the mother of a small child and Felicitas was pregnant, "big with child." As property, black women had no claim on their own bodies nor on those of the children they bore. Whether according to capital demands or simply the caprice of the slaveholders, they similarly endured separation from their children who could be killed or sold at the auction block, a kind of death unto itself.

In 81 C.E. Domitian (51-96) passed a law "that no Christian, once brought before the tribunal, should be exempted from punishment without renouncing their religion."[47] Thus it was said that the lives of the early Christians "consisted of 'persecutions above ground and prayer underground.'" Likewise, the subjugated Africans had to renounce their tribal religions; their daily lot was mitigated by prayer in the brush arbors ("hush harbors")[48] surrounding the plantations where they worked.

Individuals within both communities responded similarly to their oppression: intensely devoted to a newfound God, some accepted their fate stoically, others cheerfully. Ignatius, for example, wrote to the church at Rome that he prayed for "the joy of the beasts prepared for me . . . that I may attain unto Jesus Christ."[49] Some fled, others resisted. Eusebius reports that in 66 some members of the persecuted sect left Jerusalem for a place called Pella, beyond Jordan.[50] Runaway slaves traveled the Underground Railroad or followed the ever-constant Polaris to points north. The earlier Christians resisted chiefly through *apology*, reasoned defense of their faith.[51] The illiterate slaves resisted through numerous acts ranging from insubordination to sabotage to armed rebellion,[52] while literate blacks, free and otherwise, engaged in apology that was indeed a defense of black faith and an appeal to the reason and humanity of whites. David Walker's (1785-1830) *Appeal to the Colored Citizens of the World* (1830), which advocated armed resistance and inspired insurrections mounted by Harriet Tubman, Nat Turner and John Brown, was of this genre. Knowing that he was targeted for death, Walker demonstrated the same passionate commitment as the early Christian martyrs, stating,

> If any wish to plunge me into the wretched incapacity of a slave, or murder me for the truth, know ye, that I am in the hand of God, and at your disposal. I count my life not dear unto me, but I am ready to be offered at any moment. For what is the use of living, when I am already dead?[53]

Some martyrs "were obligated to pass, with their already wounded feet, over thorns, nails, sharp shells, etc., upon their points, others were scourged until their sinews and skins lay bare."[54] Ex-slave Mary Reynolds testified:

> Shoes was the worstest trouble. We weared rough russets when it got cold, and it seem powerful strange they'd never git them to fit . . . We prays for the end of tribulation and the end of beatings and for shoes that fit our feet.[55]

Both groups were fledgling Christians, yet many people accepted their lot as martyrs in keeping with their belief in Christian pacifism. Although they did not frequently renounce their faith, this escape option remained open to the martyrs.[56] Yet the commitment and the pacifism borne in their hearts were rooted in that community's conscientious rejection of sacred violence and in its thoroughgoing adventism. Just as Jesus' death *once for all* signaled the end of scapegoating in religious life and discourse, so baptism signified immersion in this consciousness, and the Eucharist its reenactment. As Jesus' return was imminent, it made political and religious sense not to resist the armed might of the forces arrayed against them.

But confessing slaves could not similarly renounce the skin color that made their subjugation in North America possible. In and beyond slavery, pacifism was posited as a theological mandate to which they were enjoined to submit through the use of brute force; through prohibitive laws and social structures designed to keep them ignorant and materially impoverished; and through the imposition of the hermeneutics of sacrifice, inherited from the cult of the martyrs, to subjugate them psychologically and spiritually. In Christianizing the slaves the white slaveholders taught, "Slaves obey your masters," willfully disconnecting the biblical injunction from its historical context and directly connecting the hermeneutics of sacrifice to their putatively divinely sanctioned authority. Thus, in effect and in kind, white people and the white power structures undergirding slavery reinvented the conditions and terms of Christian martyrdom in the slave community. Eschatological and apocalyptic dimensions in black faith, liturgy and rhetoric mirror the melodramatic responses in the confessions and experiences of the early church.

THE WAY OF SACRIFICE
AND THE AFRICAN AMERICAN RESPONSE

Despite the dualistic disdain for the body characteristic of Hellenistic thought in that age, the earliest Christian kerygma affirms that the body was the vehicle of God's descent to earth. Since God was in Christ, feeding, healing and even raising up physical bodies from the dead, the body gained in stature from the association. It became a metaphor for the church, providing paradigms for the spiritual and material well-being of the people. Patricia Cox Miller posits that:

> in the Christian asceticism of late antiquity, the body was perceived to be problematic, not because it was a body, but because it was not a body of plenitude. Although Christian theologians . . . had embraced the dichotomous Platonic view of the composition of the human person, they could not devalue the body to the level of prison completely if they were to affirm the positive valuation of the created world in the biblical book of Genesis, one of the central texts for anthropological speculation. Further, as Brown has observed, "Through the Incarnation of Christ, the Highest God had reached down to make even the body capable of transformation."[57]

In the martyrdom movement the human body was singularly regarded as that province over which individuals have control, relative to the claims of the state. But when Christianity received the patronage of its erstwhile enemy, the church was compelled to redefine its mission. With this change in circumstance, the emphasis on the surrender of life in the martyrdom movement was transmuted into the physical discipline associated with the ascetical movement, which established communities of work and worship that emphasized service and self-denial in the imitation of Christ. However, as Wimbush states:

> The term *ascesis* does not in itself mean more than training or practice, a conscious or intentional posture toward one's world into which one works oneself, the exercise of one's self-understanding. The fact that asceticism [conceived as] the various forms of abstinence usually associated with monasticism, is only one such way to relate to one's world suggests the broader context in which traditional asceticism is to be understood.[58]

The ascetical impulse continues to exert a powerful influence on Christian piety. Through the period of the martyrs, the ascension of Constantine I (c.285-337) and his patronage of the church; through the rise of the ascetical movement and the privatization of Christian faith, the hermeneutics of sacrifice posited "the surrender or destruction of something prized or desirable for the sake of something considered as having a higher or more pressing claim"[59] as a mandate for authentic Christian witness. Dramatized in the Crucifixion of Jesus and in the bodily experiences of the martyrs; illuminated in the Sermon on the Mount[60] and illustrated in the activities of the ascetics, the hermeneutics of sacrifice has been imposed by various Christian thinkers in the form of appeals to agape (or sacrificial love),[61] enemy-love[62] and (radical or) nonacquisitive love.[63]

In Reinhold Niebuhr's love/justice dialectic, agape is the controlling ideal in all human relations, although in matters of government, justice—or mutual love—should adjudicate. To seek justice is to seek "proximate solutions" to the "insoluble problems" of human social and political life. For Niebuhr, the way of sacrifice is amply and poignantly demonstrated by Jesus' death on the cross. In the thought of Walter Wink, the Sermon on the Mount[64] purports Jesus' "Third Way" of nonviolent, humorous confrontation of oppressive authority, whose proffered remedies (for example, turning the other cheek) are preposterous responses concealing subversive theological significance. Wink proposes that "enemy-love" is the test of authenticity for Christian faith.[65] René Girard posits that the impact of Jesus' ethic of nonacquisitive love has been to discredit the "mimetic violence" that has been the force driving human civilization, for which scapegoat theologies and attendant sacrificial rites arose to provide a measure of control.

Girard argues that the story of Cain and Abel (Gn 4:1-16) provides a prototype of relations between nonsacrificial and sacrificial cults in the primordial history of ancient Israel. He notes one distinctive thing about Cain: he does not have the "violence-outlet of animal sacrifice at his disposal"—a fact that increases his mimetic desire (because his offering of fruit is not accepted) and predisposes him to violence toward his brother.[66] Animal sacrifice in Israelite/Jewish tradition thus constituted a system of checks and balances to the human proclivity for violence, placing a relative, positive value on human blood/life and even higher value on the communal life of humans through the sustaining of blood-ties facilitated by the outlet of sacrifice. In Girard's apologetic Jesus' principled response to the principalities of his day—namely, his refusal to acquiesce to violence—points humankind away from sacred violence and toward a future of nonacquisitive love for God and neighbor.

All of these expositions are compelling because they indict everyone universally in sin and call everyone to love. Yet such moral "leveling" in fact places the moral onus on oppressed people. Privileged exegeses of the Sermon on the Mount and other texts and the categorical exclusion of violence, particularly as a countermeasure against oppression, ironically deploy a scapegoat mechanism that enables oppressor classes to maintain their privilege *by any means* while they proscribe the kinds of liberative options that may be taken by those whom they have already violently disempowered.

Reflecting on their situation in the light of the Christian message, slaves and free blacks posited alternative theological reckonings of the meaning of Christ's suffering and their own suffering. Having only a limited exposure to the scriptures, some believed that, like the white race, the black race was elected–not for beatitude, as many settlers had believed for themselves–but for suffering. To their minds suffering was God's means of achieving their submission to the civilizing hand of Christianity. Accordingly, slavery was the will of God for the once-heathen Africans. On the surface, this is the theological impetus of Phillis Wheatley's (c.1753-1784) *On Being Brought from Africa to America* (1768).[67] Through the various messages she relays, Wheatley reveals the complexity of what black people thought about their condition in light of the dissonances between Christianity as whites told it to them and as *they* experienced its graces. Drawing on biblical writ, the then-fifteen-year-old Wheatley compares the heathen "Negros" and the mythical enemy-brother "Cain,"[68] a comparison that was propagated in the mission theology of white American settlers and which black abolitionist and Christian apologist David Walker vehemently denounced in his *Appeal*:

> But where or of whom those ignorant and avaricious wretches could have got their information, I am unable to declare . . . I have searched the Bible as well as they . . . and have never seen a verse which testifies whether we are the seed of Cain or of Abel. Yet those men tell us that we are the seed of Cain, and that God put a dark stain upon us, that we might be known as their slaves!!! Now I ask . . . who act more like the seed of Cain by murdering, the whites or the blacks? How many vessel loads of human beings have the blacks thrown into the seas? How many thousand souls have the blacks murdered in cold blood, to make them work in wretchedness and ignorance, to support them and their families?[69]

American whites who have thoroughly imbibed the motif of conquest prominent in covenant theology often identify themselves completely with the victors and black people with either villains or victims. By the same token blacks identify with victims in the Bible, by choice and by conditioning. Barely more than a generation after slavery W.E.B. Du Bois echoed Wheatley's assessment of the salvific implications of the black witness in America, asking of God: "Is this Thy Justice, O Father? that guile be easier than innocence and the innocent be crucified for the guilt of the untouched guilty?"[70] In the reproduction of primordial history in the experiences of Jesus, the martyrs and the African American community, the innocent/Abel/Jesus/martyrs/blacks became

identified with the guilty party and the truly guilty/Cain/religious au-
thorities/Roman Empire/whites were absolved–by God, no less–and
were the preferred passengers on "th' angelic train" in Wheatley's poetry and in Du Bois's Jim Crow South. As righteous Abel was sacrificed
on the altar of Cain's egoism, so Christ Jesus was "made to be sin *for us*"
(pro nobis), that is, for sinful humankind, in the inchoate doctrine according to which Jesus, who "knew no sin" was "made to be sin" so that
Christians throughout the ages "might be *made* the righteousness of God
in him." Operating out of this sacrificial theological understanding,
Wheatley, in effect, offered up the innocent African American community–also "made to be sin, who knew no sin"–as "an offering in righteousness" for the Refiner's fire, attempting, I think, authentic Christian
witness in a hostile world. But, in truth, black bondage was a propitiation for the white refiners' fire in slavemaking and slaveholding America,
of which the "melting pot" is an apt symbol.

An unfortunate implication of this sacrificial theological understanding of the import of the black presence in America is the persistent
belief that Africans have contributed nothing to Western Christianity.
Africans are well-represented among the early Christian martyrs, ascetics and early church fathers; Tertullian, Cyprian, Origen and Augustine
fundamentally shaped Western Christian doctrine. Jeremiah Wright
observes:

> [Wheatley's] poem has been heralded by white politicians and
> publishers since its appearance, and has been taught to African
> American children in most American literature textbooks. Many
> devout Christians believe that, before Christ, most Africans were
> mere "pagans" and after Christ, Africans on the continent received
> Christianity from the hands of European Christian missionaries.
> Many believe that Africans held in bondage in this country re-
> ceived the only Christianity they knew from the hands of south-
> ern white evangelists.[71]

That Wheatley was significantly informed by and about Christian
sacrificial tradition is seen in her attribution to "mercy" her deliverance
from pagan, sinful Africa. Unconscionable as this may seem in an age
of pluralism, the propitiatory nature of Jesus' death affirmed in Christian tradition resonated with the penal quality of life conditions in slavery. Some blacks reasoned, as Jesus Christ was victimized and ultimately victorious, it was Christian to be victimized and to be requited at
the end, evincing both the evangelical tendency to level all people morally and a theodical intent in their responses to slavery and white racism. Wheatley mused:

How Jesus' blood for your redemption flows.
See him with hands out-stretcht upon the cross;
Immense compassion in his bosom glows'
He hears revilers, nor resents their scorn:
What matchless mercy in the Son of God!
When the whole human race by sin had fall'n,
He deign'd to die that they might rise again,
And share with him in the sublimest skies,
Life without death, and glory without end.[72]

Come, let us all with the same vigour rise,
And take a prospect of the blissful skies;
While on our minds Christ's image is imprest,
And the dear Saviour glows in every breast.
Thrice happy saint! to find thy heav'n at last,
What compensation for the evils past![73]

Quite possibly this compensatory understanding of black suffering gave rise to a passive impulse in black spirituality that is mirrored in the spirituality of other Christian communions. Yet many blacks, including Wheatley herself, viewed Christ's suffering as a manifestation of God's love for the world and their own suffering as occasion to manifest God's love in and for their world. Thus Wheatley's theology was not only sacrificial, it was also *sacramental*: she sought to mediate the presence of God to whites through and despite her experience of being a woman, black and enslaved in America—*through* her experience, because her gifts of poetry and *being* itself witnessed to the creativity and character of God; *despite* her experience, because she was, in her very being, like Jesus himself, despised and rejected by the socially, politically and economically powerful. Although her blackness offended whites and her womanhood scandalized the male-centered society, her literary gifts situated her as an agent and garnered her an audience. Moreover, they testified, as every gift does, to the power of God to make evident through faith "things not seen." This deeply rooted sacramental understanding of the significance of the black Christian witness as an artistic witness and as a witness of faith in the sovereignty of God is reflected in the melodrama of black liturgies, music and confessional utterances and in the writings of black theologians, some of whom, like Wheatley, extol a sacrificial praxis and some of whom decry it. It also demonstrates the power of an ethic of love that has existed in the African American community almost from its inception.[74] Although pacifist, the sacramental perspective was not passive but active: it deployed the moral agency of black people who would not let white violence circumvent their right to worship God and love others. Jesus revealed himself to be the fountain and source of this love ethic in a vision granted to Sojourner Truth, which her white friend Olive Gilbert recounted:

> "Who are you?" she exclaimed, as the vision brightened unto a form distinct, beaming with the beauty of holiness, and radiant with love. She then said, audibly addressing the mysterious visitant—"I *know* you and I *don't* know you." Meaning, "You seem perfectly familiar; I feel that you not only love me, but that you always *have* loved me—yet I know you not—I cannot call you by name." When she said, "I don't know you," it moved restlessly about, like agitated waters. So while she repeated, without intermission, "I know you, I know you," that the vision might remain— "Who are you?" was the cry of her heart, and her whole soul was in one deep prayer that this heavenly personage might be revealed to her, and remain with her. At length, after bending both soul and body with the intensity of this desire, till breath and strength seemed failing, and she could maintain her position no longer, an answer came to her, saying distinctly, "It is Jesus." "Yes," she responded, "it is *Jesus*."[75]

Truth would often recall this vision, embroidering on the details and indicating the degree of magnanimity found in this African American love ethic in her sermon (which was the basic theme of every one of her sermons) "When I Found Jesus":

> Praise, praise, praise to the Lord! An I begun to feel such a love in my soul as I never felt before—love to all creatures. An' then, all of a sudden, it stopped, an' I said, Dar's de white folks dat have abused you, an' beat you, an' abused your people—think o' them! But then there came another rush of love through my soul, an' I cried out loud—"Lord, I can love *even de white folks*!"[76]

For proto-womanists Wheatley and Truth, the love ethic was premised upon goodwill toward all people, even those who were their oppressors. Yet it is equally important to say what it was *not* for these Christian women. It was not that which Niebuhr commended in the African American community as a "morality of disinterestedness," which he ignorantly claimed kept the slaves from rising up against their former "masters"[77]:

> Every effort to transfer a pure morality of disinterestedness to group relations has resulted in failure. The Negroes of America have practiced it quite consistently since the Civil War. They did not rise against their masters during the war and remained remarkably

loyal to them. Their social attitudes since that time . . . have been compounded of genuine religious virtues of forgiveness and forbearance, and a certain social inertia which was derived not from religious virtue but from racial weakness. Yet they did not soften the hearts of their oppressors.[78]

Whatever Niebuhr meant by "racial weakness," the African American love ethic redounded to the ability of black people to survive, be free and express themselves in the various inimical contexts of white supremacist America. June Jordan offers yet another interpretation of Wheatley's poem *(On Being Brought from Africa to America)* that affirms Wheatley's agency and provides an insight on the poet's seeming acquiescence to the notion of black "racial weakness" in the light of her obvious talent and perspicacity:

> It's simple enough to track the nonsense about herself "benighted": *benighted* means surrounded and preyed upon by darkness. That clearly reverses what had happened to that African child, surrounded by and captured by the greed of white men. Nor should we find puzzling her depiction of African as "Pagan" versus somewhere "refined." Even her bizarre interpretation of slavery's theft of Black life as a merciful rescue should not bewilder anyone. These are regular kinds of iniquitous nonsense found in white literature, the literature that Phillis Wheatley assimilated, with no choice in the matter. But here, in this surprising poem, this first Black poet presents us with something wholly her own, something entirely new: It is her matter-of-fact assertion that "once I redemption neither sought nor knew," as in: Once I existed beyond and without these terms under consideration. *Once I existed on other than your terms.*[79]

In the context of the struggle for civil rights, Niebuhr might have invoked sacrificial love as the duty of privileged whites. But by urging whites to seek out "proximate solutions" to the "insoluble problems" of human political life, he undercut their obligation to honor the full humanity of black people, betraying his own social location as a member of the privileged classes. As a white male counseling oppressed blacks to be nonviolent, he equivocated their absolute right to be free from white oppression. Thus, in his thought, as in others, the hermeneutics of sacrifice is inherently weighted to the disadvantage of oppressed people. This is nowhere more clearly exemplified than in the bodily experiences of the martyrs and the black slaves who were killed and exploited for the social, political and economic benefit of societies that held them in utter contempt.

CONCLUSION

Christianity's enduring emphasis on the passion and death of Jesus is attributable to the fact of persecution and martyrdom in the early church. The ignominious fate of their leader created a political scandal that members of the suspect community sought to overcome by reinterpreting the significance of the sacrificial rites in the Jewish faith and practice from which their faith derived. Although Jesus was crucified for sedition, his followers construed his death as *the* Atonement—a blood sacrifice, offered, *once for all*—that signified both a divine rejection of sacred violence and a call to a life of service within the community of believers. Faith in the righteousness of the Way of Jesus (whom they also called the Christ, the messiah of Jewish expectation) and hope in his imminent return gave to these first Christians the ability to endure the experience of persecution and thereby imitate him. The deaths of the martyrs (or witnesses) were considered positive examples effecting the ultimate in the imitation of Christ *(imitatio Christi)*.

Despite tensions between Christians and Jews, Jewish resistance provided a paradigm for the church's response to the death of Jesus and to its own persecution. Although the Roman emperors sanctioned their rule with the common belief that "the basis of the political order lay in the divine realm,"[80] this same belief had always provided the impetus for Jewish political resistance, which was characterized by messianic consciousness, nationalistic zeal, religious exclusivism and the glorification of martyrdom.[81] In order to maintain the illusion of peace,[82] Rome really needed to *manage* the risks that such Jewish resolve posed. Thus, the state permitted the Jewish people (and its other subjects) to practice their inherited sacrificial rituals, as long as other aspects of their civic deportment did not challenge the state's authority. As Christians began to develop their identity apart from the Jews, they refused to participate in the Jewish rites as well; they were censured and eventually expelled from the synagogues.[83] The church attempted to overcome the scandal of the cross, not by distancing itself from the seditious implications of Jesus' life and message but by affirming the salvific witness of his death, appropriating the cultic symbols of Judaism and combining them with their messianic claims. In so doing they also ascribed to him divine attributes that were never a part of Jewish expectation. To the Jewish people the religious implications of the apotheosis of Jesus was as scandalous as the political position of the Christians.

As an emergent sect within Judaism, Christianity at once challenged Jewish religious authority and intensified the Jewish challenge to imperial authority with its claim of Jesus' ultimacy. For the Christians, who claimed no particular province or sphere of dominion, nationalistic zeal translated into missionary zeal for the Way of Jesus; religious exclusivism obtained, albeit with social, political and economic implications for the widespread empire. The state responded to the Christian menace with persecution. Although mainly local and sporadic, the suppression of Christianity throughout the Roman Empire led to a cult of martyrdom that, like slavery in America, lasted for nearly three centuries.

For the early Christians, the glorification of martyrdom also derived from their Jewish heritage, which provided models for witnessing their faith and coping with their world. But through the Christian rejection of animal sacrifice the act of martyrdom was purported to be a rejection of sacred violence that rather melodramatically internalized and perpetuated it. Jesus' crucifixion and the church's experiences of persecution and martyrdom led Christians to reappropriate the language of victimization and scapegoating in their theological discourse. The emphasis on martyrdom evolved over time into a hermeneutics of sacrifice. Codified in scripture, the hermeneutics of sacrifice has dramatically affected the lives of oppressed Christians. In the African American experience, it was an ideological tool used to impose the cross of slavery.

African Americans' suffering is near fully paralleled in that of the martyrdom community, yet the tendency among black people has been to identify wholly with the suffering of Jesus because the story made available to them–Jesus' story–tells of his profound affinity with their plight. Like the martyrs, they are committed to him because his story is their story. Jesus' death by crucifixion is a prototype of African Americans' death by *circumscription*. This circumscription does not simply entail being proscribed within a class of servants to whites, as in slavery and the post-slavery labor force; it involves a history and ongoing experience of social and political interdiction, brutality and death at the hands of white people and white power structures. Embracing the cross, transmuted into an ethic of love by the historical Christian emphasis on sacrifice and by their own understanding of themselves as sacramental witnesses, very many African Americans in and since slavery found the power they needed to survive, to be free and to express themselves. In the process they affirmed their innocence, refuted the claims of white supremacists, sanctified their own suffering and situated themselves within the cosmic drama as victims-becoming-victors.

Chapter 2

There Is a Fountain

Sources of Reflection on the Cross
in Black Theology and Womanist Theology

Oh! precious is the flow
that makes me white as snow;
No other fount I know
Nothing but the blood of Jesus!
    —Robert Lowry
        (1826-1899)

O, precious blood of my dear Redeemer! O, gaping wounds of my crucified
Saviour! Who can contemplate the sufferings of God incarnate, and not
raise his hope, and not put his trust in Him?

                                        —Richard Allen
                                            (1760-1831)

Through tribulations deep
The way to glory is.
        —Jarena Lee
            (b. 1783)

Slavery's brutality and that which followed it illustrate why the cross remains the central motif in the spirituality, liturgy and God-talk of African American Christians: their unrelenting suffering instituted and perpetuates the discourse of *theodicy*, the attempt to reconcile belief in the goodness and power of God in the face of evil and suffering. Black theologians have referenced three sources that attest to the pervasiveness of the theme of theodicy in black peoples' lives and to the completeness of their historic identification with Jesus' suffering: *slave religion*, *black radicalism* and the *Black Church*. Slave religion and black radicalism are the historical matrices that issued forth in the Black Church, black theology and womanist theology. Although womanist theologians acknowledge black women's particular experiences as discrete sources of reflection on their cross, proponents of both disciplines reflect critically upon prospects for freedom and justice for African Americans in their God-talk in order to appropriate the redemptive possibilities in the story of the cross/the event of the Atonement.

SLAVE RELIGION

Slave religion was sourced by two major streams: *Evangelicalism,* and the prior religious experiences of the displaced people, evinced in the *reprise of Africanisms* in the rites and liturgies of the Black Church, from its "hush harbor" origins to its present.

Evangelicalism

Despite their own political insecurity and attenuated religious ties to Europe, America's settlers sought to imbue the land and peoples they had vanquished and enslaved with an ethos of civility and piety. But in order to quench their thirst for empire and continue in the profitable enterprise of slavery, they needed to manage risks posed by native and black resistance, in the same way that Rome needed to manage risks posed by first-century Jews and other nationalists among the peoples whom that Empire had conquered. A Roman proverb shrewdly observed: "Quot servi, tot hostes"[1]—All slaves are enemies. This was a valuable lesson quickly learned by colonial slaveholders. Like the Romans, they were not always successful in their endeavors to maintain the illusion of peace. Like Roman legions among the peoples in territories they had occupied, British militia leavened the American populace, regulating the social and civic affairs of whites, displacing and annihilating native peoples and intimidating free blacks and slaves in an effort to preclude insurrection on the part of activist black denizens and their abolitionist friends.[2]

Nonetheless, from the inception of the slave trade Christianity had been useful in inculcating docility in some of the African peoples. Following the successful conclusion of the Revolutionary War (1775-1783) and the achievement of nationhood, Christianization was an even more important factor not only in the control of blacks but also in the ethical justification of slavery. With its emphasis on scripture as the revealed word of God and arbiter of competing human claims, Evangelicalism was effective in achieving both these aims. According to its tenets each individual is accountable to a personal piety that derives from a literal-istic appropriation of the Bible. This hermeneutical strategy morally leveled people irrespective of social and economic location by providing a standard of objective, sacral authority for the inchoate nation.

Having a distinctly Anglican core, institutionalized in the Baptist, Methodist, Presbyterian, Disciples of Christ and Protestant Episcopal denominations, American Evangelicalism coincided with the rise of Pietism in England and other parts of Europe. Informed by this admixture of religious traditions in the founding of Virginia, it also portended the beginning of *southern* (as distinct from *northern*) American culture, according to church historian, Donald Mathews.[3] Evangelicalism was not, however, delimited by southern borders but extended throughout the nation, fundamentally shaping American orthodoxy, imposing a standard of piety that was morally leveling for all persons in Christian communion, including those slaves admitted on the basis of white paternalism.[4] As a class critique evangelical piety mitigated both the effects of poverty among southern agriculturalists of diverse national origins and the elitism of northern industrialists, giving group identity to the former and censuring the latter.

By emphasizing scripture as story and the cross as its central event and by taking an equivocal stand on the issue of black bondage, proponents of Evangelicalism reinforced the visceral theodical impulses that fundamentally shaped the slaves' religious response to the reality of oppression. Scripture gave to the slaves points of identification with Jesus and other biblical victims. The theodical thrust of its stories functioned to establish a compensatory mechanism in black and *American* religiosity that mitigated class conflict between (the many) poor and (the few) wealthy whites. Evangelical preaching—emphasizing sin, salvation and the need by *all* for conversion—gave an egalitarian dimension to the character of American worship, to which the revolutionary fervor of the settlers gave social impetus and a political basis. Owing in part to this egalitarian impulse in Evangelicalism, African Americans responded by converting (from Islam and indigenous religions) to Christianity in large numbers during the first Great Awakening (1730-1760) in the nation's religious consciousness.

After economic power consolidated in the northern states, these became the locus of abolitionist activity as an extension of the egalitarian impulse in Evangelicalism. During this period, as the concept of nationhood congealed, some northern, white, evangelical church officials challenged the validity of slavery, notably, the Methodists. Yet even they equivocated about the right of blacks to be absolutely free, thus containing incipient conflict between themselves and southern slaveholders. Meanwhile, apologists urged the slaves to imitate Christ substantively, through personal sacrifice[5] as their bounden duty.

Despite the tension between North and South, Mathews believes that the slaveholding ethic was as "natural" an extension of evangelical piety as was abolitionism, in that it was an outgrowth of historical Christian triumphalism against "paganism." He argues that the scope of personal responsibility among slaveholders was conceived as a "mission to the slaves," a mission which began in earnest around 1830, following upon the second Great Awakening (1800-1830):

> Churchmen believed that the Church's primary mission in the New World was to bring all inhabitants—Indians, Africans, Europeans— under the rule of religion as outlined in the 39 articles and the book of Common Prayer. If they had stopped there they might have been more successful in America; but they did not. They identified their church with the perpetuation of a hierarchical social system . . . Rather than evoking an elemental feeling of commonality, the sermons stated as clearly as possible the rules of social conduct.[6]

Evangelical Methodists achieved wide results among blacks in both regions. Mathews states that the Methodist Episcopal (ME) Church in most southern cities was a black society with a few white members who held power and protected black worshipers from hostile authorities. William Jacob Walls reports that, as discerned "from journals and reports of early missionaries sent to America by [John] Wesley . . . the black membership of the John Street Church [New York City], in the beginning, was principally slave."[7] Evangelicalism was thus neither a southern nor a white phenomenon but rather reflected the undeniable participation of northern and southern folks—black and white—in common religious exercise.[8] Mathews writes that Evangelicalism was *black* to the extent that black people created the measure by which its egalitarian spirit could be judged, through the appropriation of the promise to "preach liberty to the captives." For a number of slaves and free blacks, Methodism adequately fulfilled that promise through the spiritual freedom its moral rigor engendered. As one among many denominational byproducts of Evangelicalism, Methodism purported to be a "spiritual movement within the temporal environment."[9] Richard Allen, a former slave (and future founder of the African Methodist Episcopal Church), explained the Methodist appeal:

> I was confident that there was no religious sect or denomination would suit the capacity of the colored people as well as the Methodist; for the plain and simple gospel suits best any people; for the unlearned can understand, and the learned are sure to understand; and the reason that the Methodist is so successful in the awaken-

ing and conversion of the colored people, the plain doctrine and
having a good discipline.[10]

Notwithstanding Methodism's spiritual appeal, it was John Wesley's
antislavery stand, integral to the denomination's doctrine and codified
in its Discipline, that raised up prospects for temporal freedom in the
slave community. Carol George affirms that these holistic implications
of Methodism accounted for its early popularity with Allen and other
African Americans as much as its pietistic theology.[11] In point of fact, a
Methodist abolitionist (Freeborn Garrettson) helped Allen to procure
his freedom when he preached a sermon based on these words: "Thou
art weighed in the balance, and art found wanting" (Dn 5:27). Allen's
guilt-stricken master then gave him opportunity to purchase his freedom.[12] Thus,

> For Allen, Methodism was not merely the sum of its attributes—its
> organization, Discipline, theology and style of worship—rather it
> was a way of life, a wholly new regenerative and revitalizing expe-
> rience. And an integral part of that experience was the emphasis
> on antislavery, not as a mere afterthought, but as a basic denomi-
> national doctrine. Eighteenth-century Methodism seemed no more
> likely to be separated from its policy on slavery than the itinerant
> preacher from his horse and saddlebags. So strong was denomina-
> tional concern in this regard in 1784, that written into the Disci-
> pline was a plan to expel from membership all those who bought
> or sold slaves except for the purpose of freeing them. Eventually,
> it is true, this policy would be challenged by those who disagreed
> with it—including Southern planters and Northern laborers—but
> when Allen accepted Methodism its official position seemed in-
> controvertible.[13]

Thus, as an integral part of its mission and theology, Methodism addressed the overwhelming theodical concern of African Americans during slavery: reckoning with the reality of bondage, physical and spiritual, accordingly with their temporal conditions and the evangelical
ethos. However, unlike the unswerving commitment of the Pennsylvania Quakers, Methodist support for black freedom was disingenuous,
for it devolved upon the affirmation of white supremacy in the polar-
ized American context. Although tension between northern and southern Methodists over the issue of slavery eventually resulted in schism,[14]
the early aims of its program of Christianization were clearly related to
the need of whites in both the North and the South to (1) inoculate
themselves against the threat of black revolt; (2) delimit social intercourse between the races; and (3) assume control of the spiritual destiny

of slaves and free blacks alike. White Methodists prohibited blacks from staying late at meetings and meeting among themselves, and imposed the paternalistic and legal requirement that a "proper white person" be appointed their leader.[15] Recounting the earliest origins of the African Methodist Episcopal Zion Church, Bishop Walls sketches some of the tensions black preachers in the ME Church experienced during its formative years and highlights the ways in which social and legal proscriptions conflated with the aims of white churches and confirmed the fears of white citizens:

> Circumstances for black preachers in the Methodist Church were much more crucial than the Baptists, although large numbers of Negroes joined the movement from its beginning in 1766. The black Methodists, in the meantime, were developing ministers in the white congregations who began to organize churches. They were licensed to preach, but were denied ordination until the General Conference of 1800 passed a limited ordination rule for African preachers. It is recorded that progenitors of the Mother AME Zion Church, in New York City, were meeting privately as early as 1780. The state law of New York had prevented Negro groups from holding open meetings since the Insurrection of 1712.[16]

Although white worshipers relegated black worshipers to second-class citizenship in their churches, Methodism, in principle, generated hope of freedom among African Americans. Thus, when Richard Allen formed the first free African Church in 1787, he united in Methodist connection despite the discrimination black Christians had experienced in St. George's ME Church (Philadelphia). Following upon his efforts, the AME Church was established in 1816. Yet, while Allen evinced a certain contentment with the evangelical thrust of Methodism, he resented slavery, holding his theological conservatism in tension with a theo-political radicalism born of the black experience. His ability to affirm the sovereignty of God and human agency reflects the theodicy project that has characterized black people's quest for meaning in a context of oppression and masked the rage[17] belying black piety in and since slavery:

> Will you, because you have reduced us to the unhappy condition our color is in, plead our incapacity for freedom, and our contented condition under oppression, as a sufficient cause for keeping us under the grievous yoke? I have shown the cause, I will also show why *they appear contented* as they can in your sight, but the dreadful insurrections they have made when opportunity has offered, is enough to convince a reasonable man that *great uneasiness and not contentment is the inhabitant of their hearts. God himself hath*

pleaded their cause; He hath from time to time raised up instruments for that purpose, sometimes mean and contemptible in your sight, at other times He hath used such as it hath pleased him, with whom you have not thought it beneath your dignity to contend. Many have been convinced of their error, condemned their former conduct, and become zealous advocates for the cause of those whom you will not suffer to plead for themselves.[18]

Evangelical apologists for slavery compounded black suffering by undermining the egalitarian principles of the nations' sacred documents and by approving the inequities of the social hierarchy through the use of literalist[19] hermeneutics. In 1857 the Rev. Frederick A. Ross (1796-1883), then pastor of the Presbyterian church in Huntsville, Alabama, accused a Philadelphia abolitionist of dismissing the "BIBLE" and the "God of the Bible" and advocating "an abolition Bible, an abolition Constitution . . . and an abolition God"–all subject to the principle of equality found in the Declaration of Independence. Responding to an abolitionist tract entitled *The Church and Slavery* by the Rev. Albert Barnes (1789-1870–then pastor of First Presbyterian Church), Ross cited the biblical relations of husband/wife, parent/child, master/apprentice, master/hireling and master/slave as ordained hierarchical relationships.[20] In accordance with biblical proscriptions, sin constituted willful violations of these prescribed relationships. This conception of sin embodied the social parameters within which white people as well as slaves and free blacks were to comport themselves. Respect for the person and property of whites was the linchpin of the moral and legal codes of every state of the Union. According to Kenneth Stampp:

At the heart of every code was the requirement that slaves submit to their masters and respect all white men. The Louisiana code of 1806 proclaimed this most lucidly: "The condition of the slave being merely a passive one, his subordination to his master and to all who represent him is not susceptible of modification or restriction . . . He owes to his master, and to all his family, a respect without bounds, and an absolute obedience, and he is consequently to execute all the orders which he receives from him, his said master, or from them." A slave was neither to raise his hand against a white man nor to use insulting or abusive language. Any number of acts, said a North Carolina judge, may constitute "insolence" -it may be merely "a look, the pointing of a finger, a refusal or neglect to step out of the way when a white person is seen to approach. But each of such acts violates the rules of propriety, and, if tolerated, would destroy that subordination, upon which our social system rests."[21]

Moreover, "the codes were quite unmerciful toward whites who inter-fered with slave discipline," as the rapacity of anti-abolitionist fervor in the South demonstrated.[22]

Thus, the moral and legal codes of slavery gave the reverence due to God to whites, with priority given to the authority and persons of white males. Their preeminence was to be reflected in all social relations, including those with white women. As early as the seventeenth-century anti-miscegenation laws prohibiting sexual relations between white women and black men permitted white men to have sexual license with black slave women.[23] The sexual encounter between slaveholder and female slave was a form of terrorism designed to intimidate the slaves and to minimize resistance. Black men, being property, had no rights to protect or provide for their families, similar to those assumed by white men. Rape was thus an effective tool for the humiliation of the entire slave community, children, wives and husbands. White males attempted to avoid this kind of humiliation by prohibiting sexual relations be-tween black males and white females, accomplishing through legal fiat their right to exploit black women sexually[24] and to sell or force into concubinage and prostitution their own children begotten of slave women. Linda Brent, a mulatto slave woman slated for concubinage with her master, described the fate of mixed-blooded children. If a white woman bore the child of a slave:

> In such cases the infant is smothered or sent where it is never seen by any who know its history. But if the white parent is the father instead of the mother, the offspring are unblushingly reared for the market. If they are girls, I have indicated plainly enough what will be their destiny . . . Slavery makes the white fathers cruel and sensual . . . it contaminates the daughters . . . And as for the col-ored race, it needs an abler pen than mine to describe the extrem-ity of their sufferings, the depth of their degradation.[25]

In addition, the spinning of myths about the gentility of white women became a new art form in nineteenth-century "romance" novels.[26] The characteristics of submissiveness, delicacy, purity and innocence ascribed to white women—in juxtaposition to the putative moral laxity and sexual crudity of black women—belied the deeply misogynistic and racist roots from which they originated. All of these biblical, legal and social at-tempts to control women's sexual agency reveal as much about the idola-trous theoretical underpinnings of white paternalism as did slavery, because they inured white men against any threat to their moral, legal and social standing. Thus, although it putatively sought to provide level moral ground for all persons in Christian communion, Evangelicalism confirmed the hierarchical ordering of the slavocracy through its biblicist theology and its failure to indict both the institution of slavery and its sexual abuses, paradoxically offending evangelical propriety. According to Isabella Lucy Bird Bishop:

> In the South the preaching is still the same . . . earnest and Evangelical. There, as elsewhere, the pulpit seeks to convince men of sin, and that the Gospel is blessed in the South I do not doubt any more than that its progress is unhindered by one important omission. The Southern ministers denounce drunkenness and other vices; dishonest dealing, worldliness, the love of display, &c; but the sin of Slavery, and the sins which arise out of it, pass unrebuked. We hear of other sins as elsewhere; but the one terrible system which denies to 4,000,000 human beings the right of indissoluble marriage and the sacredness of the parental tie, which sustains an iniquitous Slave-trade, which vitiates alike public and private morals, this the pulpit protects and fosters.[27]

In the slavocracy the uncertain status of slave marriages highlighted the absoluteness of white authority and assisted whites in the reification of class lines. Similarly, in post–Constantinian Christianity, prohibiting slave marriages added a sacralizing mystique to the church's authority. The practice demonstrates the early foundations of class bias in Christianity. G.E.M. de Ste. Croix states:

> Although the Christians laid great emphasis on the importance of monogamous marriage and the sinfulness of sexual intercourse outside it, the Christian Empire did not provide for legal marriage between slaves, any more than the pagans had done. This need not surprise us. The antebellum South was deeply religious, but no single state legislature ever tried to legitimise slave unions and thus give them a greater chance of permanency, and they always remained subject in practice to the master's whim.[28]

Like other religious movements Evangelicalism reflected "mankind's" primordial disdain for the human agency of womankind. Note this in the social roles to which white women were circumscribed on the basis of biblical proscriptions and social conventions: "*Wives*, submit yourselves unto your own husbands" (Eph 5:22; Col 3:18). Evangelical preachers employed literalist readings of the Bible in order to justify both slavery and women's oppression. bell hooks relates:

> In fundamentalist Christian teaching woman was . . . the bringer of sin into the world. Sexual lust originated with her and men were merely the victims of her wanton power. Socialization of white

men to regard woman as their moral downfall led to the development of anti-woman sentiment. White male religious teachers . . .
[appointed] themselves as the personal agents of God, [becoming]
the judges and overseers of woman's virtue. They instigated laws
to govern the sexual behavior of white women, to insure that they
would not be tempted to stray from the straight and narrow path.
Severe punishments were meted out to those women who over-
stepped the boundaries white men defined as woman's place.[29]

Despite the egalitarian impulse in Evangelicalism, church hierarchies,
black and white, continued to bid women "keep silence in the churches"
(1 Cor 14:34) and excluded them from the priesthood. When Jarena
Lee (b. 1783) first petitioned then-pastor Richard Allen for a license to
preach, he was able to affirm her gifts by allowing her to exhort the
saints on occasion, yet he refused to sanction them officially.[30] When
Allen became bishop of the newly-formed AME Church and Lee petitioned him again, he could find no biblical or ecclesiastical precedent
for allowing women more freedom.[31] Employing the same exclusionary
hermeneutics as those who had circumscribed him in the ME Church,
he missed an opportunity to witness to the right in his common cause
with black women. His response, patterned after white power dynamics
relative to blacks, helped to lay the foundation of paternalism as the
basis for sexism in the African American community and the Black
Church. To the extent that Early American white women, the slaves
and their descendants imbibed evangelical mores concerning sex and
sexual roles, Evangelicalism, along with their relative lack of agency,
subjected them to a profound dualism concerning sex, defined throughout Christian tradition as the prima facie cause of the fall.[32] This dualism is in itself a cross, the bars of which are prurience and prudishness,
preoccupation with which has issued forth in a thriving pornography
industry in which children, women, black people, gay men and lesbians
are doubly exploited in consequence of their economic needs and the
images that are projected concerning them.

Although the literalist biblical hermeneutics in evangelical theology
pervaded the entire culture and shaped social relations between blacks
and whites, slaves and slaveholders, women and men, white church
officials enjoined women and slaves to submit to biblical authority
through the hermeneutics of sacrifice. Was the biblicist ethos in which
America was shaped institutionalized in the fundamentalist movement
of the early twentieth century in order to perpetuate misogyny and black
subjugation? Although the absolutism of the fundamentalists ostensibly
sought to protect the *Bible* from assault, it was actually white, patriarchal
privilege that such a hermeneutical strategy protected.

In many respects Evangelicalism was a response to Deism. This significant religious and philosophical development came to prominence
during the eighteenth-century Enlightenment, an era characterized by
belief in the powers of human reason and culturally marked by innovations in politics, science and theology. Little explicated is the connection between the rise of Deism and the African slave trade. The key to
understanding this link lies in Deism's influence on the development of
the American social and political character. Deism was an abreaction to
the religious intolerance in Europe that had spurred many to leave their
homelands for America in the first place. Thus, despite the wide appeal
of Evangelicalism, some of Deism's major tenets were deeply rooted in
the American psyche. Nonetheless, proponents of both Evangelicalism
and Deism colluded to make and keep Africans enslaved. Evangelical
apologists justified slavery on the basis of biblical authority. Alterna-
tively, deists claimed that humankind required the consistent application of reason in order to adjudicate their affairs, in opposition to evangelical "enthusiasm" regarding claims of divine revelation. Fundamentally,
deists considered the idea of God moot, God having abandoned human
history, counter to Judeo-Christian affirmations of the active providence
of God on behalf of the people of God. The theological significance of
the rise of Deism within this historical time period lies in the fact that its
doctrine of God permitted the ongoing enslavement of African people,
not only because it denied the providence of God—and hence, the *sovereignty* of God over human, temporal matters—but also because it elevated
one group of humans at the expense of another, like the justification of
the enslavement of the Jewish people in the Babylonian cosmogony,
which asserted that human beings were created to be slaves of gods.[33]
Although some did oppose slavery on the basis of the religious and
political claims they had made for themselves against the British crown,
many settlers, deist and evangelical alike, defended slavery because of
the economic benefit and social power it afforded them. Mathews explains the irresistible appeal of slavery despite the fact that it contra-
dicted the settlers' own revolutionary fervor:

> As a result of this active rebellion, they began to form a sense of
> bondedness and special mission, which at one time led most of
> their radical spokesmen to seal the authenticity of their revolution
> by attacking slavery. This revolutionary and romantic gesture failed
> to achieve social change because evangelicals themselves wanted
> prestige and influence and wanted also to achieve power on the
> basis of their own estimation of themselves and the economic tools
> at their command. Unfortunately for blacks, one of these tools was
> slavery and most evangelicals channeled their resentment against

non-evangelical slaveholders by claiming that they could at least in theory make the slaves a more integral and stable part of the community than could non-believers.[34]

Holding sway, as it did, during the height of the international slave trade and influencing American politicians such as Benjamin Franklin (1706-1790), Thomas Paine (1737-1809) and Thomas Jefferson (1743-1826), the religious and philosophical ramifications of Deism helped to strengthen the foundations of paternalism that characterized relations between white men and white women, white people and black, slaveholders and slaves in America. Pseudoscientific theories of gender and race,[35] spun in the climate of rational inquiry fostered by the Enlightenment, buttressed the paternalistic theses of evangelical apologists. Of women, one of Deism's foremost proponents, German philosopher Immanuel Kant (1724-1804), declared:

> A woman is embarrassed little that she does not possess certain high insights, that she is timid, and not fit for serious employments, and so forth; she is beautiful and captivates, and that is enough. On the other hand, she demands all these qualities in a man, and the sublimity of her soul shows itself only in that she knows to treasure these noble qualities so far as they are found in him.[36]

Regarding African peoples Kant cited his contemporary, skeptic David Hume and offered his own assessment, reflecting the very great disdain that whites held toward the mental capacities and religious practices of the blacks, whom Jefferson and others were in the process of enslaving and legislating out of personhood and representation in the New World.[37] By disparaging blacks' humanity, Kant justified slavery. By naming their religious practices *idolatry*, he reinforced evangelical opposition to the Africans' presumed "paganism" as a rationale for Christianization:

> The Negroes of Africa have by nature no feeling that rises above the trifling. Mr. Hume challenges anyone to cite a single example in which a Negro has shown talents, and asserts that among the hundreds of thousands of blacks who are transported elsewhere from their countries, although many of them have been set free, still not a single one was ever found who presented anything great in art or science or any other praiseworthy quality, even though among the whites some continually rise aloft from the lowest rabble, and through superior gifts earn respect in the world. So fundamental is the difference between these two races of man, and it appears to be as great in regard to mental capacities as in color. The religion of fetishes so widespread among them is perhaps a

sort of idolatry that sinks as deeply into the trifling as appears to be possible to human nature.[38]

In contrast to the deists, evangelicals, in effect, denied that human beings could usurp the authority of God by emphasizing human sin and unworthiness, classic theological themes that were part of American orthodoxy. Yet, although white evangelicals criticized the humanist tenets of Deism, they most certainly imbibed the patriarchal and racial supremacy that substantively undergirded it, themselves partaking in the idolatry of Deism's proponents through the paternalistic compromise they made with blacks. The idolatry in Evangelicalism is reflected both in northern slaveholders' refusal to abandon slavery until it was no longer profitable for them and in southern slaveholders' willingness to fight a war to perpetuate it.

Like Deism, Evangelicalism provided theoretical underpinnings for the notion that the slaveholders were God's appointed agents. Unlike the deists, who abused the insights of science in order to effect domination, white evangelical ministers deployed the hermeneutics of sacrifice in their proslavery arguments. James Furman, a Baptist clergyman from South Carolina stated: "We who own slaves honor God's law in the exercise of our authority."[39] Thornton Stringfellow of Richmond, Virginia, urged upon the slaves "blind compliance" to God's will, stating that "God gave special aid [to whites] to effect slavery" as part of the divine plan to bring pagan Africans under the civilizing influence of Christianity.[40] David Hodge of New Jersey advised wives, children, slaves—all like subjects—that their bondage was "service owed to God."[41] He opined that the early Christians submitted to the authority of Rome "until the mass of the community became Christians, and then they revolutionized the government."[42] He enjoined blacks to do the same. Obviously he was not referring to the martyrs. Fortunately, activist Africans did not heed him.

The Reprise of Africanisms

The academic study of the reprise of Africanisms in black worship has generated intense debate over the extent of the influence of prior religious experiences on slave religion and the subsequent development of African American spirituality. Melville Herskovits and E. Franklin Frazier have clearly delineated the poles of this debate.[43] Herskovits, on the one hand, affirmed the reprise of Africanisms in the openly expressive nature of black worship in, for example, the use of antiphonality, the "call and response" motif in the music, confessional utterances, sermons and litanies of black worship. Frazier, on the other hand, contended that the trauma of enslavement, the Middle Passage and the brutal conditions to which the slaves were subjected on this side of the Atlantic were sufficient to erase nearly all historical memory of their experiences in Africa. I will not rehash the Herskovits-Frazier debate on Africanisms, neither in degree nor in kind. Rather, I will indicate some of the cultural-anthropological, theological-anthropological and political implications of the retentions for African Americans.

As an aspect of worship the phenomenon of "shouting" (which black theologian James Cone describes as "religious ecstasy")[44] has inspired debate about its relative value to the community. Proto-womanist, anthropologist and folklorist Zora Neale Hurston explains the African origins of shouting and its privatistic appropriation in the American context:

> There can be little doubt that shouting is a survival of the African "possession" by the gods. In Africa it is sacred to the priesthood or acolytes, in America it has become generalized. The implication is the same, however, it is a sign of special favor from the spirit that it chooses to drive out the individual consciousness temporarily and use the body for its expression.[45]

Generalizing from Hurston's cultural-anthropological perspective, the contextual reappropriation of spirit possession by African American Christians connotes the slave community's search for empowerment by the Holy Spirit. It is an example not only of how they created a distinctive culture and identity for themselves, but also of how they contributed to the *American* cultural identity as it was being shaped and reshaped in the privatistic evangelical ethos.[46] In the relative openness of evangelical worship the phenomenon of shouting was/is common among charismatic whites as well, because evangelical preachers required/require an emphatic "Yes!" to the salvific power of Christ, to the redemption and release presumably wrought in the event of the Atonement. Moreover, the stress on individual conversion invited/invites a melodramatic response. Nonetheless, as Cone states:

> White intellectuals often identify shouting in the black church with similar events in white churches, trying to give a common sociological and psychological reason for the phenomenon. Such an approach is . . . grossly misleading . . . How is it possible to speak of a common sociological and psychological reason for religious ecstasy among blacks and whites when they have radically different social and political environments, thereby creating different psychological and religious orientations? It is absurd . . . to contend that the Ku Klux Klansman and the black person who escaped him are shouting for the same or similar reasons in their

respective church services. Because whites and blacks have different historical and theological contexts out of which their worship services arise, they do not shout for the same reasons.[47]

Shouting among the slaves and their descendants was/is literally and figuratively a *seizure* of human agency and artistic freedom, a melodramatic response to the absurdity of their life conditions. Frequently derided for its melodramatic character, this seizure of agency and freedom, albeit within a given structure of religiosity, has informed nearly all liturgical aspects of black Christian communions in and since slavery. Hurston affirms the artistic intent of black worshiping communities:

> Beneath the seeming informality of religious worship there is a set formality. Sermons, prayers, moans and testimonies have their definite forms. The individual may hang as many new ornaments upon the traditional form as he likes, but the audience would be disagreeably surprised if the form were abandoned. Any new and original elaboration is welcomed, however, and this brings out the fact that all religious expression among Negroes is regarded as art, and ability is recognized as definitely as in any other art. The beautiful prayer receives the accolade as well as the beautiful song. It is merely a form of expression which people generally are not accustomed to think of as art.[48]

It is generally conceded that African American Christians founded a movement within a movement on the privatistic framework of evangelical spirituality. Yet it is certain that the slaves did not come empty-handed to the process of owning Christianity. They came with their own beliefs, customs and self-understandings in relationship to God. Some converts sought to maintain the communal impetus in African cultural mores and oral traditions through storytelling and distinctive preaching, and by inventively employing the call-and-response motif in their music to express their existential predicament.[49] However filtered their former customs may have become over time, they can yet provide cultural identity, sustenance and continuity—in short, *power*—for black Christians, to the extent that they willingly connect with the communal impetus in their African heritage. The "ring shout," for example, was a cultic ceremony done in a counter-clockwise dance fashion in various places in Africa.[50] The "holy dance" (characteristic of worship in "sanctified" churches) and the *toye-toye* (a communal, celebratory dance of southern Africans) are modern adumbrations of the ring shout, which signal times of refreshing and empowerment for the people of God. Similarly, openly expressive praise reflects back on black spirituality in

slave society, which was conditioned not merely by the relative openness of evangelical spirituality but also, perhaps fundamentally, by African peoples' penchant for art-making. The late Father Engelbert Mveng,
a Cameroonian theologian, Jesuit priest and activist in the African
negritude movement, described African art as

> a cosmic liturgy and a religious language . . . [that establish] a per-
> manent link between the destiny of humanity and that of the cos-
> mos . . . and [that] enable human beings to examine the visage of
> the cosmos and read of the names of those who are allied with life
> and those who are not.[51]

Mveng, who was a student of European and African art, and was
himself an *artiste extraordinaire*, stated that, although there is no universal understanding of what is constitutive of art, African art consistently
celebrates the "victory of life over death" and reflects the degree to
which art and art-making must be regarded as more than optional, having social and political exigency for those who are habituated to the
threat of imminent death. Certainly this was the case for the African
slaves, who, with few opportunities for uncircumscribed self-expression,
generated distinctive, melodramatic liturgics, stretching their spiritual
agency and bespeaking a critical awareness of their alliance with life in
the midst of a world controlled by those who were not so allied. Like
the melodramatic rhetoric and practices of the earliest Christians, their
worship embodied a posture of resistance to acculturation and expressed
their determination to control their own spiritual destinies rather than
to allow themselves to be controlled by the imperial powers. For the
persecuted believers in the first century, and for African Americans
during and since slavery, the significance of worship, conceived as art
and art-making, lay/lies in its power to refresh and strengthen the community for the protracted struggle between life and death.[52]

During slavery black peoples' continued association with Africa and
all things African, concomitant with white disparagement of the same,
provided rationales for the justification of slavery and Christianization
as antidotes to paganism. This reaction to African religions is consonant
with Christian triumphalism; yet, by narcissistically (or not at all) refer-
encing the historical antecedents of Christian antipathy to other religions (namely, persecution and martyrdom), the white, male control-
lers of religious discourse have convinced nearly everyone of the
inferiority of all non-Christian religions, especially African ones. An
unfortunate theological-anthropological implication of this posture contributing to low self-esteem among African American Christians is the
persistent belief that the people from whom they derive and who look
like them have contributed nothing to Western Christianity. Africans

are well-represented among the early Christian martyrs, ascetics and early church fathers. Tertullian and Cyprian were from Carthage, Origen from Alexandria, Augustine from Thagaste and Hippo, all cities of North Africa. It is presumed by most European scholars that North Africa in the patristic era was multiracial, and thus the simple fact that they are North Africans neither proves nor disproves their blackness. Yet eurocentric scholars and artists refuse to examine their assumptions and admit the possibility that they were *black* Africans. Regardless of which race one ascribes to these thinkers, it is important to affirm that they were Africans. This has implications for how their work is to be interpreted. For example, the fact that African theological anthropologies have a communal focus and traditionally place humanity at the summit of creation[53] signals the need to redeem Augustine from Western interpreters who make him a champion of individual salvation and an opponent of human agency and freedom.

Jeremiah Wright proposes that yet another infelicitous consequence of Christian exclusivity is that some *African Americans* are convinced of the inferiority of African tribal religions and African retentions.[54] Although I have attested to the keenness of Wheatley's hermeneutical insight, it is nevertheless distressing that she used such self-abnegating language to describe her former religious preparation in witnessing sacramentally to the character and creativity of God as a Christian. A little more than a century later W.E.B. Du Bois derided the Africanism of "shouting" among black Christians, referring to it as "the frenzy."[55] The syncretistic practices of blacks have caused still others to question whether African American Christianity is in fact Christian or if African retentions and other elements of slave religion caused it to become something altogether different from what the founder intended. In his book *Black Religion* Joseph Washington described "Negro religion" as a "mess of pottage," precluded from genuine Christian engagement because its "problems of inheritance" stunted its development.[56] This pole of the debate obfuscates the already hybridized nature of the Christian religion. It belies the African foundations of the central myth, which draws from the Osiris/Isis/Horus cycle of myths out of Egypt to tell its tale of a dying God and a rising Son, and it draws as well from Jewish sacrificial tradition to tell of a Lamb "slain from the foundation of the world" to evoke the sacred memory of the Israelites' escape from slavery in Egypt. Thus, to the extent that African Americans accept a de-historicized Christianity to inform their appreciation of themselves, they are culturally disempowered. Recent black theologies, African and African American, affirm the dynamic, organismic nature of religious tradition.[57] Some have explored African religions and retentions for the value of their cultural and political witness and the difference they make for the proclamation of the gospel. I agree that, to the extent slave religion kept

Africanisms alive, Christianity has been culturally and spiritually en-
riched. Although the slaves and their descendants did not retain their
customs in toto, their filtered customs transformed Christianity in the
American context, as Christianity transformed Osirian and Jewish myths,
as Judaism transformed Babylonian myths, and so on.

Through brute force, paternalistic compromise and the hermeneutics of sacrifice, European Americans called upon African Americans to
surrender their labor, their agency and, perhaps most critically, their
identity. The issue of identity is captured in a question posed by one of
the most poignant spirituals ever to emerge out of the antebellum period:

> Lord, how come me here?
> Lord, how come me here?
> Lord, how come me here?
> I wish I never wuz born.
>
> Dere ain't no freedom here.
> Dere ain't no freedom here.
> Dere ain't no freedom here.
> I wish I never wuz born.
>
> Dey treat me so mean here.
> Dey treat me so mean here.
> Dey treat me so mean here.
> I wish I never wuz born.
>
> Dey sol' my chillun away.
> Dey sol' my chillun away.
> Dey sol' my chillun away.
> I wish I never wuz born.

Although the rejoinder paints the slaves in a faithless light, they continued to search for religious meaning in the inimical contexts of their
lives and to try to make sense out of the cross they bore. The plight of
the slaves informed their search, which was enabled in part by paternalistic compromise. Nevertheless, insight for the successful negotiation of
their needs for survival, liberation and self-expression came from the
whole of their experience. All of the religious and theological impulses
that shaped American religious consciousness were sources in the development of slave religion, including the proprietary understanding of
religion fostered in covenant theology and the doctrinal commitments
of Evangelicalism (in opposition to Deism). The same liturgical rites,
disciplinary codes, theological formulae and creeds that shaped white

evangelical piety informed black spirituality. Out of these came social, legal and moral codes of conduct that devolved upon the disingenuous imposition of the hermeneutics of sacrifice.

The focus on the cross of Jesus in evangelical hymnody remains a singularly important means by which the hermeneutics of sacrifice is culturally transmitted:

> Oh! precious is the flow
> that makes me white as snow;
> No other fount I know
> Nothing but the blood of Jesus!

Despite the culturally abnegating language in this and other evangelical hymns, African Americans substantively deepened the import of the evangelical focus on the Atonement by relating Jesus' story to the story/stories of their lives. With this premise, citing Hurston's sermon,[58] womanist ethicist Katie Cannon attests to the theodical, self-affirming, creation-affirming intent in black people's embrace of evangelical theology, exegeting this confession, "He died for our sins, wounded in the house of His friends":

> This fundamental religious lore embodying African American people's understanding of evil and suffering implies that human sins committed against humanity are in flagrant opposition to Divine Goodness. The evil that we do unto one another inflicts wounds not only on Jesus but on all of creation. The mountains fall to their rocky knees and tremble like a beast. The veins of the earth bleed. The geological strata falls loose and the chamber of hell explodes. In "The Wounds of Jesus" the redemption story begins with creation and ends with consummation at Calvary.[59]

Through worship as *resistance art* the slave community testified to the existence of an immanent, embattled God, identifying the Divine Warrior with Jesus, finding in his message and his example worthy reasons for which to live and die. In response to evangelical hymn writer Isaac Watts's query, *Are Ye Soldiers of the Cross?*, they sang, and their descendants still sing *We Are Climbing Jacob's Ladder, Soldiers of the Cross, I Am on the Battle-field for My Lord* and *I'm a Soldier in the Army of the Lord.* Following the slaves' example, African American worshiping communities in postmodernity find pause to celebrate both the embattled God and the ongoing "human adventure under the gaze of God"[60] in a world still dominated by "those who are not" allied with life. What persuaded them to become or remain Christians? It was not academic reflection on the stultifying dogmas of Evangelicalism, which understood the Atone-

ment as *the* culminating event in the divine plan for the *spiritual* salvation of humankind yet had little or equivocal regard for the temporal
plight of whole groups of suffering people. Rather, it was the slaves'
ability to relate their collective story to the story of the cross. The existential contradiction between the desire to be righteous and undeserved
suffering generated the theodicy project, which continues to have currency among black and womanist theologians who, as progeny of slaves,
work diligently to end the unremitted suffering in their communities.

Nevertheless, I did not explicate mission theology (the interplay between Evangelicalism and Deism) and its effect on the American religious psyche in order to privilege its assertions or assert its primacy in
defining African American spirituality. Rather, I sought to accent the
proscribed nature of black existence, to which the slaves, free blacks
and their abolitionist friends were compelled to respond with all the
resources at their disposal, including Christianity as mediated through
the creeds and as posited by southern catechists, including their intellectual faculties and native piety and practices. The slaves and their
descendants transmuted all the raw elements of their experience into a
unique theological formulation that enabled them to express themselves
in a melodramatic manner consistent with their alliance with life, bespeaking the endemicity of art to their African souls. That said, I do not
wish to imply that their art-in-worship merely involved/involves human agency, or that it necessarily entailed/entails sham or pretense,
especially where it regards the phenomenon of shouting. Consistent
with the African conception of Spirit possession, the propensity to shout
comes from the contemplation of God's goodness and power as they
manifest themselves in the lives of devotees, that is, it comes from the
fact of *being seized* and empowered by the immensity that is God.

In light of white brutality in the administration of chattel slavery,
mission theology, vis-à-vis paternalism and the hermeneutics of sacrifice, (1) emboldened whites in making rank assertions about the Source
of their power, and (2) accommodated their perceptions about their
own morality. It was these to which the slaves responded, *theodically*
reckoning with white idolatry in their spirituality, liturgy and God-talk.
All of these things assisted the African American community in devis-
ing a critique of white Christianity and facilitated the emergence of the
Black Church.

Slave religion challenged the paternalistic thesis; perhaps that meant
singularly challenging slaveholders' understanding of themselves as
God's appointed agents. Nuancing God's *sovereignty* as a dimension of
theodicy is key to understanding African American spirituality that
emerged out of this ethos of idolatry. It begs the question of who, indeed, has power. Overwhelmingly, the slaves and their descendants
ascribed power to One who was, like them, situated in a context of

idolatry, who similarly suffered and bled and died and who, as they had in their African past, celebrated the victory of life over death: Jesus, God-Incarnate, God-Embattled, God-manifesting-love to the weak and downtrodden and to the undeserving as well. These descriptors, all of which derive from scripture, are the points of identification with Jesus that informed their ways of witnessing to the world *that* God is, *who* God is and, especially, who God is *not*. Slave religion was born of a creative impulse; it was a means for black people to express themselves artistically and to make of themselves acting subjects among whites who thwarted their agency. Informed by the hermeneutics of sacrifice inherited from Christian tradition and imposed by slave catechists, slave religion generated a distinctly African American love ethic as *theodical relief* from white oppression, wittingly and unwittingly opposing the idolatry inherent in the paternalistic ethos of the "Christian" slavocracy.

BLACK RADICALISM

Many slaves readily connected the institution of slavery and their ill-treatment to white religious duplicity. They saw clearly the connections between Jesus' story and their reality, yet chose willingly to walk in the way of sacrifice by maintaining an ethic of love in an ethos of injustice. Some were able to level critical voices against white Christians. As one female slave stated to her mistress concerning the slaveholders' morality in relation to the slaves' morality, "You no' holy. We be holy. You in no state of salvation."[61] This assessment was based not on imputed righteousness ("justification by grace through faith" [Rom 3:24]) but on the innocence of the slaves and the empirical evidence of their oppression by whites. The theme of innocence was an obvious link between the stories of the slaves and that of Jesus. In the narrative *Life of William Grimes*, the protagonist, having been falsely accused of stealing, compared his pending fate to that of Golgotha-bound Jesus, alluding to Jesus' innocence and affirming his own:

> When I considered him accusing me of stealing, when I was so innocent, and had endeavored to make him satisfied by every means in my power, that I was so, but he still persisted in disbelieving me, I then said to myself, if this thing is done in a green tree what must be done in a dry? I forgave my master in my own heart for all this, and prayed to God to forgive him and turn his heart.[62]

Grimes quoted Luke 23:28-31. There Jesus prophesies the doom of his persecutors, exhorting the crowds who are bewailing his pending crucifixion to "weep not" for him but for themselves. Like Jesus, Grimes was able to forgive his persecutor and to demonstrate the power of the love ethic to sustain him in his personal distress and give him a "morally superior vantage point" relative to his oppressor. But as Raboteau notes:

> Grimes is, of course, alluding to the sacrifice of Christ and identifying himself with Jesus, the archetypal "Suffering Servant," who spoke the words concerning green and dry wood on his way to death on Calvary. From this morally superior vantage point, Grimes is able to forgive his master. Note, however, the *element of threat* in the question: "if this thing is done in a green tree [to the innocent] what must be done in a dry [to the guilty]?" *Those who are guilty, those who persecute the innocent, will be judged and punished. The threat of judgment becomes more explicit when it is recalled that the full context of the words that Grimes quotes is a prophecy of destruction.*[63]

Significantly, the passage Grimes quoted comes after the cross has been deputed to Simon of Cyrene ("Black Simon"); because of its sacrificial implications it attests to African Americans' apprehension of the love ethic that ostensibly defines Christianity. Raboteau cites Grimes's story as an example of slave spirituality that affirmed the role of forgiveness as a crucial element in human redemption and that was capable of accommodating itself to traditional beliefs informed by the hermeneutics of sacrifice. Yet he also exposes the double-edged nature of Jesus' and Grimes's inquiries, which raise the issue of justice (as fairness) as a central component of the ethical grid of Christianity and of African American religious thought. As in Richard Allen's discourse masking black rage, Grimes's narrative indicates that, although the love ethic counseled sacrifice and forgiveness, it also raised prospects for justice, which, in that context, meant freedom or liberation. For Jesus, it meant vindication. If the Roman proverb "Quot servi, tot hostes" (All slaves are enemies) is true, the critical nature of Grimes's inquiry demonstrates that black radicalism is, and always has been, endemic to the project of black liberation and is the second edge of the sword of whatever Truth is to be found in the African American love ethic.

The love-justice ethic has deeply influenced the spirituality of all constituencies of the African American community engaged in the religious/theological enterprise in and since slavery. Accommodationist, pacifist and radical proponents of the love ethic have stressed two possibilities for achieving justice: (1) as that to be attained in the hereafter, or (2) as that to be dispensed in the here and now.

In order to cope with the realities of slave existence some slaves worked within the system. They averred that although slavery was cruel, "being placed in that situation, to repine was useless; we must submit to our fate, and bear up, as well as we can, under the cruel treatment of our despotic tyrants."[64] Like the hapless Grimes, accommodationists in and since slavery awaited the realization of freedom and justice in the hereafter. Others actively agitated for them in the here and now. Remaining pacifist, they proffered a different interpretation of the love-justice ethic. While the former countenanced love in order to shore up their passivity, evincing a *sacrificial* theology, self-understanding and praxis, the latter counseled the love-justice ethic as a way of *sacramentally* witnessing to the goodness and the power of God, evincing God's proleptic activity in their persons. Pacifist activists did not discount eschatological dimensions of the question of justice but worked to eradicate injustice through nonviolent means.

In fairness, *sacrificial* may not be the right nomenclature for the slaves accommodating words and actions that, on surface, cannot be deemed critical. Yet, as the conservatism of the Black Church suggests, it is clear that many of their descendants (1) do not acknowledge that Christianity is subject to a history of interpretation that perpetuates their subjugation, and (2) have internalized the hermeneutics of sacrifice in a manner devoid of reference to their social, political and economic locations. What appears to be accommodationist in the context of slavery often portended *survival* and enabled *self-expression*, both of which are part of the black liberation project and even foundational to it. Frequently, as a strategy, it belied the slaves' duplicity, covering up their engagement in illicit or radical activities. But as a religious premise, the accommodationist attitude (1) affirmed redemption as a promise to be realized eschatologically, which moreover (2) betokened the sovereignty of God and (3) faithfully appropriated the belated victory in the story of Jesus.

Radical activists sought to destroy inequities in the system through resistance and rebellion, proffering armed struggle against whites as a legitimate option for blacks in pursuit of freedom and justice. Nat Turner (1800-1831), Gabriel Prosser (d. 1800) and Denmark Vesey (d. 1822) emulated the messianic character of Christ as "protagonist for social change,"[65] mounting insurrections that, for them, posed no contradiction to their Christianity. Like Jesus and the martyrs, these men were betrayed and subsequently slain for their commitment to the cause of their downtrodden people. Similarly, Harriet Tubman, a Zion Methodist, saw no conflict between her faith and her activities as a conductor of the Underground Railroad, as a scout for Union forces and as a participant in numerous slave revolts. Unlike Turner, Prosser and Vesey, she was able to thwart her intended martyrdom by evading capture. As heirs of evangelical biblicism as well as the covenantal theology of the early settlers, these African Americans drew parallels from their collective experience and that of the Israelites, eliciting the participation of a broad base of African Americans in the insurrections they mounted to throw off the yokes of their oppressors. Vesey, in particular, who was also associated with the Methodist church (AME), employed the stories of the Exodus and the conquest of Palestine in order to support an emphatically Christian radicalism that subsisted in a distinct identification with Africa and an ethic informed by the biblical proposition that human beings are made in the image of God and have an inherent right to be free.[66]

The radical ethic necessitated revolt; it did not thereby countermand the love ethic. Avowedly radical activists sought vigorously not to separate the love ethic from demands for justice in the here and now. Rather, their particular brand of activism provided an alternative impetus for the love ethic: it was to be focused on the black community itself. Although this focus is generally associated with twentieth-century nationalist ideologues, David Walker had a thoroughly historicized consciousness that presaged the development of black nationalism, the black intellectual tradition and black theology. Although he counseled slaves to be circumspect until the most opportune times to take back their divinely bestowed freedom from slaveholders, Walker made it abundantly clear that he was counseling neither passivity nor pacifism:

> It is not to be understood here, that I mean for us to wait until God shall take us by the hair of our heads and drag us out of abject wretchedness and slavery, nor do I mean to convey the idea for us to wait until our enemies shall make preparations, and call us to seize those preparations, take it away from them, and put everything before us to death, in order to gain our freedom which God has given us. For you must remember that we are men as well as they.[67]

Walker was among the first to identify black self-hatred as a hindrance to black unity and empowerment. In his *Appeal to the Colored Citizens of the World* he vehemently denounced miscegenation as a barrier to African American men's and women's solidarity in the struggle against their collective suffering:

> I would wish candidly before the Lord, to be understood that I would not give a *pinch of snuff* to be married to any white person I ever saw in all the days of my life. And I do say it, that the black man, or man of colour, who will leave his own colour (provided he can get one, who is good for any thing) and marry a white woman, to be a double slave to her, just because she is *white*, ought to be treated by her as he surely will be, viz, as a NIGER *[sic]*!!![68]

Walker condemned as "*ignorant* and *deceitful*" the actions of a slave woman who reportedly helped an injured slave driver regroup in time to rally support for the recapture of several escaped slaves. He astutely connected the woman's pastoral instincts to the biblical hermeneutics of sacrifice: "I cannot think it was anything but servile deceit, combined with the most gross ignorance: for we must remember that *humanity, kindness* and the *fear of the Lord,* does not consist in protecting *devils.*"[69] To dispute this kind of thinking he declared that the enemies of justice ought to be destroyed, because they are enemies of God. Affirming human agency, confirming justice as that to be dispensed in the here and now, Walker added even more pointedly:

> If you commence, make sure work–do not trifle, for they will not trifle with you–they want us for their slaves, and think nothing of murdering us in order to subject us to that wretched condition– therefore, if there is an attempt made by us, kill or be killed.[70]

In and since slavery black radical ideologies have been based essentially upon religious premises and have evoked religious responses from the African American community. Nonetheless, activists in nearly every social arena sought to demonstrate the fallacy of assumptions of black ontological, spiritual and intellectual inferiority by addressing or uncovering the historical forces that precipitated and even necessitated black suffering. A number of thinkers advanced seminal critiques of the American economic system. Walker's *Appeal* was itself an early denunciation of agrarian capitalism[71] that helped abolitionist leaders to channel their activities into more militant responses.[72] Although his views are most often unflatteringly labeled as accommodationist, Booker T. Washington (1856-1915) sharply criticized black delimitation within the American labor force, which was beset both by immigrants and creeping industrialization, yet not the capitalist system itself.[73] Elijah Muhammad, (1897-1975) on the other hand, strongly identified with the nationalist cause, yet similarly posited an alternative economic impetus for black people, situated *within* the parameters of capitalism.[74] This economic and political conservatism was in keeping with the Muslim belief in the eschatological deliverance of Allah. Today, the Nation of Islam under the leadership of Louis Farrakhan subscribes to black self-help through entrepreneurship, in imitation of the American economic system.[75] In light of its historically conservative political engagement and the stated purpose of the recently held Million Man March on Washington (16 October 1995), *atonement,* I would argue that the Nation of Islam sees itself as a *sacramental* witness to the sovereignty of God in a still idolatrous American context.[76] Although many black women supported the March, still others viewed the organizers' renewed focus on manhood as yet another in a series of historical attempts to sacrifice black women on the altar of black male egoism.[77] The use of the language of *atonement* and the appeal to black women to stay at home in support of the men invoked the spirit of surrogacy, which is, according to premier womanist theologian Delores Williams, that structure of domination that characterizes black women's oppression in and since slavery.[78]

Throughout their history, African American women have engaged in the art of survival and in acts of resistance, seeking political redress for their oppression through abolitionist activity, through agitation for both civil rights and women's rights, and through their responses to the peremptory challenges of Black Power advocates. In white male-dominated America, white women, too, agitated for change in their social and legal status, linking their movement with black liberation struggles and injecting moral authority in their bid for suffrage and women's rights. Lucretia Mott and Elizabeth Cady Stanton–along with Frances Ellen Watkins Harper, Sarah Douglass, Harriet Forten Purvis, Margaretta Forten, Sojourner Truth, Sarah Parker Remond, Mary Ann Shadd Cary, Frederick Douglass, Charles Remond and William Lloyd Garrison–were staunch supporters of abolition *and* women's right to vote, a right that was also denied to black men within the American racist, patriarchal setting.[79] However, in the postwar frenzy to garner additional votes from the southern electorate, the constitutional right to vote was extended first to black males. At the opening convention of the Equal Rights Association in 1867, Stanton repudiated black male suffrage at the expense of white women with racist venom, referring to black men as "Sambos" whose "hour" had come.[80]

Some black women within the abolitionist and women's movements accepted black male suffrage to their exclusion because racism was the prima facie cause of their degradation; most notably, Frances Ellen Watkins Harper viewed the extension of the vote to black men as a strategic step toward the empowerment of all black people, supporting what was called the "Negro suffrage" side of the debate.[81] Sojourner Truth reluctantly agreed to this strategy as well; still, as one of the more daring members of the National Women's Suffrage Association, she made an unsuccessful attempt to vote in the 1860s.[82] Through subsequent machinations state and local government officials and white citizens' councils in southern states aborted black male suffrage. For black women struggling to give birth to a "well baby"–to a viable communal existence–the focus on black "manhood first" in the press to gain citizenship was the "beginning of sorrows" (Mt 24:8; Mk 13:8, AV) engendering sexist division in the African American community.

Sojourner Truth is an excellent example of a pacifist whose spirituality did not inhibit but rather reinforced her criticism of the hierarchical social and political realities of her day. After her release from slavery in 1827, she became actively involved in the abolitionist and women's movements, speaking extemporaneously from platforms shared with (fellow Zion Methodist) Frederick Douglass and others. With the passage of the Fugitive Slave Act in 1850 and the handing down of the infamous Dred Scott Decision (1856), in which the Supreme Court decided that black people, not being citizens, have no rights that whites are bound by law to respect, Douglass despaired of any hope in the prospects for black freedom. Sojourner Truth, from one such audience, leveled him with a one-line sermon: "Frederick! Is God dead?"[83] Truth believed that the "freedom movement was the secular counterpart of spiritual salvation."[84] She was as active in the struggle for women's rights as she was in the struggle for African Americans' rights. Although the record of her work is piecemeal, there remain extant letters, speeches and anecdotes recorded by friends and co-workers, from which emerges the image of a woman of dramatic and powerful faith, who testified as a *sacramental* witness to the goodness and sovereignty of God, against countervailing notions of patriarchal and racial supremacy in antebellum and postbellum America.

THE BLACK CHURCH

In *The Social Teaching of the Black Churches* Peter Paris states:

During the past two decades, black scholarship has exhibited a revisionist character. This contrasts with earlier scholarship which tended to focus primarily on the impact of severe environmental forces on the race. In spite of the usefulness of such studies, they nevertheless depicted the victimization of the race and wholly disregarded the way in which blacks have sought to change their environment. Since victimization implies a condition of passivity, acquiescence, and forced obedience, the "new breed" of scholars has been diligently demonstrating that blacks have functioned in every historical period as agents of change in spite of the extreme environmental constraints upon them. Their capacity to find alternative ways of thinking and acting in such situations evidences the tenacity and resiliency of the human spirit in encounter with life-threatening conditions. The preservation of the power to think and act, rather than merely obey and adapt, is necessary for the preservation of human life per se.[85]

Without question the Black Church has been that institutional vehicle by which African Americans have demonstrated their power of being, thinking and acting out of the theodical, human agency–affirming intent that Paris described. What started as the "invisible institution" in the brush arbors ("hush harbors") of the southern slavocracy and extended to the free African societies in the north was to be the only *concrete* benefit realized from paternalistic compromise with slaveholders.

Seven major denominations comprise historically black churches, exclusively controlled by African Americans.[86] In their study C. Eric Lincoln and Lawrence Mamiya omit persons in predominantly black congregations, albeit in white denominations, and smaller, independent black denominations. Building on the more inclusive work in the landmark study by Benjamin Mays and Joseph Nicholson,[87] I include all of these in my view of the Black Church as a body of believers with common practices and utterances that signify their collective apprehensions of the Divine and the attendant duties of humankind.[88] While I agree with Williams's assertion that the Black Church is "invisible,"[89] that, theologically speaking, its full reality is *not yet,* its historical function confirms its visibility and relevance on personal and communal levels. I *have* experienced proleptic manifestations of the Black Church on many worship occasions, in, for example, the singleness of purpose during prayers for the sick; in preaching moments that are peculiarly prophetic, poetic and inspiring; and in songs and testimonies, during which the confessional utterances that have sustained African Americans all along their collective journey are vocally recovered. I believe that within the confessional utterances, especially, may be discerned (1) that doctrine of God which is the distinctive theological focus of the Black Church and which demonstrates a theodical intent of the black Christian community; and (2) a doctrine of humanity that (a) assumes the moral onus is humankind's and (b) affirms a dialectical relationship between love and justice. These qualities are consistent with the prophetic tradition's views on the nature of God in the Israelite/Jewish and New Testament communities. Like them, African American Christians throughout their history affirmed that, in both the *doing* and *not doing* of love and justice, humans signify the nature of their acquaintance with God. The ethical import of the relationship between love and justice is reflected in the Early Christian and slave communities' need for justice (as fairness) and in their self-reflective capacities to temper their demands for justice with love for their enemies, consistent with synoptic presentations of the ethic of Jesus. Among African American Christians the spiritual and political aim of the love-justice ethic is the survival and liberation of the community, a colloquy of believers with accommodationist, pacifist and radical understandings of how they are to be achieved.

The Black Church *visible* has been a veritable stage on which African Americans could determine their particular roles in the cosmic drama as agents of love and justice. Its history is replete with examples attesting to its preeminence in advancing black peoples' spiritual and political liberation. Inspired by Richard Allen, James Varick, Frederick Douglass, Sojourner Truth, Henry McNeal Turner and others in the early development of Black Church and civic movements, black theologians in the 1950s and 1960s interpreted the biblical history of Israel and the ministry of Jesus as signs of God's intention for them to live in spiritual, ecclesial communion *and* in a just society:

> When blacks investigated their religious history, they were reminded that their struggle for political freedom did not begin in the 1950s and '60s, but had roots stretching back to the days of slavery. They were also reminded that their struggle for political justice in the United States had always been associated with their churches. Whether in the independent northern churches (AME, African Methodist Episcopal Zion, Baptist, etc.) or in the so-called invisible institution in the south (which merged with the independent black church after the Civil War) or as members of white denominations, black Christians have always known that the God of Moses and of Jesus did not create them to be slaves or second-class citizens.[90]

Nevertheless, the enduring Christian emphasis on "love" evinces the conservative theological underpinnings of the Black Church, as sourced by white Evangelicalism, in which the theme of love was often considered as a thing quite apart from the question of justice. As we saw in the Early American context, slaveholders preached the love-minus-justice ethic (the hermeneutics of sacrifice) to the slaves in order to foster in them passivity and a privatistic understanding of Christian faith and witness. Not many slaves accepted this signification of the gospel message but rather found in it the impetus to resist their oppression in forceful and often imaginative ways. After slavery and the era of Reconstruction ended, however, a "deradicalized"[91] Black Church appeared at a time when physical violence against blacks was at an all-time high and structural inequities became firmly entrenched in labor relations and social policy. Rayford Logan has referred to this period as the "nadir" of the black experience.[92] Little wonder if the majority of blacks responded to white oppression by incorporating the language and tenor of sacrifice in their liturgical expressions, outnumbered, out-resourced and incapable of formulating an adequate reaction to the violence of that epoch. This very fact informed King's radical ecclesiology in his own context, although his theology was laced with sacrificial language. Yet, as Cone has stated, "the acid test of any ecclesiological statement is whether it has taken sufficient account of the actual world in which liturgical confessions are made."[93] Many black worshipers in post-modernity utilize this type of language in their confessions and hymnody, not in an attempt to counterpose a pervasive sense of white violence, but in their attempts to apprehend the doctrines of evangelical Christianity.[94]

To some radical activists during and since slavery, evangelical Christianity was and is synonymous with black suffering and the individualism that hampers the development of black unity and nationhood. These are vital ideals if the practical goals of black liberation are to be achieved; that is, if African Americans are to stop their collective suffering and become self-determining, independent of the goodwill of whites. In the 1950s and 1960s, Malcolm X and Albert B. Cleage Jr. argued that the love ethic to which Martin Luther King Jr. appealed and to which he connected his movement evinced these conservative theological underpinnings of the Black Church. King and others in the Civil Rights movement advocated black empowerment through integration, nonviolence and broader economic participation within a religious ethos that honored the evangelical tenets of Christianity. Minister Malcolm and Cleage advocated black empowerment through separation and conscientization. They counseled responding to white violence with self-defense, and they favored economic independence through the payment of reparations to blacks for slavery. They regarded the church, the Black Church in particular—with its emphases on the cross/Atonement, conversion and shouting—as the major purveyor of insidious individualism. They preferred the communal impulse in the teachings of the Honorable Elijah Muhammad and Marcus Garvey, which was employed in other nationalist groups such as RAM (Revolutionary Action Movement) and the Black Panthers and in the socialist philosophy of Marxism.

Nevertheless, like King, other radical voices of that period knew that the most effective way to galvanize the community for social and political change was through the physical resource of the Black Church. Remaining *within* the church, they criticized black Christians' commitment to what was presumably the theology of the slaveholders. Despite the cogency of their critique, in the social and political upheavals that characterized the times, black theologians used the grand impetus of the Black Church–based Civil Rights movement to further their nationalistic agenda and develop more effective ways for African Americans to engage in thinking and talking about God, love and justice. In July 1966 the National Committee of Negro Churchmen (NCNC, later, NCBC—the National Committee of Black Churchmen) issued the first systematic response to the polarities manifesting in the Civil Rights and Black Power movements.

Curiously, although black theology's early proponents were concerned church leaders, the Black Church was presumed to be less a source in the construction of black theology because it (1) was conceived

as a response to the theology of white churches (which effectively counseled an apolitical agenda by ignoring the practical needs of oppressed
blacks); (2) was critical of the conservatism of the Black Church; and (3)
took shape as a discipline in the academy. Consequently, to those who
do not recognize that Evangelicalism furnished the raw material for black
theological reflection, black theology has made few inroads to the Black
Church that the church has adequately acknowledged. However, according to Cone:

> There are those who would say that black theology has nothing to
> do with the black church, because it is an academic discipline that
> is taught in seminaries and universities (mostly white) and thus
> unrelated to the spiritual and worshiping life of the black Chris-
> tian community. There are others who would say that black theol-
> ogy is the prophetic voice of the black church, calling it back to its
> liberating heritage, thereby enabling it to become a more effective
> instrument of black liberation. With these two sharply different
> versions of the importance of black theology to the black church,
> it is clear that some misunderstanding (if not antagonism) does
> exist regarding the acceptance of black theology in the black
> church.[95]

J. Deotis Roberts stated the dilemma of black theology more suc-
cinctly: "Black theology began in church and community. It has since
had its main seat in the academy. To the extent that black theology has
lost its strong anchor in the black church, it may be said to be uprooted
from its source of life."[96] Gayraud Wilmore argued that black theology
failed to become a mass movement because the elitism of the middle-
class black men articulating it prevented them from locating the "springs
of action in the religion of the masses,"[97] that is, in the *spiritual* resources
of the Black Church, as King had. During the first phase of the black
theology movement (1964-1969) black theologians were responding to
Washington's *Black Religion*, in which he questions the validity of syncretistic practices in the Black Church in light of its claim to be Christian. Wilmore states that the flurry of apologetic activity that issued forth
in the NCNC statement really betokened the entrenched shame that
black theologians had for their history, heritage and perceived lack of
an intellectual tradition. Although the statement called for an infusion
of black power to radicalize the Black Church's deeply Christian commitment, its authors could not wholly break with the evangelical impulses they criticized relative to the integrationist movement because it
had likewise fundamentally shaped their understanding of the faith.

Black theology is a product of the radical impulses that have always
been present in the Black Church visible and which have underlain or

accompanied the community's perennial attempts to reconcile faith in the goodness and power of God with the seemingly limitless capacity of whites to make black people suffer. On this view, since black theology is a theology *of* the church, black theologians need to mine the insights of the Black Church in order to represent faithfully its love-and-justice-affirming traditions. Cecil Cone posed this critique of black theology as articulated by his brother, James Cone, stating that he had not adequately sourced the religion of the Black Church but relied too heavily on the insights of European "classical" theology to articulate his agenda of liberation.[98] In his first attempts to rectify this Eurocentric bias Cone relied upon the musical traditions of the antebellum Black Church, as in reflections on the hidden meaning of the spirituals in slave culture, to confirm the existence of critical dimensions in black faith.[99]

Although the recovery of meanings has proven invaluable to the African American community because these meanings affirmed black agency against countervailing images of servile passivity, this emphasis on the spirituals has left untapped other insights of the Black Church since slavery that attest to its critical acumen. To wit, the distinctive confessional utterances found in black hymnody, reprised in song after song, have not been exegeted.[100] In addition, although the Black Church is very Bible-centered, its particular history of interpretation has not been lifted up. This task is vital to the further development of black theology. Often scholars take for granted that African American Christians are bound to one meaning of scriptural texts. Yet this is not simply a problem of black epistemology. African American biblical scholar William H. Myers notes that source critical and other Western hermeneutical approaches to biblical interpretation emphasize the notion that a text has only one legitimate meaning, usually conceived as *the* orthodox meaning.[101] These meanings are authenticated to predetermine the way biblical texts can be interpreted and appropriated; thus, Western, liberal interpretative tradition is as proscriptive as that of other literalists. This contributes to an acute "hermeneutical dilemma" for African American exegetes. While black biblical scholars affirm the value of the tools they have garnered, at the same time Western approaches exalt one world view over all others and are not able to help black people address the questions raised in their contexts. Myers proposes an "evolving solution" to this hermeneutical dilemma.

As part of this evolving solution I propose the use of confessional utterances to unlock hidden meanings of texts for African Americans. They may confirm the traditional meanings of texts, as in the saying "God is good—all the time," which is consistent with the biblical poet's understanding that the "steadfast love of God never ceases" (Lam 3:22). Or they may be text-amplifying in a way that demonstrates theodical intentions, or they may be human agency-affirming. For example, the biblical exhortation to "watch and pray" is restated time and again in the Black Church as "watch, *fight* and pray." Others reflect on the quest for justice in human relations: "(There is a bright side, somewhere) *Don't you stop until you find it.*" A favorite contingency employed by many African Americans in sermons and songs is the statement, "*If* you live right, heaven belongs to you." African Americans continuously affirm the sovereignty of God with utterances such as "God never fails"; "God will make a way out of no way"; "God is God all by Himself." Some of these utterances are not unique to the Black Church; they may have a common origin in white evangelical hymnody and confession. But in the Black Church they are theodical statements that reject the attempts of self-made gods to usurp God's dominion in black peoples' lives. Generated in an ethos of idolatry and injustice they function as mantras to focus the spiritual energies of the black body of Christ, and to reassure the black oppressed that white oppressors do not have all power and that white oppression does not have the last say. They are faith statements indicating their belief that God will take care of their needs expeditiously. They are denials of their ultimate dependency upon whites.

Consonant with Dwight Hopkins's proposal that black theologians display a renewed emphasis on black religion as a source for doing theology,[102] I suggest that there are many more such artifacts that can be lifted up out of the Black Church. Exegeted, these can become sources in the fortification of black theology, among them: "Jesus is a heart-fixer, mind-regulator, habit-breaker"; "He may not come when you want him but he'll be right on time"; "He's alright." These confessional utterances capture the ambiguity with which African Americans understand Jesus' relationship to the Divine and the delicacy with which they seek to protect the Divine reputation.

In its incipient and modern manifestations the Black Church visible was a forum and a point of departure for addressing the community's spiritual and political concerns. Despite the Black Church's remarkable struggle to affirm black agency, it has not waged theodical war against the literalism of the Bible on behalf of African American women with the same consistency. Rather, as the womanist critique of the Black Church has pointed out, the male leaders of its hierarchy have utilized the same exclusionary tactics that slavery apologists for white churches used to maintain docility among the slaves, appealing to the hermeneutics of sacrifice and resorting to literalism to preclude black women's full participation in church and society.[103]

Like the slaveholding church, the Black Church in postmodernity has implemented paternalistic compromise with women, who comprise as much as 85 percent of its constituency. Recognizing this, many, if not most, of the denominations have relaxed their policies concerning women's participation by allowing them to function in offices other than the pastorate. This role is usually reserved for charismatic men who govern on the basis of the messianic expectations that the Black Church has historically placed on its leaders. As a womanist, I favor non-messianic models of ministry; nonetheless, the policy is punitive to those women who have been gifted and called to such positions of leadership. Moreover, the focus on black "manhood first" in the churches repeats oppression in the community by disregarding the ontological implications of black women's suffering. Such a focus denies that the rapacity of sexism is as insidious as racism. Black men who employ this stratagem for empowerment collude with culture and society to obfuscate the psychosocial, economic and political effects of black men's suffering on black women. Falsely dichotomizing the collective experience of black oppression, they elevate the concept of "manhood" to the level of ultimate concern. Thus, in the praxis of paternalistic sexism, black male leaders in the church emulate the idolatrous values of the dominant white culture.[104]

I have discerned at least two negative implications of paternalistic compromise with women for the Black Church in postmodernity. First, although the Black Church is "invisible" or "not yet," there is the increasing danger of perishing relevance for the Black Church visible. In *The Prophethood of Black Believers* J. Deotis Roberts describes the church as the "organ of the spirit."[105] He avers that "the mission and ministry of the black churches" is to "provide a powerful means to enrich, empower, and provide hope for the black poor and all conditions of black folk."[106] Because the Black Church does not exist for itself, it must continually ask itself if it is being faithful to the aims of the One and ones for whom it does exist. The spiritual heritage of survival and liberation in the stories of African American men *and* women is an appropriate starting point for the search for ongoing relevance and credibility in a context of oppression.

The second negative implication of the Black Church's paternalistic compromise with women (and black women's acceptance of it) is that the sexist conditions it sustains create existential and moral dilemmas for women, often forcing them to choose between the sanctity of their humanity and their love for the church. Sometimes it is difficult to adjudicate the demands of both because these issues conflate with the issues of survival, liberation and self-expression. Although these dilemmas can never be finally resolved, womanist theologians empower black women who work in the church through the injunction to love themselves, *regardless.* Early black theologians were relatively silent regarding sexism. Since it is also a theology *for* the church, black theology needs to bring to bear prophetic insights that derive from its engagement with other marginalized groups, both *within* and *outside* the Black Church and the African American community.

CONCLUSION

Paternalism in the slavocracy reproduced the idolatrous ethos of the Roman empire, which found its ultimate expression in the apotheosis of the emperor. The paternalistic thesis failed to take seriously the dehumanization of the slaves and the concomitant apotheosis of slaveholders in their own estimation. As Evangelicalism was a search among whites in the South for communal identity, some effect redounded to their relationships to black people, to the extent that they considered them human. I agree with Donald Mathews that the slaveholders' estimation of the economic tools at their command seduced them into thinking that they were God's appointed agents. I would say forthrightly that their estimation of *themselves* was tantamount to idolatry. The illusion of white transcendence—the self-delusion of entire peoples—was achieved and has been maintained through the use of force to arrogate every good thing of this life for white consumption (houses, land, mineral resources). It is reflected in their willingness to subdue everything (rainforests, oceans, creatures) and all peoples; in the way they use the institutions they have developed (banks, schools, churches) to maintain their privileges and deny them to others; and in their penchant for building lasting monuments to white supremacists in order to sacralize their memory and reinforce the notion of their everlasting goodness. To conspire to deny the humanity of whole peoples is to arrogate the authority of God. But that which is gratuitously asserted can be effectively denied. It is to this that the enslaved and marginalized blacks responded in the implicit theodicy of the love ethic generated in and propagated since slavery. Their responses had critical dimensions that sought to disabuse whites of their divine pretensions. In truth, the ability of blacks continuously to affirm God was an *anthropodicy* that black theologues generated because they wanted to believe in God's good intentions for them and sought to protect the notion of God's power and sovereignty.

Jesus, some said, "never said a mumblin' word" against the religious and political authorities who crucified him and persecuted his followers. Yet during slavery, Reconstruction, the era of Jim and Jane Crow and the rise of the Civil Rights and Black Power movements, many black Christian and non-Christian religious liberally embraced strategies of *resistance* in their confessional stances and political activism against white church-and-state-sanctioned exploitation. Some activists were pacifist, promoting the goal of liberation through peaceful engagement with whites. Others were radical, promoting black liberation by any means, including force, as circumstances demanded. The actions they undertook to ensure their survival and secure their freedom bespeak an attitude of faith in the rightness of their actions and in the providence of

God; of hope in the truthfulness of American justice claims; and of love for themselves and their humanity. But beyond an indefatigable attitude of faith, hope and love, their activism testifies to the thoroughgoing resentment that all African Americans hold toward their cross, the bars of which are slavery and discrimination. Moreover, it denotes the various and sundry ways they have sought remediation, while simultaneously maintaining the parallels between their suffering and that of Jesus, and overwhelmingly embracing the salvation proffered in him.

Despite black peoples' willingness to escape the fate of Jesus, the Crucified One, no single social, political, cultural or economic critique predominates in the African American religious community because any such critique is inseparable from the moral and theological issues of slavery, ongoing brutality and discrimination, and these issues are resolved variously by a diverse people. Nevertheless, a fortuitous consequence of the heightened political consciousness of African Americans effected by pacifist and radical black activists of the 1960s is that black theologians and womanist theologians entertain both eschatological and proleptic dimensions of the question of justice.

Chapter 3

The Scandal of the Cross

Reconciliation, Nationhood and Liberation
in Black Christology

Christianity has always insisted that the cross we bear precedes the crown we wear. To be a Christian, one must take up his cross, with all of its difficulties and agonizing and tension-packed contents and carry it until that very cross leaves its marks upon us and redeems us to that more excellent way which comes only through suffering.

— Martin Luther King Jr.

The crucifixion convinced the Disciples that the Nation was doomed to extinction. When they stood in the distance and looked at Jesus upon the cross, they were convinced that they had lost the only leader who could bring individuals together and make a Nation that could stand independent and free. So the Disciples were demoralized. They watched the crucifixion, and said, the movement is dead. The Nation can no longer exist. The only individual who had the power of revolutionary leadership has been killed. And they fled.

— Albert B. Cleage Jr.

[Jesus'] death is the revelation of the freedom of God, taking upon himself the totality of human oppression.

— James H. Cone

And I, whither shall I cause my shame to go?

— Tamar, daughter of King David

Christology is the primary doctrine or teaching of the church regarding Jesus of Nazareth, whom the church affirms as Christ, the messiah of God. It is the record of the church's perennial attempts to answer Jesus'

71

question, "But, who do you say that I am?" (Mt 16:15), beginning with the simple confession of the primitive church that "Jesus is Lord," through the creedal formulations of the Nicene and Chalcedonian Fathers, to the assertion of black theologians that "Christ is black" and those of womanist theologians that "Christ is a black woman" and "God is as Christ does." Contemporizing the relevance of Christ's gospel for African Americans in their context, black theologians reformulated Tertullian's classic question, "What has Athens to do with Jerusalem?," asking, "Who is Jesus Christ for us today?" According to Cone:

> Who Christ is was controlled by the Greek view of what God had to do to save man. Few, if any of the early Church Fathers grounded their christological arguments in the concrete history of Jesus of Nazareth. Consequently, little is said about the significance of his ministry to the poor as a definition of his person. The Nicene Fathers showed little interest in the christological significance of Jesus' deeds for the humiliated, because most of the discussion took place in the social context of the Church's position as the favored religion of the Roman State. It therefore became easy to define Jesus as the divinizer (the modern counterpart is "spiritualizer") of humanity. When this happens Christology is removed from history, and salvation becomes only peripherally related to this world.[1]

Reflecting on their own cultural particularity and historical-political context, black theologians questioned the validity of existing christological constructs in determining what constitutes both saving knowledge and a saving praxis for black people in America. Martin Luther King Jr. both held and transformed traditional notions of christology and the related doctrines, most notably, *Atonement,* which reflects on the salvific work of Christ to *reconcile* God with humankind (and humankind with humankind); and *ecclesiology,* which reflects on the purposes of the church. Albert B. Cleage Jr. radically reappropriated Christian tradition, disputing the privatistic premises of Eurocentric biblical interpretation of the significance of Jesus and their relevance for black salvation, the goal of which was black *nationhood.* James H. Cone proposed more centrist christological views relative to these two positions, affirming the primacy of black salvation, which he equated with social, economic, political and spiritual *liberation.*

These pastors/preachers/scholars were critically aware of the relationship between white biblical interpretations and black suffering. Each was immersed in the theodicy project that has characterized the black Christian witness. Although each attached singular significance to human agency in the accomplishment of the community's salvific or liberative goals, they supported their theodical claims with the biblical paradigm of the Exodus and Jesus' words in the Lukan passage, "The spirit of the Lord is upon me" (Lk 4:18), citing these as evidence of Christ's will to liberate the oppressed.

THE SOCIAL CONTEXT OF BLACK CHRISTOLOGY

Following the Civil War and Reconstruction agriculture remained the chief economic activity of the South. Whites could no longer legally compel black men and women to work for them,[2] yet because they retained virtually all of the economic power, they remanded their erstwhile chattel to subservient positions—as farm workers and domestics— in the post-slavery work force. In the South the division of labor remained the same as it was in slavery but, for the first time, whites were forced to make contractual arrangements with those originally slated for bondage in perpetuity. Like the biblical Amnon, Tamar's half-brother and rapist, who tried to cast off the implications of his dreadful deed by rejecting her and then subjecting her to a worse fate (of desolation),[3] whites ended slavery but continued demoralizing blacks into the twentieth century through economic exploitation, discrimination and lynchings both criminal and legislative.[4] In the years following 1915 and 1940 the failure of black banks, the collapse of the cotton market and the fear of white vigilantism prompted massive numbers of blacks to migrate North,[5] significantly reducing the number of available black farm workers and the capacity of agrarian capitalism to remain at the center of the American economy.

Within these historical parameters Wilmore situates the deradicalization of the Black Church,[6] a phenomenon he attributes to (1) the decline of the influence of AME Bishop Henry McNeal Turner (d. 1915); (2) the deterioration of race relations due to rising white mob violence, Jim Crow laws and the resurgence of scientific rationalism;[7] (3) the rise of Marcus Garvey (1887-1940) and the Universal Negro Improvement Association (UNIA); (4) evangelical "ferment in black religion" that spawned the Holiness and Pentecostal movements and that issued forth in an abundance of fundamentalist churches; and (5) the retreat from the radical cause by black "mainline" churches[8] due to (a) economic factors, (b) competition from secular organizations that arose to address the temporal needs of blacks, and (c) their small number relative to rural-oriented, revivalistic churches.

In 1914 several members of my mother's extended family established one of these rural, revivalistic holiness churches, the Church of God by Faith (incorporated in 1923).[9] In the mid-1950s my mother, a few of her siblings and my elder siblings moved from Florida to western New England where, a few years and three siblings later, I was born. In 1965 my mother married my stepfather, who had been her childhood friend. He was stationed at Westover AFB near Springfield, Massachusetts, and transferred to Seymour Johnson AFB near Goldsboro, North Carolina. The military was then and remains one of the few corridors to social, economic and political empowerment for black men. It was yet another phenomenon that diminished the ability of southern agrarian capitalism to thrive. Nonetheless, when I was a child, and even today, plantation labor constituted and constitutes a major portion of southern economies that draw heavily on a labor pool of black and Latino people (many of whom are also of African descent) and that replicate many of the working conditions of the Old South. A veritable *cross* of unremitted suffering in these communities results from extremely low wages and from undignified, unsafe conditions at these work sites.

Thus, "the longest and most durable labor Blacks have performed within the American experience [is] in the area of agriculture."[10] Manning Marable states:

> From the American Revolution until the eve of World War I, about 90 percent of all Black people lived in the South. As late as 1940, 77 percent of all Blacks resided in the former slave states, while only 27 percent of all white Americans lived there. The majority of Black male workers ploughed and planted the fields, harvesting the annual yields of cotton or corn, usually for the benefit of an absent white landlord. In 1910, 57 percent of all Black men and 52 percent of all Black women workers were farmers. Eight percent of the men and 42 percent of the women were employed as domestics or personal servants. Only one sixth of the Black population worked in manufacturing or industries.[11]

At the turn of the century primary voices in the black radical tradition criticized the circumscription of African Americans in a servant class and the structuring of American society and economy in ways that perpetuated black dependency on whites. A number of thinkers reflected on the ways evangelical religion contributed to this structural dependency by encouraging blacks to regard their condition of servitude as their divine lot or, alternately, by separating their history, skin color and the sociopolitical structure that devolved upon them from the question of how and who Jesus saves.

African Americans were nevertheless able to foster a collective awareness of the causes and consequences of their plight and sought solutions that comported with their religious and theological sensibilities. These were, however, shaped in and informed by the privatistic evangelical ethos which had always associated Christ with white authority. Breaking with this tradition, in the 1960s, black theologians Cone and Cleage picked up on the theme of blackness as a positive category in their academic reflections. The seeds of this resistance are found in the thought of early black nationalist Robert Alexander Young. "Blackness" gained wider acceptance in religious usage when, in the late nineteenth century, Bishop Henry McNeal Turner of the AME Church declared that "God is a Negro" in response to the growing conservatism of the AME Church and African American community.[12] An influential bishop in the North Carolina conference, he denounced the leadership of Booker T. Washington, whose sphere of influence was likewise in the South (where most African Americans lived). Washington proposed black uplift through vocational training, promoting conciliatory Christian views based on the Puritan work ethic.[13] Turner and others regarded his views as obsequious. Yet it was Washington who grew in public stature after the passing of Frederick Douglass (1817?-1895) from the political scene.[14]

Turner had little faith that the American socioeconomic context would permit African Americans to participate as free and self-determining beings therein. During the early phases of his ministry he called for land reparations to blacks in payment for slavery and eventually called for a return to Africa. Marcus Garvey focused on Turner's theme of blackness, taking special care to affirm the biological blackness of Christ and the ontological worth of African Americans, thereby injecting a systematic cultural critique of American society in the discourse on black liberation. Turner and Garvey vigorously supported emigration to Africa as the most promising prospect for justice.[15] W.E.B. Du Bois (1868-1963), who emigrated to Africa in his later years, echoed Turner's theme of blackness, as did a very young, very strident, Minister Malcolm X (1925-1965), two generations after Turner's demise. As an heir of the radical tradition, Malcolm similarly called for reparations and separation for blacks during his tenure in the Nation of Islam.

In spite of the economic and cultural critiques generated by Turner and other black religious radicals, the deradicalization of the Black Church was due, in no small measure, to the influence of the hermeneutics of sacrifice, whose authority was deeply entrenched in the *American* religious consciousness. During the post-Reconstruction period black Christians turned to the Bible but had few tools for interpreting it. Although radical activists in the Black Church and wider community proffered seminally critical views of the Bible[16] and white Christianity, they were not enough to dissuade the black masses from their commitment to evangelical doctrine.

For African Americans the postbellum Reconstruction period (1865-1877) and the period following were crucial times, and the conditions to which they were subject cried out for remediation. Like the early church, the fact of persecution and martyrdom in black history made a decisive impact on the way the victimized and scapegoated Africans variously interpreted Jesus' mission for authentic witness in the American context. The early Christians asserted the salvific meaning of Jesus' death by reinterpreting Jewish sacrificial rites to indicate the means by which their redemption was accomplished. Recasting the role of the Messiah/ Christ in the Jewish people's hope of redemption, in the process, they spiritualized the meaning of Jesus' ministry for Christians for centuries to come.

In and since slavery, Christianity, as sourced by Evangelicalism, spiritualized the import of Jesus for African Americans. Christology, referenced by the hermeneutics of sacrifice, encouraged many slaves and their descendants to leave white authority unchallenged or constrained them to veil whatever challenge they did or could pose. Prompted by their own survival needs in an extremely hostile environment, very many black people did and do accede to unfair and arbitrary standards in the dominant society. Yet in and since slavery Christianity, informed by such experience as the guiding norm of black theological reflection, empowered and empowers others to resist their circumscription. Out of this history of accommodation and resistance to the cross in the African American experience the Civil Rights and Black Power movements[17] emerged in the 1950s and 1960s, promoting, respectively, integrationism and nationalism as the social and political means to effect black salvation. Both these positions historically have been informed by the variegated portraits of Christ/Jesus in scripture and Christian tradition.

Integrationists were led by a coalition of civic organizations and the Black Church. They opted for full participation in American society, employing a praxis of nonviolent resistance to state policies of racial hegemony. They appealed for black empowerment on the basis of African Americans' violated civil rights, relying on the principles of moral suasion and the goodwill of white enforcers of civil and moral law. Nationalists favored separation from whites, advocating land reparations and separate cultural activities and economic and educational institutions, appealing on the basis of black peoples' violated human rights. Religious leaders in both groups engaged the question of theodicy, apropos to the inimical context in which the community sought its salvation/liberation.

As a community mediator, as a nation builder and as a religious leader, the black preacher was and is expected to be the living embodiment of the black activism sparked by the egalitarian and pietistic social ideals informed by Evangelicalism yet forged in the crucible of slavery and race oppression.[18] For many African Americans and their activist friends, no one before or since has done this more effectively than the Baptist minister, theologian and Christian martyr, Martin Luther King Jr.

MARTIN LUTHER KING JR.

In the American South of 1955 separate but unequal schools, restaurants, amusements, water fountains and toilets were available for whites and blacks, who were at that time derisively termed *coloreds*. Public transportation, too, was segregated: blacks paid the same fares as whites but had to sit at the back of the bus, filling up the colored section from the rear. On the afternoon of 1 December 1955, in Montgomery, Alabama, a white bus driver ordered Rosa Parks and three other blacks to surrender their seats selected in this way to an inconvenienced white passenger. The others moved on; Parks sat immovable. Thus the first boycott signaling the renewed press for equality was sparked by the first sit-in of national note and was perpetrated by a single, weary black woman. As womanist theologian Delores Williams puts it in her now well-known saying, "If Rosa Parks had not sat down, Martin King would not have stood up."[19]

And stand up he did, proclaiming the love of God for the "least of these" (Mt 25:31-46), those black citizens who wanted to participate in American life as social and political equals with racist whites, who responded with still more violence. Tracked down (as he said of Parks) by the *Zeitgeist* (the spirit of the times),[20] King began publicly articulating the grievances of African Americans, spearheading a boycott of the segregated bus system at the behest of Montgomery's black civic and religious leaders. King and his cohorts in the Montgomery Improvement Association (MIA) were the first group since the abolitionists to organize a mass movement that confronted the racially stratified conditions with demands for integration with the force of evangelical doctrine. (Although Garvey's movement was larger and employed Christian symbolism, its philosophy was separatist and its Christian associations derived from the African Orthodox Christian Church, which reinterpreted Catholicism. And while people in mainline black churches were also activists in the freedom movement, civic leaders like A. Philip Randolph did not systematically apply evangelical doctrine to the ideological task of solving the problem of segregation in the railroad and other industries in the manner of King.)

As the son of a Baptist minister and as a minister-in-training, King was well-grounded in the doctrinal commitments of Evangelicalism. He was also concerned about its individualistic theological focus and the implications that focus held for African Americans in their political context. While a student at Crozer Theological Seminary and Boston University, King became acquainted with the socialist philosophy of Karl Marx (1818-1883) and the corporate ideals of the Social Gospel movement.[21] He was especially impressed with Walter Rauschenbusch (1861-

1918), whose concretized Christology in Hell's Kitchen bore more similarity to the deeds of the Jesus of history, unlike any that could be attributed to the Christ of faith promoted by liberal demythologizers of his day.

Ever the existentialist, King was looking for practical solutions to remedy the collective plight of his persecuted people. He admired his elder contemporary Reinhold Niebuhr, whose work he respected for its breadth of analysis of the problem of human sin and its remediation, structural *and* individual.[22] This work separated Niebuhr from many of his colleagues in the white churches and in the academy and accounts for the imprecise nature of the neo-orthodox label usually attached to his thought.[23] King's ability to reflect on the significance of Christ Jesus was undoubtedly enhanced by this exposure to the liberalizing, depersonalizing trends in what was essentially *white* theological discourse. Yet early in his development he saw the inadequacy of the Social Gospel movement in the "superficial optimism"[24] derived from its liberal heritage. And King diverged from Niebuhr over the issue of pacifism.[25]

Both King and Niebuhr viewed the Sermon on the Mount as a definitive text describing the "inner and transcendent" perspective of Jesus, who they believed counseled agape as the proper Christian response to the persecutorial demands of oppressors.[26] Although the Hindu nationalist and spiritual leader Mohandas (Mahatma) K. Gandhi (1869-1948) provided an actual model of the way of agape in his activism in southern Africa and India using Vedic scriptures and principles, King credited Niebuhr with influencing the development of his philosophy of nonviolent confrontation as a proper *Christian* strategy for social change in the American context.[27] Nevertheless, while Niebuhr supported King's movement and method as preferable alternatives to the more militant Black Power movement underway, he was reluctant to affirm pacifism as the response of the church in every historical circumstance. Niebuhr regarded such a subsumption of human agency as leaving little room for grace to inform and faith to discern a Christian course of action.

For King and for Niebuhr, agape was illuminated in Jesus' death on the cross. Yet in Niebuhr's thought, although agape or sacrificial love was the controlling ideal for all human relations, justice or *mutual* love was the arbiter of competing human claims. This was in keeping with his doctrine of Christian realism as the basis for government, the aim of which was to find "proximate" solutions to the "insoluble problems" of human political existence. Thus, despite the commendability of a "morality of disinterestedness" (which he attributed to American "negroes"), he demurred that the way of agape is not a "simple historical possibility" either for the powerless or for those in power:

Since this possibility does not exist, it is not even right to insist that every action of the Christian must conform to *agape*, rather than to the norms of relative justice and mutual love by which life is maintained and conflicting interests are arbitrated in history. For as soon as the life and interest of others than the agent are involved in an action or policy, the sacrifice of those interests ceases to be "self-sacrifice." It may actually become an unjust betrayal of their interests. Failure to understand this simple fact and this paradoxical relation between individual and collective action has resulted in the unholy alliance between Christian perfectionism and cowardly counsels of political expediency in dealing with the tyrants of our own day.[28]

Yet to King, Niebuhr confused pacifism with passivity, or "nonresistance to evil."[29] The pacifism that agape bespoke was the way to confront earthly powers and to mediate the real presence of Christ *sacramentally*. Said King, "Christ furnished the spirit and motivation while Gandhi furnished the method."[30] At first King proffered Gandhi's method of nonviolent, direct action as the only viable strategy for black people to desegregate the American South in a time when white southerners were violently inclined. But he came to believe that Niebuhr's views of the Christian church as a body that should not be pacifist in confronting powers subverted scriptural accounts of the meaning of Jesus' life and mission and did not go far enough in affirming his nonviolent intentions for the church. Echoing centuries of Christian conditioning vis-à-vis the biblical hermeneutics of sacrifice, King repeatedly explained the role of agape as that which motivated the movement and which characterizes the spirit and praxis of all those in whom God lives and through whom God loves:

Agape is understanding, creative, redemptive good will for all men. Biblical theologians would say it is the love of God working in the minds of men. It is an overflowing love which seeks nothing in return. And when you come to love on this level you begin to love men not because they are likable, not because they do things to attract us, but because God loves them and here we love the person who does the evil deed while hating the deed that the person does. It is the type of love that stands at the center of the movement that we are trying to carry on in the Southland—*agape*.[31]

King's pacifism could be attributed to the strong intellectual influence of Gandhi and the practicability of his method of nonviolence for African Americans. Nevertheless, his christological perspectives fundamentally comported with the scriptural and theological traditions of the

Black Church, which focused on the cross (and hence on *reconciliation* or At-*one*-ment with God) as part of its evangelical heritage, yet also emphasized the redemption of the community as part of its theodical/ anthropodical project. Through his ability to persuade many blacks (and whites) to practice nonviolent, direct-action techniques in battle against systemic racism, King, with the masses, bodily reinterpreted the hermeneutics of sacrifice as it pertained to the human agency of the despised community, in the process reorienting the way black and white Christians of today ground their understanding of the nature and work of Christ.

As we have seen throughout its history, the Black Church has expected its ministers to be actively engaged in finding ways to sustain the community, politically and spiritually. Yet it also promoted individual piety in keeping with its evangelical heritage. This fact took on heightened significance and signification during the period of deradicalization. King embodied this paradox intellectually and emotionally in his sermons and speeches. On the one hand, he did not reject individual responsibility for sin, consistent with the emphasis on individual conversion in evangelical thought. On the other hand, he condemned the enduring apathy of the black ministers who remained "aloof" from the call to social responsibility, which he believed was also revealed in the gospel of Jesus. His early approach reflected an integrated understanding of the public and private aspects of the theodical, reconciling and liberating aims of religion:

> A religion true to its nature must also be concerned about man's social conditions. Religion deals with both earth and heaven, both time and eternity. Religion operates not only on the vertical plane but also on the horizontal. It seeks not only to integrate men with God but to integrate men with men and each man with himself. On the one hand it seeks to change the souls of men, and thereby unite them with God; on the other hand it seeks to change the environmental conditions of men so that the soul will have a chance after it is changed. Any religion that professes to be concerned with the souls of men and is not concerned with the slums that damn them, the economic conditions that strangle them, and the social conditions that cripple them is a dry-as-dust religion. Such a religion is the kind the Marxists like to see—an opiate of the people.[32]

Some King scholars cite the differences between his published writings (many of which were ghostwritten yet give evidence of his theological training and perspectives) and the private spirituality evinced in his sermons and unpublished statements (which demonstrate the primacy of his Black Church experience).[33] I agree with Lewis V. Baldwin that it is unnecessary to separate public and private aspects of his spirituality, because the cultural legacy of King includes both and because both informed the development of his position on nonviolence.[34] Nevertheless, in agreement with Cone, I believe that the subtlety of the impact of the Black Church on his intellectual development can best be understood by those who know its interpretive traditions. It can also be recognized in his inventive re-tooling of confessional utterances. In the epigraph for this chapter, for example, King expands upon the saying, "no cross, no crown," commonly signified in the Black Church.

Yet King was not merely demonstrating his academic prowess.[35] He was responding to the social, political and economic conditions to which the majority of African American Christians were then subject and the theodical/anthropodical impulses that arose therefrom. Moreover, his approach was informed by the veiled rage and radical critique that lay back of the conservatism of the Black Church. In a 1963 interview with noted black psychologist Kenneth B. Clark, King stated:

> There isn't a lot of time; time is running out, and the Negro is making it palpably clear that he wants all of his rights, that he wants them here, and that he wants them now . . . The shape of the world today does not afford us the luxury of slow movement and the Negro's quest for dignity and self-respect doesn't afford the nation this kind of slow movement.[36]

King and the other Christian leaders of the Civil Rights movement focused on African Americans' collective need for liberation, concurrent with radical activists in the community. Priorities of the movement included suffrage and access to social services, which entailed an end to Jim Crow discrimination in education, employment and housing. Employing strategies of sit-ins, marches and boycotts, King and the masses lodged peaceful protests against the exclusionary tactics of southern state police, local police and elected officials who denied blacks the opportunity to exercise these basic rights.

King came to proffer nonviolence as a complete way of life for African Americans, because he believed that "ends are pre-existent in the means." He also viewed the biblically derived mandate of nonviolence as symbolical of faith in and praxis of the "beloved community." He began a theological revolution in the church, academy and society. Utilizing the historical Jesus as a guide and emphasizing the model of the church as the beloved community, his movement synergized the doctrines of ecclesiology and Christology, signifying the church as the *body of Christ* doing the will of God in America and in the world.

Nevertheless, to his radical detractors, such as Albert Cleage and Malcolm X, the love ethic to which King appealed and to which he consistently connected his nonviolent ethic evinced the conservative theological underpinnings of the Black Church as sourced by Evangelicalism. Despite King's repeated warnings to the churches about the real danger of irrelevancy coming from these theological foci; despite the fact that the movement sprang from the grassroots and that its gains furthered blacks socially and politically, they interpreted King's focus on integration as having primarily privatistic religious/theological import. Despite his confrontational brand of activism, they interpreted his nonviolent message and movement as passive embodiments of black theological dependence on whites, who had, under the admonitions of evangelical piety, no compelling theological reasons to relinquish their social and political privilege relative to African Americans.

Many black people could not affirm King's message of nonviolence. Some committed themselves to fighting injustice by any means necessary. They pointed to the system's violence against poor black people and to the physical violence of whites against marching hordes of peaceful protestors. As the students in his movement became increasingly aware of the need for cultural pride and self-direction, political and economic empowerment became their major objectives. The Student Non-Violent Coordinating Committee (SNCC), which was an offshoot of the SCLC and the other integrationist organizations came increasingly under the influence of the rising Black Power movement, proponents of which criticized King's oft-cited proclamation that "unearned suffering is redemptive." This notion echoed Wheatley's and Du Bois's theodical concern that black people are "chosen" to suffer. In King's thought it evinced teleological and eschatological dimensions of the question of justice. The teleological aspects bore implications for the way he believed the church was to comport itself and realize proleptically its status as the beloved community. The eschatological aspects derived from the historical tendency of the Black Church to appropriate the whole story about Jesus, including his experience of the cross and his belated victory at resurrection.[37] Nevertheless, the centrality of the cross in nearly all Christian discourse and liturgies altogether obscures the teleological and eschatological issues in a practical way, because it historically facilitated the imposition of the hermeneutics of sacrifice. In this little ditty Black Power advocates ridiculed the implications of the hermeneutics of sacrifice for black people in the racist American context:

> Too much love
> Too much love
> Nothing kills a nigger like
> Too much love.[38]

Black Power advocates injected into the Civil Rights movement a crucial perspective that challenged the authority of oppressors to define them, delimit their world or interpret scripture on their behalf. We cannot understand the life of King without appreciating those critical persons who informed his thinking, especially Malcolm X, who was also slated for martyrdom, but whose locus of discourse was in the North. There, violence against blacks took less overt forms of social and political marginalization but, as in the South, had deadly sociopolitical and economic consequences. Malcolm's *political* solution was self-defense, or *non*-nonviolence, which King equated with violence and which he rejected as suicidal. His *theological* solution (as given by Elijah Muhammad), separation from white mainstream society, was practically impossible because in the integrationism-nationalism dynamic most blacks were inclined toward integrationism.

Although King became more conscious about the interconnectedness of the civil-rights struggle and the third-world struggle for human rights, he never surrendered his commitment to the philosophy of nonviolence but extended its scope and applicability to whites. Yet due to the cogency of the Black Power critique and the intransigence of whites, he came to affirm "blackness" and to call for "separation" as a temporary measure to overcome the powerlessness of the African American community, admitting in reference to the increasingly influential Malcolm X, "Maybe he does have some of the answers."[39]

Faced with the conditioned proclivity of African American Christians *not* to resist white violence, other Black Church leaders asked, "How can I be Black and remain Christian?" Radical spokespersons in the inchoate black theology movement condemned the hermeneutics of sacrifice whites used to interpret King, whose radical import was evident in the fact that he confronted whites on terms of equality more effectively than anyone else had.[40] They recognized that the most effective way to galvanize the community for social change was through the Black Church. Although they criticized church folks' commitment to what was presumably the theology of the slaveholders, black theologians used the grand impetus of the church-based movement to further their nationalistic agendas and to develop their epistemological platforms.

ALBERT B. CLEAGE JR.

Like the southern integrationist King, Cleage was born (1911) into the relative comfort and privilege of the black middle-class, the son of a prominent physician, in Indianapolis, Indiana. Like King, he would become one of the most outspoken opponents of black oppression. Both their social statuses, locations of discourse and religious traditions affected their analyses of the problems of blacks and the means available to resolve them. While Cleage appreciated the sincerity and dedication of King, he nevertheless denounced the equivocal, reformist approach to white society that King and the SCLC employed in their pursuit of civil rights and broader participation for blacks in American social and political processes. In the years just prior to King's public ministry, Cleage was pastor of the Central Congregational Church (1951-1967) in Detroit, Michigan, a black congregation within a liberal, white denomination (Congregationalist, or the United Church of Christ).[41] Like King, Cleage would remain in the Christian church while developing his agenda of black liberation. Yet, unlike King, who would not endorse black empowerment by *any* means, he would champion black Christian nationalism and become one of its foremost proponents.

Mark Chapman attributes Cleage's nationalist fervor to the influence of Elijah Muhammad[42] and his Nation of Islam (NOI) in the black religious community. Situated within the nationalist strand, Minister Muhammad's development of the NOI was an abreaction to white supremacy in the received theological traditions of the Black Church. According to Chapman, Cleage believed that the success of the NOI lay in the fact that Minister Muhammad vocalized many of the subtexts that already existed in the collective black unconscious, which, though comprised of the views of people with varying faiths, was essentially Christian. Despite the cogency of the love ethic that typically characterized the response of the community to oppression, the socioeconomic and political factors contributing to its alienation belied the claims of justice and inclusivity in the covenant theology upon which King relied in order to articulate his critique. Cleage and other nationalists came to question also the spiritual freedom or salvation putatively found in the rhetoric and tenets of evangelical faith that undergirded King and the masses who followed him:

> No actual power was needed to perpetuate the Black man's enslavement. Everything that could be done to liberate the Black man had already been accomplished at Calvary two thousand years ago. The Black man needed to do nothing himself except accept his lot and be washed in the blood of the Lamb and be made white like snow (in preparation for the life to come). So, then, if you are Black you can be poverty-stricken, you can be brutalized, and you can still be saved. Your children can be discriminated against and denied a decent education, and you can still be saved. You can live in a neighborhood from which all the decencies of life have been taken and you're still saved. It was this kind of primi-

tive Christianity which Black slaves received from their White slave masters.[43]

Early in his career Cleage took seriously the Muslim critique of American Christianity as a "white man's religion." The impact of this nationalist critique on his thought was underscored by his having met and befriended Malcolm X in 1963. At that time Cleage was involved in the leadership of the Detroit Council for Human Rights (DCHR), a northern-based group that was trying to duplicate in that locale the efforts of the SCLC to engage churches in the task of empowering the community politically. The DCHR organized the Detroit Freedom March, rallying 200,000 blacks in support of King.[44] Following this, they attempted to organize the *Northern* Christian Leadership Conference, which was to parallel the SCLC. Cleage was put off by the conservatism of other pastors in the DCHR, especially the chairman, C. L. Franklin, who dissociated himself from the radical activists Cleage had invited to participate in the Conference, Conrad Lynn and William Worthy of the Freedom Now Party.[45] Chapman reports that after Cleage left the DCHR, he joined with GOAL (Group on Advanced Leadership) to form the Northern Negro Grass Roots Leadership Conference (note that this title privileges no particular religion). This is when he met the fiery Muslim leader.

Although Malcolm X would come to exert a profound influence on his rhetoric and thought, Hiley Ward states that Cleage's concept of nationalism comported less with the Muslim theological focus and more with that of Black Power, which had a decidedly economic emphasis:

His main thrust is with Black Power which hits whites more directly in their own backyard and at the office. Money, jobs, opportunities of all sorts are channeled to blacks, most certainly in all black areas. His nationalism is understood only in connection with his concept of economic power. Further, he does not raise the specter of messianic leadership as the Muslims and the Moors have done. In this matter-of-fact approach, he sees the struggle in less redemptive terms. He doesn't like the word redemption, and I have heard him use it only in scoring King's idea of suffering nonviolent redemption. Cleage has room for a messianic emphasis; but it is historical, in terms of the Messiah of the Gospels.[46]

Although Cleage admired Malcolm X greatly, the "failure of nerve" on the part of the Detroit pastors made one thing abundantly clear to him: despite its history of activism, the Black Church had no *theology* to support its actions.[47] Yet, given the fact that the African American community was then and remains now overwhelmingly Christian, the anomalous position of the NOI made evident the necessity of remaining in the Christian church, if Cleage and other northern ministers who were being positively influenced by the rumblings of black power were to build up faith in the possibility of black *nationhood* in their constituencies. Thus, any *black* theology that was going to engage the black masses in a liberative praxis needed to be recognizably Christian. Chapman states:

> Cleage liked the nationalist focus of the Black Muslims and respected their ability to reform the lives of troubled youth who had become involved with drugs, alcohol, and crime. But Cleage also realized that the masses of African American youth would neither accept the Puritan ethic of the Nation of Islam nor completely renounce the Christian heritage of their parents and grandparents. He therefore sought to develop a Black Christian Nationalist movement that fused the black nationalism of Elijah Muhammad and Malcolm X to an African-American Christian base.[48]

Inspired by the increasing militancy of the student vanguards of the Civil Rights movement, motivated by the worsening conditions in the communities that erupted into the riots of 1964 and that saw the assassination of Malcolm X (1965), Cleage joined with other ministers who had issued the first statement embracing the concept of black power and linking it with their Christian witness in 1966, the National Committee of Negro Churchmen. Cleage espoused a different theological position than most of the signatories on the NCBC statement, who spoke in conciliatory terms, often qualifying their views on violence by citing traditional Christian values to support their claims. Ever the militant, Cleage had been impressed by Garvey's reappropriation of Christianity in order to carry out his Pan-African nationalistic agenda. It soon became evident that, in Cleage's thought, the goal of nationhood permitted no rapprochement between blacks and whites, liberal and otherwise. This was confirmed for him in the Detroit riot of July 1967, during which dozens of black people were killed. Earlier that same year he had renamed Central Church the Shrine of the Black Madonna, and it came under the structure of the African Orthodox Christian Church (the Catholic tenets of which Garvey had used to propel his movement).[49] In the process, Cleage transformed its liturgical traditions and stretched the liberal intent of its former denomination. Although he voiced many of the same criticisms of white religion as the NOI had, Cleage, with Garvey, argued that Christianity was historically the black man's religion. He set about recovering the liberative import of the gospel for black people, dramatically reappropriating the privatistic premises of scriptural interpretation and of the nature of salvation in slaveholding religion.

As the community had identified it, white supremacy was the cross in the African American experience. With few exceptions its leaders, integrationist and nationalist, remained committed to the Christian faith. Affected by the nationalist critique, principals in the incipient black theology movement embraced the concept of black empowerment. But unlike many of his predecessors in the earliest black nationalist traditions, who qualified the meaning of Jesus' blackness (as did some later black theologians), to Cleage, Jesus is literally, biologically, the *Black* Messiah, as he had also been for Garvey.

For Cleage, blackness is an absolute religious value[50] that challenged the anthropological assumptions of white supremacy in the received theological traditions of the Black Church in the American context. Although these traditions are imbibed by African Americans and have putatively sustained the community, Cleage recognized that at the same time they were abnegating to the community's self-image. Although the Black Church had been a forum to attend to the community's need for ontological affirmation, Cleage and other ministers influenced by black power asserted that it was now "without consciousness of its responsibility and potential power"[51] to assist the community in the ongoing fight for liberation. Nevertheless, he also implicated the community in its own immolation:

> That white Americans continue to insist upon a white Christ in the face of all historical evidence to the contrary and despite the hundreds of shrines to Black Madonnas all over the world, is the crowning demonstration of their white supremacist conviction that all things good and valuable must be white. On the other hand, until black Christians are ready to challenge this lie, they have not freed themselves from their spiritual bondage to the white man nor established in their own minds their right to first-class citizenship in Christ's kingdom on earth. Black people cannot build dignity on their knees worshiping a white Christ. We must put down this white Jesus which the white man gave us in slavery and which has been tearing us to pieces.[52]

Yet, as J. Deotis Roberts pointed out, the emphasis on a black madonna was alienating to the evangelical, largely Protestant sensibilities of some African Americans:

> Some Blacks have a problem with the "Black Madonna" for sociological as well as theological reasons. Sociologically, the black

madonna is associated with the female-headed family pattern. This family pattern has resulted from oppression in a white racist society and is not of African origin. It is believed by these critics that this pattern of family life must be overcome if black nationalism is to be a success. Therefore, Cleage's Shrine of the Black Madonna together with the symbol of the black madonna convey the wrong message. Theologically, most Blacks are Protestant (Methodist or Baptist). The black madonna, associated in their minds with the meaning of the virgin Mary for Roman Catholics, is not attractive to them.[53]

In 1968 Cleage published *The Black Messiah*, a collection of sermons in which he expostulated a transformed, literalist hermeneutics that has as its key the unfolding or revelation of black nationhood in scripture. He disavowed the privatized nature of evangelical religion, which morally leveled all persons in Christian communion but which did not challenge the social, economic and political structures of domination in the American society. To Cleage, these things constituted saving knowledge: (1) awareness that Jesus and the biblical world that attested to him were, historically, biologically black (this meant that Jesus was a black Jew living in Palestine among a black Jewish people); (2) that Jesus' agenda had nationalistic import and had little if anything to do with the Atonement doctrines that have so much currency in black churches; thus (3) salvation was a corporate project, not an individualistic one. A saving praxis required ultimate loyalty to black people, which is the sine qua non in Cleage's thought, according to the African American ethicist Riggins Earl.[54] Yet in the wake of slaveholding religion, learning how to be faithful to one another necessitated a revolution in religious values. For Cleage, this meant, in part, discarding those liturgical traditions in the Black Church that served no purpose other than to betray its foundation in white paternalism and to incur white disdain. While Cleage recognized the historical theodicy project and the struggles of the people to find creative agency in their various contexts, he nevertheless derided some of the liturgical practices of African Americans. He questioned, for example, the validity of shouting, since, to him, its privatistic import detracted from the mission of black nationhood and the task of organizing for revolution.

> The church and slave Christianity has perpetuated our individualism. We don't have any sense of being a people fighting our problems together. We're waiting for God to save us individually. We're running up and down the aisle shouting and singing and hoping that Jesus will speak to our individual needs, not the needs of Black people. We do not really ask God to help us change the basic con-

ditions under which Black people live. This is the weakness of the
Black church. It was a survival instrument. It helped maintain san-
ity, but it destroyed the possibility of a united Black Liberation
Struggle.[55]

Cleage's particular disdain for this reprised Africanism, as Wilmore
has pointed out, is reflected in the shame most black theologians felt at
their inherited traditions. Nevertheless, I would argue that Cleage stands
within those black intellectual and liturgical traditions that I have already described as *apologetic* and *melodramatic*–apologetic, in that their
practitioners sought to defend the faith by transforming it; melodramatic, in that they accomplished their transformations by stretching the
received story of and about Jesus all the way out to its artistic conclusions for the purpose of achieving community. For Cleage, the incarnation in the story of Jesus referred to the birth of the Black Nation, that
God would be *born* and *borne* in the members of the Nation; the ministry
of Jesus provided models for bringing blacks into the Nation; his death
and resurrection symbolized that there was nothing more important to
God than black nationhood. Thus a saving praxis also included the possibility, even likelihood, of violent revolution. In sharp contrast to King,
he made no disclaimer about violence, whether conceived as self-defense or as protracted struggle on the part of the oppressed. Rather, as
Jesus' passion story demonstrated the profundity of his commitment to
the Nation, he purported a *sacramental* witness in the concept of *nationhood*, demonstrable in the loyalty of black people to one another. With
his nationalist counterparts in the non-Christian forces of the Black Power
movement, he brokered a love ethic wholly redirected toward the African American community. Thus, for Cleage, *reconciliation* was a matter
between blacks on all levels. It was part of their neighborly obligation
to one another and part of their collective obligation to learn about and
reconnect to their African heritage of Christianity:

> Black people must understand that only within the Black nation
> do we turn the other cheek. We turn the other cheek only to a
> Black brother, or a Black sister. We do not turn the other cheek in
> any other situation, and it's my firm conviction that this is what
> Jesus was talking to Israel about in the first place, because Israel
> was engaged in the same kind of liberation struggle against the
> White Gentile world. The teachings of the Bible must be reinter-
> preted for the benefit of Black people so that the church can be-
> come useful in the liberation struggle . . . Only if we can redis-
> cover the historic roots of Christianity and strip from it the mystical
> distortions which are not basic to the concept of nation as revealed
> in the Old Testament and in the teachings of Jesus, will we be able

to bring the Black Christian church into the liberation struggle and make it relevant to the lives of Black people.[56]

Cleage is no fundamentalist; he does not accept the mythological worldview of the Bible, yet, through his selective canon, he maintains a consistent hermeneutical perspective on the significance of Jesus for black revolution that is literalist in its import (that is, he intends an exclusionary policy toward whites and projects this through scripture). He rejects sacrifice altogether, whether conceived as the mission of Jesus or as any imposition coming from *outside* the African American community.

When we march, when we take it to the streets in open conflict, we must understand that in the stamping feet and the thunder of violence we can hear the voice of God. When the Black Church accepts its role in the Black Revolution, it is able to understand and interpret revolutionary Christianity, and the revolution becomes a part of our Christian faith. Every Sunday morning when we preach from the Old Testament, or when we preach about Jesus, we seek to help black people understand that the struggle in which we are engaged is a cosmic struggle, that the very universe struggles with us when we fight to throw off the oppression of white people. We want black people to understand that they are coming to church to get the strength and direction to go out and fight oppression all week. We don't pray for strength to endure any more. We pray for the strength to fight heroically.[57]

As salvation or liberation was the proper work of the church engaged in Jesus' mission, it was the responsibility of the church to organize the community for social action. This corporate conception of salvation made it possible for any black person to be involved in the work of the church, confessing Christian or not. Hence, Cleage was prepared to ordain Stokely Carmichael and others from the radical, non-Christian arm of the Black Power movement, to give them the sanctuary of the church in case of draft. Cleage understood the community as besieged, like the early church, and called for a martyrdom ethic among blacks in violent resistance to any state-sanctioned oppression. This would evince the peoples' faith in their right to achieve nationhood:

Maybe you have taken communion lightly. But the broken bread is the symbol that we are willing as individuals to *sacrifice* ourselves for the Nation. The wine is the symbol that we are willing to shed our blood for the Nation. So when we come together, it's as though we are around a table united, a people, a Nation . . . And this is what baptism is. When members come into the church, we baptize members who have not been baptized, as well as those who would like to be baptized again, because they want to be baptized into the Nation. We baptize into the Nation in the Name of the Father, the Son and the Holy Spirit . . . You die to all your old Uncle Tom ways, the slave ways you used to have. And you are born again . . . resurrected in the newness of life into the Black Nation . . . We are building it; some of us may die, but the remnant must live.[58]

JAMES H. CONE

Although he was born in rural Fordyce, Arkansas, to poor parents, Cone, like Cleage and King, had many foundational experiences that lend dignity to his public witness. These derive primarily from his birth family and from his lifelong, albeit complicated relationship to the African Methodist Episcopal Church. Cone and his brothers, Charles Jr. and Cecil, were raised in Bearden, Arkansas. His mother, whom he described as "one of the pillars of Macedonia" (AME) instilled in him the concept of God's justice, sovereignty and mystery,[59] defying the deadening ethos of white supremacy in which Bearden and the whole nation were immersed while illuminating the question of theodicy for Cone and his brothers. His father provided a model of uncompromising integrity for them. Mr. Cone would not allow any of the whites in the small town to address Mrs. Cone by her first name, flouting this privilege that racist whites assumed. Nor would he permit her to work outside the home, despite their poverty, not only respecting the paternalistic social mores of the times but also expressing his determination that she would be accorded the respect she was due in view of her femininity, and which he believed black people were due, simply in view of their humanity. It is important to assess the centrality of this legacy of dignity and spirituality in relation to theodical reflection in Cone's personal history,[60] because it provides a context for understanding the psychological contours of his evolving theological and christological perspectives, which hinge on the existentialist concept of *somebodiness.*[61] The early affirmation of his particular *somebodiness* fostered in him a precociousness that led to deep intellectual curiosity. In the church of his youthful experience the gospel story was signified to address these issues. A corporate conception of *somebodiness* already existed in the AME Church, the church of Allen, Lee and Turner, where Cone's intellectual gifts made room for him as a youth. At the age of sixteen he was appointed to his first pastorate. Shaped by these foundational experiences in his family and church context, he felt compelled to express his discontent with the way things were for the four hundred blacks in relationship to the eight hundred whites of Bearden.

To be put in one's place, as defined by white society, was a terrible reality for blacks in Bearden. It meant being beaten by the town cop and spending an inordinate length of time in a stinking jail. It meant attending "separate but equal" schools, going to the balcony when attending a movie, and drinking water from a "colored" fountain. It meant refusing to retaliate when called a nigger—unless you were prepared to leave town at the precise moment of your rebellion. You had no name except your first name or "boy"; and if you were past the age of sixty-five, you might attain the dubious honor of being called "uncle" or "auntie."[62]

These personal and collective experiences of affirmation and denigration elicited Cone's understanding of *liberation* as the right to realize individual and communal *somebodiness.* In his thought, liberation—for communion with God, with oneself and with others—is a teleological given; it is not a goal to be achieved but a gift resident in the fact of being human. This gift is to be "unwrapped" over the course of a human life. Through the unfolding of *somebodiness* devotees and communities purport a sacramental witness to the character and creativity of God. While this existentialist focus privileges marginalized peoples' ways of knowing, doing, reflecting and talking about God, for Cone, this continuous revelation is also the work of Christ:

> There is no liberation independent of Jesus' past, present, and future coming. He is the ground of our present freedom to struggle and the source of our hope that the vision disclosed in our historical fight against oppression will be fully realized in God's future. In this sense, liberation is not a human possession but a divine gift of freedom to those who struggle in faith against violence and oppression. Liberation is not an object but the *project* of freedom wherein the oppressed realize that their fight for freedom is a divine right of creation.[63]

Thus, liberation—personal and collective—is the proper project of humankind. It is also God's historical project, according to the biblical witness of the Exodus and Jesus' liberating ministry to the poor and despised of his time, his identification with them in the suffering of the cross and his promise of victory through resurrection. Cone was himself immersed in the renewed push for black assertion in the American context. In 1954 he was a youthful pastor when the *Brown vs. Topeka Board of Education* publicly raised white resistance to black empowerment and signalled new stirrings in black consciousness. In 1955 King launched the boycott of the Montgomery bus system. Earlier that same year vigilante whites lynched and murdered a young Chicago boy,

Emmett Till, allegedly for engaging in the "criminal" act of whistling at a white woman. The general ethos in which these events occurred fortuitously led Cone to ponder the black struggle for freedom and his place in it. The precocious Cone was still a teenager when he graduated from Shorter College and matriculated at Philander Smith, an AME Church–affiliated institution. At the age of twenty, not having been re-appointed to a pastoral charge, he took up theological studies at Garrett-Northwestern. As the Civil Rights movement gained impetus, it became more difficult for him to remain contented with this privatized, academic focus of his life.

Cone was in the Chicago area during the rise to prominence of Muslim Minister Malcolm X. However, he never met Malcolm X and did not include in his academic work the critical insights that black radicals had garnered. In the neo-orthodox ethos, there was no warrant and no permission for *black* theology, as such. Cone studied the work of evangelical theologian Karl Barth. Although Barth had had some experience confronting state powers in Nazi Germany through his relationship to the Confessing Church, the academic milieu did not permit Cone to study his own racial situation in an analogous way. Yet the neo-orthodox foundation of his theology did not simply result from classroom encounters with white theologians or from a simple appropriation of their thought. Rather, it derived from the evangelical emphasis of the Black Church that had affirmed him and that had been the church of his mother. As a pioneering black theologian Cone did not have many models for expressing the insights that came from his engagement of the ongoing theodicy project of a community in search of civil and human rights. Like King, he sought practical ways to blend the theology of his experience *and* training in order to make a relevant contribution to the discourse. In the context of the turbulent 1960s the theological task for Christian theologians was conceived as combining the central story's import with the notion of black empowerment. Yet, although Cone was impressed with the insight and achievements of King, the childhood experience that netted him the ability to articulate his anger at black delimitation and suffering and the primacy of liberation in his thought pushed him closer, in some ways, to Cleage, because he could not disavow countermeasures to white violence as a suitable option for oppressed blacks. Cone was not a signatory on the NCBC document, but he wrote a seminal article defining his commitment to Black Power in light of being Christian.[64] He seized upon the ontological implications of Black Power to articulate a systematic theology shaped by his existential questions.

Cone attaches significance to the deeds of the historical Jesus as recorded in scripture as well as to the spiritual import of the Atonement conceived as an *event*, the central event in salvific history. Nevertheless, as he interprets the event, it is useful only insofar as it gives articulation to the black struggle for meaningful existence in the context of white America. Like King, Cone comes very close to affirming the traditional story; however, he transforms its significance for blacks by affirming the ontological blackness of Christ, unlike Cleage, who makes the point about Christ's literal blackness, in the manner of Garvey. Christ, in his ontological blackness, is God's gift to black humanity, for Cone. This is not necessarily a literal affirmation of the central doctrinal claims of the story (namely, incarnation, Atonement, resurrection). Rather, as one standing within the Black Church tradition of his mother, Cone compels African Americans to articulate the nature of their faith in the power of the Christian story. In this way he affirms the liberating intentions of black people who confess faith in Christ Jesus. The Bible, as witness to Christ Jesus, is not infallible; it is *reliable,* because it is this same Jesus who provides the "necessary soul" to fight against suffering. Although Cone's capacity for theological reflection was no doubt heightened by his training, it is the *experience* of oppressed people that was and remains normative for Cone and that accounts for the enduring centrality of the cross in the Black Church and in his theology.

Critics of Cone cite the primacy of liberation in his thought, almost to the exclusion of reconciliation.[65] For Cone, liberation is foundational to the reconciliation that is also made possible by God in the work of Christ. In the racist American context the affirmation of blackness is a necessary requisite for both black people and whites to evolve into a mature, authentic freedom in which interchange between persons of equal stature makes reconciliation possible. This is consistent with a doctrine of creation in which it is God's unqualified love that bestows worth upon the human creature—outside of this creative act of God, all are equally unworthy. (This anthropological focus also situates Cone in the evangelical tradition.) But since even liberal whites do not regard blacks as equals, attempts at reconciliation before the full liberation of blacks are always at the expense of blackness. Cone states that, under white terms of reconciliation, the dignity and beauty of blackness are denied or subsumed under the value systems of white culture. The unwillingness of whites to share power with blacks, or even to regard black people as fully human, renders their talk about reconciliation an attempt by whites to free themselves from their historical indebtedness to blacks. It is also an attempt to mystify their ongoing oppression of black people. These have present consequences. The experience of oppression makes it incumbent upon blacks to fight for liberation by any means necessary. Cone says that "love for blacks means confronting whites on terms of equality." This means that blackness must continually be affirmed: (1) by blacks, who have an obligation to destroy "the white thing" (that is, white supremacy); and (2) by whites, because identification with the oppressed is a consequence of Christian discipleship, since God is on the side of the oppressed. Reconciliation is the result of God's initiative, which can only be realized when whites affirm blackness by becoming "ontologically black" (that is, by identifying with the oppressed), and by repudiating their own whiteness (that is, by refusing to accept the benefits of whiteness). To Cone, whites must be born again. Thus reconciliation is God's gift of blackness to whites; liberation is God's gift to oppressed blacks to counter "the shit of the white environment."[66]

Since reconciliation is the work of Christ, it is not the proper task, or at least not the first task of black people's theological project. For whites, personal acts of devotion consist of relinquishing the presumption of privilege that whiteness confers and becoming ontologically black. (In postmodernity, one would think that this is an option for blacks, too, because so many black people have rejected their blackness.) Cone's experience of the Black Church influenced his appreciation for and ability to resource the confessional utterances and liturgical practices of African Americans, though this became his way of responding to the criticism leveled by Cecil Cone and others. Nevertheless, because he was deeply aware of the theodical impulse of black religiosity, he did not deride the faith as others did but rather generously lifted up the traditions. Cone sees black faith as a continuous affirmation of God despite the contradictions of black existence, in every historical phase.

Black suffering remains a scandal to Cone. His ongoing relationship to the Black Church permitted growth not only in his capacity to interpret the meaning of the faith but in his political awareness. He has broadened the circle of inclusion so that he is a willing participant in dialogue with third-world theologians, black women, gay men and lesbians, as those for whom God makes an option as well, those whom God chooses because they, too, are despised and rejected. On the way to becoming the "father of black liberation theology," Cone encountered many obstacles, including graduate school professors and others who tried to control his energy and space. Yet he also received much affirmation, which he relates in the autobiographical *My Soul Looks Back.* Cone was not opposed to the concept of black nationhood as a concomitant to black liberation in the early stages of his ministry. What remains unchanged about his perspective is that he still wholeheartedly affirms the project of liberation. A universal impetus has always been present in his thought, in his reluctance to affirm the literal blackness of Christ and opening the question of Christ's option to all who are poor and oppressed. Later in his career Cone's theological focus would shift to coalition-building between the oppressed black community and other oppressed communities. For Cone, the scandal of the cross continues in the scandal of a crucified world. His ability to affirm dignity and *somebodiness* for himself was instrumental in his appreciation for others' existential desire–and need–to be affirmed in their *somebodiness*, that is, for ontological affirmation. Today Cone struggles to make their critiques of the limitations of his early, narrowly focused perspective integral to his ongoing development, although the claim for human dignity–*somebodiness*, for everyone–is inherent in his earliest thought.

CONCLUSION

Historical Christianity's focus on the cross, the experience of chattel slavery and unabated experiences of suffering and delimitation illustrate in principle the major reason cited by black theologians as to why the symbolism of the cross became and remains central in African American Christianity. Race and class oppression stand as facts of life that still require that prophetic word from black theologians. So I want to sustain the theodicy thesis of black theologians by connecting it not only to the suffering of Jesus but also to that of his earliest interpreters. I advance the theodicy thesis by making the identification with Jesus stronger, connecting it with the Christian martyrs who acted in many ways to overcome that state of siege. They did it by organizing, by *apologia*; some fled; some went willingly to their deaths. However they confessed themselves to be religious persons, one thing that comes through loud and clear–in their rhetoric, in the creative ways they responded to their oppressors' will to extirpate their religion by extinguishing their lives–is the *melodrama* with which they confessed. Like the martyrs, some blacks willingly embraced death, but others did not because they had a will to survive and it was the will of the state that they survive because slavery was their oppressors' means of income and livelihood. And so the state "killed" them in other ways. By relating their personal and communal suffering to that of Jesus, black Christians have demonstrated a theodical intent in their reflections on the significance of the life and ministry of Jesus, especially his passion and death on the cross (given their experiences and the evangelical emphasis on the Atonement as *event*). In the years just prior to his martyrdom King saw the scandal of the cross in the intransigence of white violence. For Cleage, to this day, the scandal of the cross lies in the individualism of the Black Church. Through their apprehensions of doctrine they sacralized their experiences, overturned the scandal of white "interposition and nullification"[67] of their civil and human rights and maintained belief in the possibility of redemption through Christ.

Given the mores of the times, which were affected by the ongoing war in Vietnam, the emergence of white countercultural groups and the concurrent activism of white feminists, what did the emphasis on sacrifice and group loyalty mean, practically speaking, for black women in King's integrationist and Cleage's nationalist movements? In response to white restrictions on their agency, these powerful black men restricted black women's agency through domination and paternalism. In Cleage's *The Black Messiah* a number of sermons are eulogies or paeans to prominent men in the era of black consciousness, including King, Stokely Carmichael and Malcolm X. Nearly every reference Cleage makes to women in his sermons is by way of negative example. Thus, the praxis of sexism as paternalism was ensconced in both integrationist and nationalist philosophy.[68] Although Cone did not found a movement, he literally provides the ground of thought for many black and womanist theologians because he trained many, if not most of them, directly and indirectly. (It is impossible to assess his impact even on this author.) Nonetheless, the paternalistic foundation of sexism in the African American community that Roberts revealed vis-à-vis the nationalist critique of white oppression illuminates the hyper-masculinist context in which black theology was being shaped. Paula Giddings states:

> Black masculinity was challenged by racial caste and wives who were already engaged in the work force. In the beginning, the civil rights movement had served to confirm masculine as well as racial assertiveness, but when it began to break down, that old nightmare of impotence no doubt resurfaced.[69]

Perhaps black women's historical willingness to exercise whatever agency they could wrest from the society is one reason why some people in both movements resisted Cleage's emphasis on a black madonna. The inferred threat in black women's achieving agency—to which sexism as paternalism and as domination responded—certainly contextualizes Carmichael's infamous faux pas, as does the public loosening of sexual mores during the concurrent countercultural movement among whites. But in Cleage's thought, as well as in King's, subsumption and circumscription of the particular voices, insights and experiences of living, breathing African American women were the rule. The elevation of the symbolic Black Madonna was the exception. (I observe that Garvey and Cleage, wittingly or unwittingly, may have provided a prototype for black Catholic resistance to European cultural hegemony in worship.[70]) Moreover, since racism was the most compelling aspect of black existence to King, Cleage and other black theologians, and was likely the priority of most black women as well, they simply did not address the peculiar crosses of sexism and heterosexism in the African American experience. Neither did Cone, until he was summarily challenged by black women entering the discourse. For Cone today, the scandal of the cross lies in the intransigence of worldwide white imperialism and in the refusal of the churches to become evermore self-critical and vigilant in the naming of oppression.

Chapter 4

Rethinking Sacrifice

The Challenge of Womanist Christology

I would argue . . . that the significance of Christ is not his maleness, but his humanity. The most significant events of Jesus Christ were the life and ministry, the crucifixion, and the resurrection. The significance of these events, in one sense, is that in them the absolute becomes concrete. God becomes concrete not only in the man Jesus, for he was crucified, but in the lives of those who will accept the challenges of the risen Saviour the Christ.

                                                              –Jacquelyn Grant

Christ is present in the Black community working to sustain as well as to deliver it from the multidimensional oppression that besets it. Christ is also present as a prophet, challenging the Black community to rid itself of anything that divides it against itself and to renounce any way in which it oppresses others.

                                                         –Kelly Brown Douglas

There is nothing of God in the blood of the cross. God does not intend black women's surrogacy experience. Neither can Christian faith affirm such an idea. Jesus did not come to be a surrogate. Jesus came for life, to show humans a perfect vision of ministerial relation that humans had forgotten long ago. However, as Christians, black women cannot forget the cross. But neither can they glorify it. To do so is to make their exploitation sacred. To do so is to glorify sin.

                                                         –Delores S. Williams

African American women share in the historic experience of race and class oppression with black men and other people of color; class oppression with poor white women and men; and gender oppression with all women. With black men they bore the cross of slavery and, in

99

the post-slavery work force, the stigma of the servant class. Many southern African American women (and men) still wear, in their hands, on their backs and knees, the stigmata impressed by the sun, thorns and other hazards of nature, relics of their not-so-distant sharecropping past.

In postmodernity, with all people of color, black women and men share the cross of systemic racism and the issues endemic to it, especially the thwarting of the embarrassingly simple ideal of social, economic and political parity with whites—debates over which impugn the humanity of colored peoples the world over, the deprivations of which undermine their prospects for survival, liberation and creative self-expression. With all women, black women still die daily on the cross of sexism and the issues particular to it, including physical domination, economic injustice, political marginalization and jeopardized reproductive rights—debates over which impugn the capacity of women to be full moral and social agents, the associated deprivations of which undermine the ability of women to participate fully in the imaging and construction of their own lives.

African Americans have always wrested humanity and agency from their proscribed existence, in conversation with the faith traditions they inherited from both Africa and America. From the days of slavery the very intransigence of their life circumstances helped shape the community's image of the Divine as an embattled God and its image of Christ Jesus as a liberator from the seemingly demonic forces arrayed against it. The Bible provided mirrors of their experiences in stories of exile, enslavement and Exodus. In various and sundry ways Jesus was a prime exemplar of how to live in communion with God and neighbor in a context of oppression. Inspired by the critical perspectives on the Bible generated in slavery, black liberation theologians of the 1950s and 1960s articulating these experiences and sentiments of the African American community proffered hope, not in the compensatory mechanisms of slaveholding religion, but in the design, coordination and execution of practical *liturgies* (Greek: "the work of the people")[1] that were relevant to their sociopolitical situation. Whether the task was embodying the hermeneutics of sacrifice in the praxis of nonviolence or recovering the liberative import of the gospel through nation-building or coalition-building with other oppressed peoples, black theologians regarded the ongoing work of the people in claiming and exercising their freedom as that which God intended and as that which Jesus Christ's empowerment continuously effects. In the process, and in the naming of black experience, they discounted significant portions of the lived-world struggles of black women against sexist oppression coming from outside and from *within* the African American community. In so doing black theologians signified their understanding that racism was the most compelling aspect of black existence.

Nineteenth-century white feminists criticized women's social and political marginalization, having gained moral impetus from the anti-slavery movement. Some of these early feminist theologues also addressed the androcentrism of the Bible and Christian tradition,[2] evincing critical awareness of the role of "sacred" authority in the maintenance of oppression. Twentieth-century feminists continued their work, agitating for equal rights for women, again gaining momentum from the African American experience as the community renewed its press for political empowerment and ontological recognition, that is, for civil and human rights.

Although neo-orthodox and liberal theologians addressed to some degree oppression and the structural realities that undergird it; although the influence of historical criticism provided some relief from the strictures of conservative biblicism, privileged white, male experience nonetheless provided the paradigm for "human experience" in their constructs.[3] To feminist theologians, neo-orthodoxy and liberalism left intact hierarchical models for relations between men and women, since their proponents did not problematize Christ's maleness or masculinity itself. Yet feminists did not themselves problematize the issue of race as it pertained to women's experience, and they discounted black women's lived-world struggles against racist oppression by white women outside and especially within the feminist movement.[4] In so doing they gave primacy to sexism as the most compelling aspect of women's existence.

Although the latter-day African American male theologians emphasized black liberation, the biblical stories and interpretive traditions they used likewise highlighted masculine experience. Their counterparts in the feminist movement focused on women's liberation, viewing the Bible through the lenses of their experiences as white, middle-class women and as mothers. Thus, as black women began to study theology, all of the available theological paradigms were models of empowerment for whites and/or men, and not necessarily for black women and men and their children. Nevertheless, womanist theologians today acknowledge their ideological indebtedness to black and feminist liberationists. Because of their legacy of work on behalf of struggling and faith-*full* communities, the nature of black women's task remains deeply theological. Yet the inability or unwillingness of proponents within both movements to overcome socially reinforced sexism and racism points up an ideological contradiction that remains unresolved. Frances Beale described this phenomenon in the lived reality of black women as "double jeopardy."[5] As Beale noted, black women's particular experiences yielded valuable insights that contributed to the development of liberation ideology, although in both theological movements these insights were often hidden or subsumed.

During the early stages of the development of womanist perspectives, as activist black women reflected on the proscribed nature of their lives in their society, churches and homes, womanist theology began to take shape, emerging as a distinct academic discipline in the 1980s. It was articulated, in part, in response to Alice Walker's delineation of the basic contours of womanist consciousness in her book *In Search of Our Mothers' Gardens.* In this work of nonfiction and in her portrayal of black women in her novels and poetry,[6] Walker helped black female scholars of religion to name themselves in ways that celebrate their uniqueness, providing mirrors for them to see themselves as fully capable adjudicators of the demands of their lives.

THE SOCIAL CONTEXT OF WOMANIST CHRISTOLOGY

Womanists locate resources for doing theology in the *survival* and *liberation* traditions of the African American religious community. Consistent with the christocentrism of the Black Church, the evangelical thrust of black theology, along with critical insights on racism and classism in nationalist perspectives, the theologians I have focused upon have taken on the challenge of making the good news of and about Jesus relevant to all elements of a community forged in and forging ahead in crisis, bringing their own experiences of sexism to bear, as well. Kelly Brown Douglas explores the *roots of the Black Christ* and Christ's significance for African American women. Jacquelyn Grant focuses on *Black Church* traditions that have informed African American women and sustained them in their spiritual, social and political witness, yet maintains a stringent critique of racism, sexism and classism in the society, the academy and the Black Church. While varieties of womanist theology are critical of black theologies of liberation, they do not oppose the project of black liberation; they place a more nuanced emphasis on the goal of *survival* and *quality of life* issues for African American people, male and female. Delores S. Williams expresses this view of the womanist enterprise.

Womanist theology is not focused inward; rather, it emerges out of and engages in considered reflection on the experiences of black women in relationship to black men, particularly the black men with whom we form subsets of the human community; to nonblack women; and to each other, from slavery to the present. Proto-womanist christological reflection began in slavery. I came to the enterprise as a child with an understanding of myself as a social and religious being. As such, I have rights and obligations relative to humankind and to God, who is the source of my being, the path and sometimes goad to my *becoming.* As a maturing womanist I begin again with the questions of why and how I presently claim this identity as a lens through which I see Jesus' story as a source of divine empowerment for my personal and collective becoming.

Although the family context is presumably one of safety, in which self-realization may take place, it was there that I gained firsthand perspectives on class and gender oppression, as I related in earlier chapters. On reflection, I am startled by the ways economic considerations colored interrelations between and among my parents and siblings. The crushing awareness of our racial circumscription and poverty was reduplicated in the battery that both my alienated parents inflicted on their children, and on each other. I viewed these early, violent exchanges, which would culminate in tragedy, as affronts to my godly prerogative of *becoming*. As I moved beyond the environs of family and into active roles in the society and the church, I encountered racism, sexism and classism in ways that exacerbated my inherited self-alienation, for which I sought relief–not *remedy*–in the Christian faith.

Born in 1958 I was too young in the 1960s to assess the dynamic processes shaping the American culture and the far-ranging implications they held for my *becoming*. The push for civil and human rights in public arenas; the Vietnam War; the emergence of white countercultural movements (issuing forth in the sexual revolution and the proliferation of drug cultures, religious sects, radical fringe groups, and so on); and the rise of black theology reflected the kaleidoscopic moodscape of the American civic, social and religious consciousness. The confluence of these events fostered in me and other "buppies" the notion that self-determination was a reasonable expectation for our lives. Yet this idea, intimately related to our *becoming*, was not without its contradictions in our lived experiences.

Whether or not many blacks perceived her as a symbol, the unveiling of the Black Madonna (1967) and the African American community's rejection of her illuminate the intracommunal contradictions of that social context. Black women encountered the age-old phenomenon of sexism in culturally specific ways that devolved upon their history of slavery. In light of the way white society conspired to keep black men from participation in the post-slavery work force, black male principals in the sixties movements saw this as a time of *their* uplift. The emphasis on "manhood first" relegated black women's concerns to secondary status. Many black women acquiesced to this exclusionary posture of integrationists (such as Stokely Carmichael in his early days as chief spokesperson for SNCC), which complemented the paternalism of nationalists (like Black Panther leader Eldridge Cleaver, who first sounded the battle cry of manhood), despite the fact that both groups devalued women's worth as political and moral agents. Yet in an era that saw dramatic increases in both the sexual availability of white women and single female-headed households in the African American community, the rejection of the Black Madonna signaled the rejection of black women as social partners. Universalism in integrationist philosophy could support black men's acceptance of white women as social partners with more integrity than nationalist paternalistic rhetoric.

In other discourse tensions stirred among the women who represented various constituencies: black/white; lesbian/bisexual/heterosexual; poor/working class/middle class/wealthy; uneducated and under-educated/educated. Black women were immersed in totalistic ontological assault in the sexism, racism, heterosexism and classism of the age of Aquarius. Then, as now, abusive men and control-driven persons raped, battered and killed them. All these phenomena provided the seedbed of womanist christological reflection, having left black women with little choice but to develop theological perspectives that pertained to their need for *bodily* redemption. The development of this crucial insight on embodied theology would become especially important for black lesbians, who had been stratified out of any consideration as partners in theological and social discourse with heterosexual women and men. Like Mary, a number of black women "kept all these things in [their] heart[s]" (Lk 2:51).

As I see it, womanism has arisen to counter several interrelated claims concerning black women that have currency in the African American community. Most commonly signified is the myth that black women, along with white men, are the most powerful persons in American society. While this relates to the fact that whites severely delimited the options of black men in the labor force, it also comports with the view, generated in slavery, that black women are licentious and capable of fulfilling every titillating imagination of repressed white men. Another claim is that the community needs to be of one mind concerning what is sexually appropriate. In light of these views women are incapable of adjudicating for the community; they are untrustworthy moral agents who must be controlled or rejected. These myths and the sexual politics that devolve upon them portend the loss of community and are the proximate cause for my personal grief and the grief I share with other womanists in postmodernity.

Womanist consciousness has enabled me to see the relegation of my concerns, and indeed, my humanity, to secondary status as a pattern to which women are collectively subjected, primarily because men are socially and ecclesially conditioned to view women as morally lax or as objects of entitlement, and not as moral agents, subjects in process of becoming. With other womanist theologians I have begun to think about the religious, social and political experiences of black women and to reflect critically on the relationship between these and white, male-centered interpretations of Christian doctrine.

Atonement Theories in Womanist Perspective

Throughout Christian history the idea that Jesus Christ died "for our sake" has been alternately rendered as "on our behalf" or "in our stead" or "in our place," highlighting the surrogacy motif in scriptural and apostolic witness concerning Jesus.[7] Surrogacy has raised concern in feminist and womanist discourse over the nature of the relationship between God and Christ, inciting a controversy that poses several issues of grave concern for traditional theories of the Atonement which purport that God *required* Jesus' death. These include the *ransom* and *satisfaction* theories, which synergized in the *substitution* theories of Protestant reformers.[8] In the early church the prevailing mythos that the world was beset by competing principalities and powers gave rise to the belief that Jesus' death was a "ransom" paid to the devil. This idea was explicated by Origen (183-253) and upheld by St. Augustine and succeeding generations of Augustinian thinkers until the twelfth century, when St. Anselm of Bec and Canterbury (1033-1109) created a major paradigm shift in Western Atonement doctrine, systematically debunking the notion that the devil was due anything. Anselm affirmed that God was due honor. In his argument, in which he tried to demonstrate the necessity of the incarnation, if human sin were neither punished nor paid, then it would be subject to no law. If sin were not punished, something disordered is forgiven in the rational order. God is not constrained by the rational order but rather works within it; therefore it was not fitting for God to forgive something that is disordered. (Despite this, human beings are mandated to forgive; they may not arrogate unto themselves the moral authority of God.)[9] Moreover, if injustice is forgiven out of mercy alone, then injustice is more at liberty than justice. This would make injustice resemble God, since God alone is subject to no one's law. To fulfill the demands of the rational order and redeem God's plan for creation, justice requires either punishment or satisfaction (*aut poena aut satisfactio*). Although it was incumbent upon humankind to satisfy the demands of the Infinite, only a God could actually accomplish this; thus it was necessary for God to become human in order to restore the honor due to Godself.

Peter Abelard was a younger contemporary of Anselm. Abelard's view of the Atonement was *subjective*; he emphasized God's acts of love as the primary and ultimate factors in human redemption. Like Anselm, he rejected the concept that the devil had any proprietary rights over humanity that God had to purchase because human beings were "simply seduced."[10] Yet unlike Anselm and Western tradition up to that time, he did not overly stress human sin and unworthiness, and he rejected the necessity of the Atonement to satisfy the demands of justice. In his *moral influence* theory God's own initiative of grace (which he equated with love) prompted God, in Christ, to act on humanity's behalf. God's actions (especially Christ's death on the cross) in turn incite a response of love toward God and neighbor by their salvific potency and example. Abelard believed that God was not constrained to act in this way on human behalf. God was free to effect human redemption in another way, for God had shown the will to remit sin simply through forgiveness. Therefore it was unnecessary that God, or Jesus, should die for sins; hence it was unnecessary for God to become human. Yet God *chose* this unique act of grace to "arouse us to very great love of God," teaching humankind by this example that "true charity should not now shrink from enduring anything for him."[11]

Martin Luther (1483-1546) and other sixteenth-century reformers resumed the "classical" model of the Atonement, which both acknowledged the existence of evil principalities and affirmed that God was the *acting subject* implementing sacrifice as well as *the acted upon object* of sacrificial rites. (Aulen stated that there is also an *objective* and *subjective* element in Anselm's satisfaction theory of the Atonement, albeit more sharply dichotomized than in the classical view. Because of the divinity and the humanity of Jesus, God is part object and part subject of the sacrifice. Nevertheless, because Anselm placed more emphasis on God's action undertaken to restore God's honor and to fulfill the demands of the rational order, his doctrine is known as an *objective* theory.) The classical view is consistent with the biblical testimony of the priestly, prophetic tradition of the Israelites concerning Yahweh and of the early church concerning Jesus. For the ancient Israelites and the Jews of the first century, Yahweh provided the system of vicarious sacrifice in order to render the people clean and fit for worship, a means whereby they could indicate the seriousness of their intentions to be in communion with God and the neighbor. God, too, is objectively changed, in that God regards the estate of sinners by reason of the bloodloss. The early church, particularly the Johannine communities, similarly reformulated the meaning of Jesus' death, attributing his death to his own agency, ascribing to him a sacramental witness to the goodness and power of God against the countervailing principalities. In the age of the Reformation a concomitant stress on human sinfulness *vis-à-vis* the righteousness of God (*iustitia Dei*) gave a penal quality to the nature of Jesus' death in the substitution theory of the Atonement. This broke entirely with the prescription of merit as the basis of salvation. Although the doing of meritorious works connoted right spiritual action in the Middle Ages, in substitution theory the righteousness of God was *imputed* to humankind on account of the work and worthiness of Christ alone.

As I have indicated, oppressed Christians of the first and second centuries generated the hermeneutics of sacrifice in consequence of the interplay of persecution and adventism. Yet, due to the waning of time and the ineluctable processes of institutionalization, the church had to revise its earliest self-definitions, bartering with state powers in order to inoculate itself against the state's abuses while carrying out its Great Commission (Mt 28:19-20). In the fourth century Emperor Constantine appropriated the Christian religion to sacralize his mission of conquest. Instead of being an instrument of salvation for the world's oppressed, Christianity became the means of worldwide imperialism. As the church became increasingly self-absorbed, its stated interest in missions aligned with the goals of the state, by which the church accrued power, authority and converts, who in turn give it a rationale for its continued existence.

Unfortunately, rather than purport a meaning of Christ's death that empowers Christian adherents to be countercultural, *sacramental* witnesses, the entrenchment of its own power and authority seems to have been the goal of the church since Constantine. In the fifth century Augustine used the weight of imperial authority to crush the Donatists in their opposition to the Catholic church. In the Middle Ages Anselm consented to the class arrangements of feudalism, using it to model the Divine-human relationship. During the Peasant Revolt of 1525 Martin Luther stood against German peasants' demands for equitable economic conditions and political autonomy in favor of "the magisterial sword and secular (Roman) law as the only bar to a relapse in barbarism."[12] In colonial and slaveholding America the church in collusion with the state imposed the hermeneutics of sacrifice because it was effective in inculcating docility among would-be insurrectionists and maintaining civil order. In the early years of the twentieth century head of state Woodrow Wilson (1913-1921) implemented Jim Crow laws in order to maintain the illusion of white supremacy and separate, unequal institutions, which, of course, included the church. In the era of civil rights and Black Power white churches roundly ignored the abuses that state authorities heaped upon the black masses. And in postmodernity attitudes laced with sexist and heterosexist innuendo and rhetoric pervade black and white pulpits, negatively affecting the enactment and enforcement of laws protecting women and homosexuals. Thus, the church is historically guilty of inflicting and perpetuating abuse, allying with oppressors and imposing the hermeneutics of sacrifice on subjugated peoples in order to justify the abusive policies of the state and of its own ministerium.

Through the historical unfolding of Atonement theories and the hermeneutics of sacrifice the Christian emphasis on Jesus' role as a surrogate/scapegoat has supported "violence, victimization and undeserved suffering"[13] and lends credence to the charge of "divine child abuse" leveled by Asian American feminist Rita Nakashima Brock.[14] It is notable, though, that the church has developed no single doctrine or teaching on the Atonement, only a number of theories that have different weight from communion to communion. Many people in black churches harmonize theories of the Atonement, in much the same way that Christian tradition harmonized synoptic and fourth gospel accounts of the life and ministry of Jesus. Given that this syncretic model emphasizes Jesus' surrogacy as the means of spiritual liberation, often without a concomitant or necessary stress on political liberation, the doctrine begs for fresh interpretation so that it might have more liberative relevance for black Christians. Womanist theologians have taken up this challenge. In the process of formulating a Christology "from below," they stress the deeds of the historical Jesus and not the idealized Christ, in keeping with the liberative traditions of the religious community.

JACQUELYN GRANT

Jacquelyn Grant, a systematic theologian and an ordained elder in the AME Church, builds upon the Johannine christological presupposition that Jesus is God-become-human. As she notes, little distinction is made between Jesus and God in the hymnody, confessional utterances and theological understandings of the Black Church. The image of Jesus as the divine co-sufferer comports with black Christians' continuous attempts to compare Christ's suffering and death with their own. Like Douglas, Grant affirms the liberation perspective that Jesus/God is on the side of the oppressed,[15] making a similar claim that the experiences of black women in slavery replicated Jesus' suffering. Thus, Christ's identification with "the least of these" in his own context meant that he identified with those who were "the least of these" in their contexts. Surviving, resisting and overcoming slavery; living in and finding ways to express themselves artistically despite the strictures of the servant class, black women encountered in the stories about Jesus One who identified with them and empowered them in and through his (1) incarnation and lowly birth, (2) ministry to the poor, sick and outcast, (3) shameful and *wrongful* death, and (4) victorious resurrection. In postmodernity Jesus' whole story remains a message of freedom for black women, inspiring "active hope" in their struggle for liberation from the burdens of the "tri-dimensional phenomenon of race, class and gender oppression."[16] Grant describes the currency of the phrase, "the least of these":

> This notion of "the least" is attractive because it descriptively locates the condition of Black women. "The least" are those people who have no water to give, but offer what they have . . . Black women's experience in general is such a reality. Their tri-dimensional reality renders their particular situation a complex one. One

could say that not only are they the oppressed of the oppressed, but their situation represents "the particular within the particular."[17]

Far from being exclusive, this anthropological claim recognizes that black women are members of several communities at once: black people, poor people (generally) and women. The reality of black women finds some of them managing their lives despite whatever prominence or lack thereof they face in postmodernity. All of them engaged in the life-and-death struggle for meaningful existence in an alien culture are vulnerable to despair and dissoluteness and require ontological affirmation. That Jesus Christ was black, as black male liberation theologians claimed, was an affirmation of blackness. Yet, as Kelly Brown Douglas has stated:

> Essentially, the Black Christ was such a thorough response to the 1960s Black freedom struggles that it was impotent in dealing with concerns beyond racism. It, like the movement that called it forth, was grounded in a social analysis focused on race. The Black Christ signaled a one-dimensional understanding of social oppression.[18]

Against this shortfall in black theology, dating back to its incipience in the historic Black Church, Grant argues:

> The crucifixion was for universal salvation, not just for male salvation or, as we may extend the argument to include, not just for White salvation. Because of this Christ came and died, no less for the woman as for the man, no less for Blacks as well as for Whites.[19]

Among womanists, Grant consistently lifts up the image of Jesus as the "divine co-sufferer." For Grant, that Jesus Christ was born, lived, struggled and died among the poor was an affirmation that his ultimate victory is theirs to appropriate. That "Christ came and died, no less for the woman as for the man" was an affirmation of black femininity, indicating that Christ's significance lay not in Jesus' maleness but in his humanity. For Grant, the bold declaration that "Christ is a black woman" carries a step further black theologians' assertion that "Christ is black" by radicalizing black women's conceptual apparatus for imaging God. More important, in helping black women view the Divine impetus in/ as themselves, her formulation takes seriously the challenge of making the good news of and about Jesus ever more relevant to African American women. Taken together, as black women are unable to do otherwise, these assertions have implications for understanding the Atonement as God's option for and empowerment of black women. They allow black women to recognize the self-identified Christ in all their particularities. Christ's empowerment of black women lends greater, not less, universal import to the gospel, since they embody all these realities.

Nevertheless, Grant does not here recognize black lesbian and bisexual women's experience of heterosexist oppression in the totality of black women's experience. This, too, is the cross in the African American experience. Grant ignores lesbian and bisexual women's situation representing the "particular within the particular within the particular" and renders them "ultimate other[s]" according to Douglas, who uses Patricia Hill Collins's terminology in her critique of Grant.[20] Douglas challenges Grant's assertion that, in postmodernity, "Christ is a black woman," not because it is inaccurate but because Grant does not go far enough in affirming the necessary *wholeness* in the African American community. Douglas offers a *sociopolitical analysis of wholeness* with a fourfold intentionality not to oppress on the basis of race, sex, sexual preference or class. This is consistent with the slave community's commitment to continuing Jesus' ministry in the margins and Douglas's proposition that "God is as Christ does."[21] For Grant and Douglas, this activity includes the incarnation, ministry, sacrificial death and resurrection.

KELLY BROWN DOUGLAS

The history of the church is replete with christological controversies; perhaps no controversy has undermined the oneness, apostolicity, universality and holiness of the church's claims[22] more effectively than the issue of how Christ and, by extension, God is to be imaged. Kelly Brown Douglas, a systematic theologian and an Episcopalian priest, has explicated the emergence of the "Black Christ" in African American nationalist thought as a precursor to the development of a constructive womanist Christology. The nationalist offering of the Black Christ focused on the recognition or reimaging of God/Jesus as biologically black.[23] According to Douglas, Robert Alexander Young gave one of the earliest arguments for the blackness of God, whom Young believed would send a messiah to redress the wrongs blacks experienced in slavery. This messiah would be "born of a black woman." Douglas states that AME Bishop Henry McNeal Turner was among the first to identify the need for blacks to image God in the likeness of themselves, ascribing an ontological significance to the community's reimaging project. Whereas Young and Turner more directly linked the issue of Christ's/God's blackness to opposition to oppression, Marcus Garvey was one of the first to affirm blackness as a biological characteristic of the historical Jesus.

Despite these early attempts to state the significance of God/Christ in relationship to blackness, the Black Christ did not emerge as a formal category for theological reflection in the *liberation* approach until Black Power met with black theology. Contemporizing the relevance of the gospel for the oppressed, black theologians in the late 1960s framed their christological question in this way: Who is Jesus Christ for us today? Although their responses varied, they emphasized Jesus' suffering and stated mission of liberating the oppressed (cf. Lk 4:16-20) as those factors that characterized the essence of his identity, which led many of them to conclude that Christ is black.

Although Douglas locates the earliest warrants for the Black Christ in slave religion, for the slaves, the concept had less to do with Jesus' presumed biological race and more to do with those with whom he identified during his lifetime and who they were: the poor and despised. The slaves ascertained the good intentions of the Black Christ toward them in the stories of the liberating God of the Hebrew Bible and those of Jesus, whose ministry healing, feeding and spiritually affirming the marginalized resonated deeply with their needs. Salvation in slave religion was related to a commitment to continuing this liberating activity.

The slaves' focus on Jesus' liberating ministry was in clear contradistinction to the slaveholders' focus on the *incarnation* of God in the "White Christ," an archetype generated through cultural imperialism, as whites narcissistically appropriated the historical antecedents of Christianity and disingenuously imposed the hermeneutics of sacrifice on the non-Christian Africans and those who came to choose the Christian faith. Slaveholding religion stressed the incarnation of God in Christ for the purpose of reconciling humans to God through his atoning death. This Anselmian emphasis on God's act rendered Jesus' earthly ministry of little importance relative to the gift of salvation, which was "automatic" after conversion and which counterposed his liberating actions on behalf of the poor as "a standard for Christian actions."[24] This incarnational approach comports with Johannine Logos theology and the Pauline stress on "justification by faith" (*sola fides*), since Martin Luther (1483-1546) the cornerstone of Protestant theology. Douglas cites the Lukan gospel as important evidence of Jesus' liberating ministry. While the other synoptic gospels similarly relate Jesus' liberating acts, they are peculiarly in evidence in the gospel of Luke. The slave community responded affirmatively to these stories and traditions. Moreover, Jesus' own experience of suffering was a reflection of the slaves' suffering, as Douglas attests:

> Essentially, through the cross the slaves' experience and Jesus' experience converged. The suffering of slavery and the suffering of the cross were synonymous. The crucifixion confirmed to slaves

that they were one with Jesus, and more importantly, that Jesus was one with them.[25]

As outlined in chapters 1 and 2, the cross became the central motif in the liturgies, hymnody and confessional utterances of African Americans because the symbolism provided tangible parallels to the historical sufferings of the community. Yet this identification does not sufficiently account for the christocentrism of the contemporary Black Church, which heavily references the cross as part of its evangelical heritage. Still, in referring to the christocentrism of the Black Church, I do not simply imply a "high" Christology that is laced with the doctrinal presuppositions of evangelical faith and that focuses on the incarnation, as opposed to a "low" Christology that accents Jesus' liberating works. Rather, both understandings are taken together in a way that exponentially increases the significance of Christ Jesus' story for African Americans.

What accounts for the slaves' and their descendants' peculiar blend of high and low Christology based on incarnational *and* liberation approaches to understanding the nature of Christ Jesus? I maintain that, as the slaves were privy to both these aspects of Christian tradition, they had a theodical stake in lifting up the divine-human dynamic in the story. Christian tradition early sought to harmonize fourth gospel and synoptic accounts of this import of Jesus' mission and works, generating the hermeneutics of sacrifice as the rule of Christian conduct. I concur with Douglas's assessment that, taken alone, the incarnational thesis provided no binding moral standard upon Christians because it emphasized God's act in Christ and neither his nor our human agency. Yet through its stress on individual conversion Evangelicalism, one of the matrices of slaveholding and slave religion, promoted higher standards of holiness among Christians. Along with the imposition of the hermeneutics of sacrifice, it proposed even higher standards for the slaves in relationship to the slaveholders.

As I see it, suffering points up the need for holiness, experienced as wholeness. In this light holiness is agency; it is spiritual power for enduring, resisting and overcoming the causes of suffering. In the liberationist anthropology of my inheritance and training, the emphasis on human agency is integral to the salvific event expressed in the incarnational thesis and the salvation to be derived from following Jesus' example. Black church folks commonly confess, "He died that I might have a right to the tree of life," as the basis of eschatological hope, and offer evidence of salvation in their moral deportment: "If you live right, heaven belongs to you." A popularized version of black theologian James Cone's views on liberation and reconciliation recapitulates the community's stress on Christ's agency and human agency in the utterance, "Without liberation there can be no reconciliation."[26]

In their practice of telling and retelling parts of a *whole story* the community affirms the two natures of Christ Jesus, who charges them to be *wholly* holy and empowers them to fight their oppression. As Jesus was innocent, when the community responds to the call to holiness, highlighting its members' innocence, it exposes the egregious nature of the crimes against them and against *God*, in Christ, and confirms the ultimacy of their liberatory claims. Thus, in my and Douglas's liberationist perspective, the cross is not taken up apart from what the rest of the story affirms; namely, that Jesus was God *incarnate*, who lived, struggled and died in suffering solidarity with society's victims.

DELORES S. WILLIAMS

A systematic theologian and lay preacher in the Presbyterian denomination, Delores S. Williams matches the theme of black women's surrogacy to traditional views of the Atonement, which cite Jesus' death as a vicarious sacrifice for the sake of sinful humankind. As Williams has pointed out, surrogacy is that structure of domination that gives black women's oppression its unique character.[27] Owing to the unique ways black women's bodies have been exploited in and since slavery, naming black women's experience as surrogacy is more apt than any other ascription given by black theologians. Williams questions whether the image of Jesus as a surrogate figure has salvific power for black women, or whether by its sacralization it reinforces the exploitation that has accompanied their experience of surrogacy. She also questions with feminist scholars what Christian emphases on the sacrifice of Jesus indicate about God, raising the issue of the relationship between God and Christ in her discussion of *coerced* and *voluntary* surrogacy, linking black women's experience to their Christian self-understandings.

During slavery white men and women forced black women to provide surrogate services for them, exploiting their biological functions in order to (1) generate a steady supply of slaves for the developing capitalist economy, (2) gratify their sexual desires (although rape was also a means of social control), and (3) supply wet-nurse services for suckling white babies. Depicted as paragons of endurance, black women not only managed white people's homes—cooking, cleaning and caring for their children—but also labored, as did black men, in white-owned fields to sustain the agrarian economy of the South. The image of black women working alongside black men in the fields contrasted sharply with the standards of femininity upheld for white women, as did their alternate portrayal as sexually and morally lax. Thus, whites exploited black women's bodies, sexually and maternally, in substitution for white women's bodies; their labor, in substitution for that of white women and men as well as black men (according to prevailing norms respecting social roles). Williams labels this exploitation of black women during the antebellum period *coerced surrogacy.*

Williams describes black women's labor in the postbellum period as *voluntary surrogacy,* because whites could no longer legally compel them to work on their behalf. Although, to date, black women are still sexually exploited by white men, Williams states that such illicit sexual coupling was sharply curtailed in the postbellum period, as white men lost their legal right to rape black women, and as black men and women together sought ways to protect black women from this kind of assault. Because of the premium placed on white women's femininity and "virtue," whites sought to keep black men from meaningful participation in the labor force and relegated black women to subservient positions therein (as housekeepers, for example).[28] Many black women today (and, increasingly, other women of color) are circumscribed within this range of social roles, constituting a class of servants to white people. An important theological and social ramification of their circumscription is that black women are unable to participate more creatively in their own lives. This, too, is the cross in the African American experience. The racial caste system of the post-slavery work force presently functions as a bar to social, political and economic equality and the quality of life black women desire for themselves and their families. In postmodernity, given the way the racial caste system conspires with the criminalization of black men, both by inference and by massive imprisonment,[29] perhaps it singularly accounts for the high rates of disaffection and personal dissolution in the African American community.

Since there is little difference between *coerced* and *voluntary* surrogacy in light of the way job markets have been constructed to obstruct black women's right and responsibility of self-development, I see Williams's distinction between the two as a heuristic device that enables a historical perspective on black women's oppression and allows one to make generalizations about the cross in black women's experience.

Williams challenges the anthropological assumption in traditional Atonement doctrine that Christ died for the sake of sinners. The slaves would have no need for justification of this kind, in light of their innocence and the empirical evidence of their oppression by whites. Furthermore, she states that Jesus' life and witness condemned the degradation black women experience in their presently circumscribed and surrogate roles. Like Douglas, Williams cites the synoptic gospels as scriptural warrant for fleshing out the content of a ministerial vision, proffered in the life of Jesus, which allows black women to see that their redemption does not depend upon any form of surrogacy but upon their participation in Jesus' vision.

According to Williams, by his life, by his practice of "righting relationships" and by his ministry of healing folks physically, spiritually
and mentally, Jesus demonstrated God's intention for oppressed people
to live abundantly. In killing Jesus, the human principalities and powers
signaled their intent to kill his liberative, egalitarian vision. The resurrection represented "the life of the ministerial vision gaining victory
over the evil attempt to kill it."[30] In his life, then, and not in his death,
according to Williams, Jesus conquered sin by not submitting his moral
agency to the powers that challenged his authority to transform tradition. As theologians throughout Christian history have done, Williams
uses the language and social, cultural and political thought of her world
to transform the significance of the doctrine of the Atonement for black
women. She states:

> Black women are intelligent people living in a technological world
> where nuclear bombs, defilement of the earth, racism, sexism and
> economic injustice attest to the presence and power of evil in the
> world. Perhaps not many people today can believe that evil and
> sin were overcome by Jesus' death on the cross, that is, that Jesus
> took human sin upon himself and therefore saved humankind.
> Rather, it seems more intelligent to believe that redemption had
> to do with God, through Jesus, giving humankind new vision to
> see resources for positive, abundant relational life—a vision hu-
> mankind did not have before.[31]

At the controversial "Re-Imagining Conference" of 1993 sponsored
by the World Council of Churches,[32] Williams appraised the implications of reimaging God/Christ at the "cultural root," a project that the
African American community has historically undertaken in order to
counter the idolatrous images proffered in racist propaganda (and which
were themselves *re*images).[33] Williams herself undertook the effort to
unmask the "defects" of the community's various depictions of the
reimaged Christ. While the slaves signified a Christ/Jesus who "supported and fitted into a culture of resistance," Christ remained, nonetheless, white, powerful and male until black theologians reimaged Christ
as black. Williams lifted up, out of her own religious experience, *another*
reimaged Christ, a "relational" Jesus, who was "shrouded in poverty"
and who was "female and male indexed" (as Jesus was regarded as "poor
little Mary's son"). Yet Williams questioned the adequacy of even this
reimaged form, since it does not attend to the needs of Mary's daughters. Williams posited the need for womanist theologians to reimage
Jesus and the significance of the "Christian pageant" continuously
through the lenses of their experience, because the "androcentric tell-

ing of African American history"[34]–and Jesus' story (!)–obfuscates God's/ Jesus' empowerment of women. For example, the confession that the Spirit came through a woman's body means that "feminine is incorporated in the very being of Jesus." This example of a *re-re*imaged Jesus provides a view of the incarnation that is "serviceable" to women (empowering them to see the divine impetus in/as themselves) and that "energizes" the church, as this signification of the story provides further testimony to the character and creativity of God.

For Williams, the story of Hagar, the Egyptian slave and surrogate for Sarah (Gn 16; 21:8-21), is a compelling analogy to the experience of African American women. Hagar's story has implications not only for a communitarian survival ethic in the African American community but also for reconceptualizing the nature of God. In the story Hagar is not set free; ultimately, she is cast out. Yet she survives, along with her son, Ishmael. Their experiences belie the claim of black theology that the historical and ontological project of God is freedom for God's people and that the crowning achievement of this project is Christ's surrogacy for humankind on the cross. Rather, this story posits the survival of the black family by all means available. As in Hagar's story, so for black women, survival is effected through the resources God grants and empowers them to see. In agreement with Douglas and Grant, Williams asserts that black women cannot forget the cross because Jesus' brokenness is a mirror of their brokenness. Nevertheless, she warns African American women against glorifying suffering for its own sake because it makes their exploitation sacred.

In fairness to black men, womanists need to ask if Christianity idealizes suffering for them as well, since the suffering *community* understands itself as fundamentally Christian. In American society black men are suffering servants and scapegoats too. Many black men are effectively locked out of economic power arrangements in society. Targeted and censured by the criminal justice system, they become coerced surrogates in the prison system. Others, uneducated and under-educated, are proscribed within the same system of voluntary surrogacy imposed upon black women. Given the ways that oppression takes on a character and life of its own, black suffering is *demonarchy*,[35] posing a very real, annihilistic threat to *all* black people. Sadly, because of high incidences of absence, social and economic interdiction and disaffection among black men, black women are also compelled to act as surrogates on their behalf. Since black women are constrained to act on behalf of the community by their pressing circumstances, is this *coerced* or *voluntary* surrogacy? Sometimes it is difficult to judge whether black women respond to their communities out of love or an undue sense of obligation, fostered in the hermeneutics of sacrifice and exacerbated by inequitable social conditions. Nonetheless, because some black men shift the blame for their degradation onto "strong" black women, leading to the distorted view of African American women as "devouring mothers" or "castrating matriarchs,"[36] the polemic on surrogacy is as necessary as reimaging God/Christ as black in order to identify the correct antecedents of black disempowerment.

Grant has discussed the role of male preachers and male God/Christ-symbolism as fulfillment of absent father-figure and husband-figure for many black women. The sensual/sexual overtones in black worship are powerful indicators of this.[37] Grant implicates the historic "catastrophic emasculation" of black men by white society as a powerful underlying cause of sexism in the black community. The focus on manhood, that is, the "right" of black men to have equal capacity to "provide" for their families; the shifting of blame for the phenomenon of black male emasculation onto black women and the silence of black women so as not to divide the community; and, may we not forget, black women's existential desires to be in right relationship, all contribute to the frustrating experiences of sexism as paternalism. Furthermore, these factors lie at the root of many black women's reluctance to disclaim a relationship between Jesus' maleness and the office of Christ. This does not mean that womanists should therefore permit this state of discourse to remain unchallenged. As Douglas points out, black women's "own testimonies emphasize Jesus Christ's activities in their struggle to survive and be free, not his maleness."[38] It does mean, however, that womanists need to be sensitive to the religious and social particularities of the women they seek to empower, because these nuances exist in themselves, as well, and because black women's self-images—and indeed, their very futures—are at stake. Douglas queries:

> Given Jesus' maleness, is such an equation evident when a black church woman says that "calling God 'she' just doesn't sound right"? Does a male Jesus imply to black women that God is also male? . . . [Black male preachers] have reasoned . . . ordained clergy must also be male . . . Womanist theology must discuss the relationship between the biological particularities of the historical Jesus and the universal qualities of the Christ of faith. At stake is whether or not black women are able to see themselves in Christ and Christ in themselves.[39]

The polemic on surrogacy is also necessary to engage those black men who have not been so radically disempowered in the task of reformulating power dynamics within the African American community so as not to reproduce the reality of domination. This includes those men in privileged positions in the Black Church. Since the nineteenth century many black male pastors, following Bishop Allen's lead, have argued persistently from biblical authority, relegating women to marginal positions in the church and society. Of seven historically black churches identified by Lincoln and Mamiya, one, the Church of God in Christ, explicitly prohibits the ordination of women, subjecting them to the proof-texts, "Let your women keep silence in the churches: for it is not permitted unto them to speak; but they are commanded to be under obedience (1 Cor 14:34, AV) and "I suffer not a woman to speak nor to usurp authority over the man, but to be in silence" (1 Ti 2:12, AV). In the Baptist communions, "while there is no specific policy against the ordination of women . . . the general climate has not been supportive of women preaching and pastoring churches."[40] Since the AME Zion Church became the first black and first Methodist communion to ordain women in 1894, Methodist authorities have been decidedly more progressive on this issue; however, female ministers still have to contend for viable pastorates and denominational support. All of this reluctance to allow women full participation in the life of the church suggests an arbitrariness with which sacred authority is ascribed to the Bible in ways that validate the gifts and callings and humanity of black men but not of black women. This, too, is the cross in African American women's experience.

For Williams, self-love, *regardless,* is the sine qua non of womanist thought, because black women's roles as nurturers and sustainers of the black family and community implicate them in their own sexist oppression by black men. Yet black women do not live in a vacuum. The lived-world struggle to appropriate self-love as a critical principle is difficult. Many needs exist within the African American community, and black women have more often than not risen to meet them. For example, when brothers, lovers, husbands and friends are embroiled in the prison system, who provides for their considerable social, emotional and economic needs besides black women? When black women are unable to meet those needs, guilt often ensues because many regard their powerlessness as a failure to do their Christian duty. Nevertheless, it is incumbent upon black women to love themselves "*regardless*" if they are to participate creatively and responsibly in the quest for justice and dignity for themselves and the community.

Moreover, the impact of the plight of black men on black women and their children and the demands made on black women to be providers and paragons of strength can be psychologically devastating in light of their own interdiction and disaffection in the larger society, and can lead to a dominating display of power by those who are otherwise powerless. I view my childhood experiences of physical abuse in this light. The extent of my mother's self-alienation gives impetus to my search for the meaning of my blackness and femininity apart from the choices that society and the church proffer. Are there possibilities for service and uplift in African American communities that are non-exploitative? Grant distinguishes between "the sin of servanthood" and "the deliverance of discipleship."[41] She criticizes the Christian use of the language of service/servanthood as adequate descriptors for black women's witness because of black women's socioeconomic marginalization. The historic and ongoing suffering of black/women/people entails second-class citizenship and often implies to ruthless exegetes that they are cursed, divinely destined to be "servants of servants."[42] Thus Grant argues with Williams that surrogacy is sin:

> Christians, in the interest of fairness and justice, need to reconsider the servant language, for it has been this language that has undergirded much of the human structures causing pain and suffering for many oppressed peoples. The conditions created were nothing short of injustice and in fact, sin.[43]

Grant, who also participated in the Re-Imagining Conference,[44] decried the use of oppressive language in three areas: race relations, class relations, and sex/gender (or male/female) relations. She stated:

> It should be clear that the control of language via creation and definition makes for the control of people. It assists the process of keeping certain people in their prescribed place. It orchestrates people's feelings about themselves and about others.[45]

Yet Grant again excluded from her reflections the experience of the disempowering—even death-dealing—effects of oppressive language as it affects those involved in same-sex relations. Although she traced the history of the institutionalization of sexist/generic language, Grant reserved her strongest condemnation for white supremacy, which is, as she stated, "manifested in all aspects of life." In order to counter this evil ensconced in the language and in traditional biblical interpretations, Grant proposed a moratorium on the use of "servant language" among oppressed people.

In keeping with Walker's definition of a womanist as one who is "committed to survival and wholeness of entire people, male and female," womanist theologians emphasize community building and maintenance. The current focus on the recovery of the black community is, in part, the reason Grant posits the necessity of the deliverance of discipleship as a model of empowerment for those who have not been considered disciples. This ought to be the case whether a devotee is female or male, homosexual, bisexual or heterosexual, whether one is empowered or disempowered in this class-stricken culture. The social, political and economic exigencies of their day to day lives demand the serious engagement of all black people in the struggle for survival and liberation from the oppression of the white power structures that dominate every sphere of public life in America. This struggle extends, as ever, to the religio-cultural sphere.

CONCLUSION

Just as male black liberation theologians and white feminist theologians attempted to redress the absence of their voices in theological discourse, womanist theologians are attempting to address black women's needs and the needs of an entire community in crisis. Although many of the historical sources in the development of black and feminist theologies inform womanist theology, the discipline recognizes black women's particular experiences as discrete sources. Womanist theologians challenge the adequacy of the Exodus paradigm that black theologians use and the critical lenses of white feminists, offering instead "herstories" from the Bible and their experiences, which state more precisely the nature of their oppression and reflect their understanding of God's participation in their efforts to survive, be free and creatively express themselves.

As clergy, Douglas and Grant and I have a different stake in the received story than non-clergy womanists. They identified the need for womanist theologians to embody the wholeness that they find in Christ Jesus, the prophet and the co-sufferer, whom they seek to mediate to the community in ever more inclusive ways. In theory this seems plausible; yet it is in fact more daunting than it appears, as womanists seek their own survival in a male-dominated profession, and as they work out their own souls' salvation. I suspect that any womanist's ecclesiastical identity has a bearing on what she is able to state publicly, whether she feels free, fears censure or whether, out of her own conditioned religious consciousness, she is reluctant to affirm what other womanists believe. As Williams has stated, womanist theology is a *variety* theology, concerned with the survival and liberation of black/women/people. It is informed by various christological traditions. Grant's typology of white feminists' christological perspectives in the book *White Women's Christ and Black Women's Jesus* is instructive for nuancing womanist perspectives. This is a task that should be undertaken by womanists collectively and by each womanist entering the discipline for herself.

Williams's challenge cuts to the heart of traditional notions of the Atonement held so dear in the Black Church. The relevance of her critique of the violence sanctioned therein cannot be overstated as African Americans reflect on the historic and ongoing *defilement* of the African American community, which is attested to in the stories of black women and men in and since slavery and the heyday of lynching. In postmodernity the blood-related issues of AIDS and black nihilism (or black-on-black violence) place the onus for ethical deliberation on the significance of Christ's blood/bloodloss squarely on the African American community. Yet defilement places the larger cosmic community at risk, as environmental rape continues unabated and the threat of global thermonuclear war–the "limits of unimaginable violence"-[46] is a very real, if hidden, palpable presence in our midst, lurking about, like the devil incarnate, seeking to devour the earth.

As postmodern Christians it is important to state forthrightly, as Williams has done, that God did not condone the violence of the cross or black women's surrogacy; nor yet does God condone this present state of affairs. But in fairness to the story, Jesus' story, Williams should allow for its multiple impact and import in its own context, for its own day. I agree with Williams that Christians need to look more carefully for the life-affirming images in the ministry of Jesus, such as the mustard seed and the fishes and the loaves. At the Re-Imagining Conference, when asked, "What is to be our theory of the Atonement?" and, "For what did Jesus come?" Williams demurred, lifting up these images as more faith-inducing than that of a suffering God:

> Those are the kinds of images we need for our religion. I don't think we need folks hanging on crosses and blood dripping and weird stuff. I think we really need to see the sustaining, the sustenance images, the faith that we are to have. The fish and loaves, the candles we are to light, that our light will so shine before people so that we can remember that this message that Jesus brought, I think, is about life, and it's about the only two commandments that Jesus gave; [they were] about love.[47]

Although Williams takes issue with the notion that God required the death of the Son, Jesus, as I do, this understanding of the significance of the Atonement belies other testimony in scripture that God indeed sent Christ, but for more honorable purposes. All three synoptic gospels record Jesus as having told the parable of a vineyard owner who sends servant after servant to inspect the site of the vineyard only to have each one shamefully and brutally mistreated.[48] Anticipating a kindlier response, the vineyard owner sends his own son, thinking "they will respect my son." Instead, the tenants murder him, incurring the wrath of the vineyard owner. In what are likely the most quoted Bible verses among Christians, John 3:16-17, the gospel writer has Jesus testifying of God that "God so *loved* the world, that he gave his only-begotten Son, that whosoever believeth in him should not perish, but have everlasting life. For God sent not the Son into the world to condemn the world, but that the world through him might be saved" (AV). Thus, synoptic and Johannine traditions allege that, if humankind is incorrigible, God's intentions are honorable (although the theodical traps posed by God's presumed omniscience are formidable and, so far, irresistible). Yet I do not offer these as proof-texts in order to exonerate God; rather, I wish to indicate what these confessions illuminate about the worlds in which they were generated. In that Hellenistic context these laudatory ascriptions of God in the Fourth Gospel counterpose a long-existing doctrine of God which stated that the supreme deity and ruler of the gods, Zeus, created human beings for toil and pain. In Aeschylus's play *Prometheus Bound*,[49] Zeus had a controversy with the protagonist and champion of humankind. Zeus wanted to destroy all humans and replace them with another, perhaps more servile race. Prometheus, whose name means "forethought," instead gave gifts to humankind, gifts of arts and sciences that raised them from the status of slaves of gods. (This common signification about humans in relationship to the Divine was present in the Babylonian cosmogony). In utter defiance of Zeus and his minions, Prometheus "stole from heaven the gods' prerogatives of fire, and gave this final gift" to the people of earth. For this act of defiance Zeus seized and bound Prometheus in fetters on a rocky mountain; Zeus then sent his messengers, Hephaistos (ironically, the god of fire), along with Power and Violence into the world to punish and ridicule humankind and its hapless helper. Countering this myth, the scriptural passages confirm what Williams seeks to affirm: "Jesus came for life" and to demonstrate the utter feasibility of life in love and honor. In light of their witness, I agree with her claim that "there is nothing of God in the blood of the cross," if she means by that there is nothing of God's *sanction* in violence.

Moreover, in the Hellenistic cosmogony, Zeus is not held to be eternal; rather, he rules among the gods by power and violence. Prometheus holds the key to his downfall; he is able to resist to the end revealing the means by which Zeus will fall. The gospel writers transmute the significance of this story for the suffering Christian communities: among them, the Fourth Gospel consistently sublimates the context of death with the promise of eternal life for believers in Christ Jesus. This spiritualizing tendency of the Fourth Gospel is significant because of its impact on the lives of African American Christians (and all Christians) and because of the images of Jesus that emerge therefrom and their import for black faith. Certainly, as their confessional utterances confirm, black people know Jesus through the testimony of John: Word, Light, Lamb, Son of God, Door, Good Shepherd, Way (and Way-maker), Friend, Sovereign Lord. The community that attested to these ascriptions about Jesus was a community under siege, that, like radical black activists, proffered agape, sacrificial love, to *itself.* "A new commandment I give to you, that you love one another; even as I have loved you" (Jn 13:34). Unfortunately, this focus is lost in the harmonizing tendencies of eurocentric biblical discourse, which in each of its attempts to find the "historical Jesus" has sought to posit monolithic views that have little to do with the liberation of African Americans and even less to do with their experience of Jesus.

The aforementioned scriptural witness comports with Jewish claims about God, namely, that God loves the people of God: "But this I call to mind and therefore I have hope: the steadfast love of the LORD never ceases, his mercies never come to an end; they are new every morning; great is thy faithfulness" (Lam 3:21-23). This contrasts sharply with the picture of Zeus in the Greek dramas: Zeus is petulant, mean, vindictive, always and forever needing to be appeased, whether through blood sacrifice or by constantly servile deportment. Throughout Israelite history the Jewish theodical project sought to protect the notion of the love of God for the people of God, the sovereignty of God over all people and all creation.[50] Moreover, in the Deuteronomistic code, each test of individual and collective suffering was construed as an opportunity to clarify the devotee's and/or the people's intentions toward God. From the Exodus through their attempts at nation-building, taking captive and being taken captive, through exile and return, this signification about God sustained the identity of the people in the various alien cultures to which they were politically subject, culminating in the priestly, prophetic understanding that *Yahweh reveres and does not require blood.*

Perhaps it is ironic, or it is a testimony to the vagaries of imperialism, that no such respect for life was imputed to Yahweh in regard to the violent conquest of the Canaanite peoples. The Christian appropriation of the Suffering Servant songs, too, indicates something about the currency of sacrifice and suffering for their own sake. Nonetheless, in historical context, servant symbolism and Canaanite oppression expose the system of sacred violence that undergirded life in the ancient and developing Near East. With the advent of prophetic messianism to address/redress its own political and military subjugations, Israel began to evince critical awareness of the relationship between sacred violence and structural violence, and to proffer redemptive themes that emphasized Yahweh's establishment of righteous rule and promise of peace among the nations. This had the effect of making Yahweh a more palatable God and reflected Israel's growing theological and philosophic sophistication. Thus, James G. Williams argues, Israel as a nation was "created through a process of becoming exceptional *vis-à-vis* the violent structures in the midst of which it came to be."[51] While this may be true in terms of Israel's development of a theology of resistance and hope, the practical implications of this statement are troubling when viewed in the light of Jesus' crucifixion and the oppression of Palestinian people in the state of Israel at present.

Most assuredly I do not wish to minimize the violence that Christian anti-semitism engenders; nevertheless, according to New Testament understandings of the Jewish leaders' complicity in Jesus' execution, the sacrifice of Jesus was a capitulation to the violent authority of Rome, a response rooted in the political insecurity of the Jewish masses, evincing the strength of neither resistance nor hope. Nor do I wish to minimize the violence perpetrated against the Jewish people in the Holocaust, which occasioned their return to Palestine, nor yet in the countermeasures used by displaced Palestinians—Muslim and Christian—bent on self-determination. I simply want to indicate the endemicity of violence in the world we know and to point out that this sense of sacrifice—*permitting injury or disadvantage to someone or something for the sake of someone or something else*—does *not* have divine sanction and is precisely a betrayal of Yahweh's insistence on righting relations.

Sacrifice understood as the surrender or destruction of something prized or desirable for the sake of something considered as having a higher or more pressing claim is not genuinely that unless it involves one's own agency. The central story's grounding in Hebraic faith and liturgy sheds light on the early church's confession that Jesus' death was *once for all.* Because God desires mercy and not sacrifice, there should never really be any reason for the act of sacrifice. Yahweh's institution of the sacrificial system and Jesus' self-sacrifice are thus construed as the disclosure of God's mercy. Despite the melodramatic quirks in the telling and retelling of this story, Judeo-Christian traditions attempt to signify God's unwillingness to trivialize the blood/life/loss of any creature. In light of this the belief that God, in Christ, shed God's own blood elevates the meaning of the *once for all* nature of Christ Jesus' death. The divine-human dynamic in the story signifies that there is *something* of God in the blood of the cross, confirming the commonly held belief among African Americans that Jesus is the "divine co-sufferer," as Grant attested. Contrary to the church's historical attempts to impose the hermeneutics of sacrifice on any people whom it or the state would subjugate, this is not sanction for anyone's or any group's victimization. Rather, it highlights the egregious nature of every historical crime against humanity and the Divinity. Thus, the cross is about God's love for humankind in a profound sense. I believe that Christians need to ponder the implications of Christ's death continuously, because the drama testifies to the exceedingly great lengths to which God goes to advise the extent of human estrangement. It is no slight on the intelligence of black women when they confess this; rather, it reflects on what they say they need and what they say Christ's real presence, mediated through the gospel, provides–redemption and release from the self-alienation and social alienation they experience in their workaday lives. Gospel singer Helen Baylor's *Testimony* is a stirring account of her deliverance from drug addiction through Christ's agency. She attests that there *is* power in the blood, even in the *name* of Jesus.

For many Christians, while the image of a crucifix signifies awareness of a God who suffers with us in our experiences of suffering, the image of an empty cross signifies faith in the possibility of our own resurrection. Williams disparages this distinction because, "too often, Christians are thereby taught to believe that something good can result from violence."[52] Yet the reality of violence in black women's lives informs their theodical attempts to ascribe *meaning* to their suffering and to affirm the divine assistance to gain victory over it. For many, the struggle is ongoing. That is not to say that "violence, victimization and undeserved" suffering are redemptive, but that suffering and merit are unrelated, just as love and merit are, and that we who suffer can be redeemed. This is the singular significance of God's self-disclosure in every aspect of Christ Jesus' walk with us. When black women can see the truth of this revelation, self-love becomes imminently possible. Williams affirms that the cross and crucifixion are "symbols of realism . . . reminders of what can happen to reformers who successfully challenge the status quo . . . [and] of the struggle that lies ahead"[53] for those who are likewise engaged. Perhaps that is redemptive for a survivalist, but for many survivors of violence, the crucifix is a supreme reminder of God's *with-us-ness* (that is, of God's decision to be *at-one* with us; or, better said, of the fact that we are already *at-one*). The empty cross is a symbol of God's continuous empowerment. This is why I believe that the continuous intercession of the spirit of Christ must become integral to womanist reckonings of Christ Jesus' significance. Not the resurrection but Christ's intercession signals the end of the gospel story and the beginning of Christ's significance for us, "on our behalf."

Chapter 5

Our Mothers' Gardens

Discrete Sources of Reflection on the Cross in Womanist Christology

What might have been? He's never far from my mind. I was reading in Scriptures where the Lord Jesus Christ was scarred. His visage, his face was marred beyond that of any other man, and Emmett came to me. I said, "Oh my God, what a comparison." The spirit spoke to me as plainly as I'm talking to you now. And the spirit said, "Emmett was race hatred personified. That is how ugly race hatred is." I said, "Oh." I had to sit down. It struck me really hard. If Jesus Christ died for our sins, Emmett Till bore our prejudices, so . . .

–Mamie Mobley
Mother of Emmett Till

Why I'm not good enough? Harpo ast Mr. _____.
Mr. _____ say, Your mammy.
Harpo say, What wrong with my mammy?
Mr. _____ say, Somebody kill her . . .
[Harpo]: It not her fault somebody kill her. It not! It not!

–Alice Walker
The Color Purple

In analytical psychology, liberation from alienation entails anamnesis, or retrieval of experience that is painful yet necessary for the healing/wholeness of the psyche. Borrowing from this insight, womanist theology recognizes reflection upon personal and collective experience as discrete sources in the construction of theological statements. Although it is varietal, womanist theology is fundamentally a theology of liberation; its discipline requires commitment to the wholeness of entire peoples, male and female. Collective anamnesis requires thoroughgoing honesty about the ways in which black women and their families have been disempowered by the social sins of racism, sexism, heterosexism/homophobia and classism. Womanists affirm the didactic value of "intergenerational dialogue"[1] with their predecessors–the slave women who first articulated the meaning of African American women's struggle to come to faith–as well as the families and constituencies to which womanists belong and from which they derive theological insight.

In the Introduction I stated that my penchant for theological reflection began at an early age, as I tried to understand the circumscription of black families in the southern work force. I intimated that my family was embroiled in a complex of issues that often resolved in domestic violence, some of which stemmed from the economic and social stress we were experiencing, some of which stemmed from both my parents' profound self-alienation and social alienation. My mother's story, in particular, is that of a woman who, for the better part of her short life and for all of my life with her, lived in deep grief over personal losses too numerous and painful to recount. Lost in a fog of addiction, after several failed marriages, miscarriages and broken relationships, she, too, was shot and killed by her lover. Her murder attests to the insidiousness of sexism within the African American community and to the truth of the radical critique of the hermeneutics of sacrifice put forth in the little ditty that some Black Power advocates sang in opposition to the Civil Rights movement, which I mentioned earlier and take liberty to paraphrase here: "Too much love . . . nothing kills a [woman] like too much love."

Building on Abelard's insight that Christ's example teaches and saves us, I believe that anyone's death has salvific significance if we learn continuously from the life that preceded it. I often resort to my mother's garden–her life story–which, for many years I regarded as a tragic tale that had moralistic theological import, at best. Whenever I have failed to heed the lessons I have learned, it reflects the fact that I had neglected to tend her garden. Sometimes, I have to admit, I very nearly forget the "rose" that she was–sweet, fragile, beautiful, funny, boisterous, quiet, complicated–much like Margaret Avery in her depiction of Shug Avery in the movie *The Color Purple*. Although her self-alienation was evident long before I was born, in light of her considerable gifts of music, poetry, intellect and humor, upon my mother's demise, I was compelled to ask Mobley's question, "What might have been?" as a grieving child. As a consequence of my own alienation, I have been compelled many times to ask Harpo's questions. As a religious person and as a scholar in the tradition of "faith in search of understanding," I search wholeheartedly for answers to them all. The personal crosses I have borne form the basis of my engagement in proto-womanist and womanist reflection on the cross in the African American experience.

As a black/woman/person with roots in the poor and working classes, I bring all of my experiences and insights to bear on my womanist theological reflection, in hope of *sacramentally* witnessing to who and what God is in me.

A WOMANIST MUSING/WOMANIST PROSE

What might have been? Why I'm not good enough? What wrong with my mammy? The above citations instance the experiences of African American males Emmett Till, a mid-twentieth century lynching victim and martyr (d. 1955), and Harpo, a fictional character in Alice Walker's controversial novel. Till was a fourteen-year-old boy accused of whistling at a white woman. When his body was discovered, he had been shot and beaten, his neck rigged with a gin-mill fan around it. Harpo's mother, Annie Julia, had been shot and killed, like my own mother, by a jealous lover. Each crime disclosed demonstrates how inextricably linked are the sufferings of African American women and men and their children. The narrator relating each fatality nods to the world of spirit: Mobley, to the Holy Spirit, out of her Christian conceptualization; Walker, to the world of dreams (Harpo has just awakened from a nightmare), out of her nonpersonalistic theism and humanistic commitments. Each in her own way, for better and worse, confirms the creedal postulation of a "communion of saints." In their accounts, death destroyed neither the love that bound each family nor the causes for the lament that went up to the Spirit-world in consequence of each victim's fallenness. Mobley's question implicates the brutality of white racism in the interdiction of a well-intended life. Drawing the comparison with Christ's suffering, she also implicates (or absolves) God, invoking the hermeneutics of sacrifice. Harpo's questions evoke the legal stipulation that would have effected chattel slavery for life: *partus sequitur ventrem,* that is, "the child follows the condition of the mother." Stigmatized by his mother's fate, he was powerless to overcome his own social alienation and win the approval of his beloved Sofia's father.

Walker's humanistic leanings and nonpersonalistic doctrine of God can be discerned in the words of Shug Avery, singer, lover and priest of sorts to Celie, the protagonist, whom Shug leads to a powerful, new understanding of who, or rather, *what* God is, apart from the silent, obdurate, white, male authority figure to whom Celie has been writing letters,[2] the medium through which the entire story unfolds. In the exchange Shug celebrates neither human agency nor God alone but a dimension of the human-Divine encounter that is not traditionally emphasized in Christian thought. Through Shug's witness to the character, creativity and oneness of God, Walker affirms the ability to delight one-self/Godself in the things and people of the created realm:

> [Celie:] Shug a beautiful something, let me tell you. She frown a little, look out across the yard, lean back in her chair, look like a big rose. She say, My first step from the old white man was trees. Then air. Then birds. Then other people. But one day when I was sitting quiet and feeling like a motherless child, which I was, it come to me: that feeling of being part of everything, not separate at all. I knew that if I cut a tree, my arm would bleed. And I laughed and I cried and I run all around the house. I knew just what it was. In fact, when it happen, you can't miss it. It sort of like you know what, she say, grinning and rubbing high up on my thigh.
>
> *Shug!* I say.
>
> Oh, she say. God love all them feelings. That's some of the best stuff God did. And when you know God loves 'em you enjoys 'em a lot more. You can just relax, go with everything that's going, and praise God by liking what you like.
>
> God don't think it dirty? I ast.
>
> Naw, she say. God made it. Listen, God love everything you love—and a mess of stuff you don't. But more than anything, God love admiration.[3]

The exchange between Celie and Shug is reminiscent of the nonpersonalistic theism of Hinduism, in which devotees worship the impersonal God Brahma yet also worship the incarnating God Krishna. As the Supreme Personality of the Godhead, Krishna is the Supreme *Enjoyer* of everything that is.[4] According to the Lord Krishna, "If one offers Me with love and devotion a leaf, a flower, fruit or water, I will accept it" (v. 9:26).[5] Although one of Western Christianity's major interpreters, St. Augustine, posited God's *dilectio* (delight) in creation and ours in God as the basis for communion with God, this dimension was overshadowed by his preoccupation with sin. A certain cherishable, devotional aspect of Christianity has been nearly lost in the Western church's continued focus on sin and its remedy, putatively revealed in Christ's death on the cross and in one's embodiment of the hermeneutics of sacrifice, which is described as the sine qua non of Christian witness and which is echoed in Mobley's understanding of the theological significance of her son's brutal death.

Mobley cites the fourth song of Deutero-Isaiah's Suffering Servant songs (Is 42:1-2; 49:1-6; 50:4-11; 52:13–53:12). Although the Servant is identified in none of them, according to Rabbi Stephen Geller of the Jewish Theological Seminary (New York City), the text possibly refers to (a) a prophet, (b) a priest or (c) a king because prophetic, priestly and royal motifs abound in the Servant songs and because all are noted "servants of God" in the Hebrew Bible.[6] The specific verse Mobley quoted simulates royal imagery by drawing its antitheses: The king is supposed to be good-looking, for example, Saul is lifted up because of his singular handsomeness (1 Sm 9:2); the Servant has no attractive features. The king has the authority of speech; the Servant does not open his mouth. Whereas the king is divinely chosen and anointed, the Servant is "inhumanly disfigured," perhaps with leprosy, a condition which suggested divine disfavor in that context. If a royal figure is involved, the passage may intentionally refer to the ritual humiliation of kings in other ancient Near Eastern cultures.[7] Some legal injustice may also be indicated (Is 53:8). The anti-royal, righteous sufferer motif runs throughout the passage. As Geller noted, the idea that the Servant suffers vicariously and performs an atoning work for the sins of the people through his death (Is 53:4-10) is a new theological development of the late-Exilic era. This climaxes in a statement that issues forth in a promise of resurrection, another new theme: "Yet it was the will of the LORD to bruise him; he has put him to grief; when he makes himself an offering for sin, he shall see his offspring, he shall prolong his days; the will of the LORD shall prosper in his hand" (v. 10). Together, the righteous sufferer motif, atoning work, death and resurrection of the Servant account for the Christian appropriation of the songs to describe the career and significance of Jesus. In Jewish interpretive tradition the Servant is usually identified as the Jewish people or a "remnant" thereof; nevertheless, the songs provided a blueprint for the *imitatio Christi* for the church in persecution and slavery, and they still guide African Americans' apprehension of Christian kerygma and doctrine.

Like the Servant, Jesus and the Jewish people, African Americans have been devalued, marred and killed by the violence of oppressors. Given their experiences of massive collective suffering, the notion that divine disfavor is operative contributes to the ambiguity with which persons in both communities understand their relationship to God. Although the love ethic in the Black Church is predicated on the theme of righteous suffering and is sustained by the compensatory mechanisms of promise, it is unclear if Mobley appeals to it prescriptively and thereby absolves God concerning Emmett's death. Yet it is abundantly clear that she recognizes the destructiveness in the human agency of those responsible. Thus, her comparison of Emmett's suffering with that of Christ's strikes me as having been made not as an inflated or sanctimonious claim but descriptively, in consequence of genuinely living in the theodical question. As one standing within the interpretive tradition of the Black Church, Mobley's willingness to be taught by the Spirit is likely an affirmation of the goodness and sovereignty of God in opposition to white supremacy. Nonetheless, the ambiguity of her statement is instructive because it is self-enjoining to a higher code of conduct.

Mobley's image of God, reflected in the face of her mutilated son, as well as Walker's conceptualization of God, recall the lattice-work what-not that graced my early home (with its dual images of Jesus crucified and Christ glorified) and my family's experience of plantation farming. Just as the cross and the croker sack evoked in me the same reaction of resentment to suffering, when I looked again on the cotton fields of North Carolina, a more attractive picture emerged from a second, skewed image of *that* crucifixion through circumscription. Like the triumphalist God, plantation labor also fascinated me, for two reasons: (1) because the element of surprise was always great among the mass of folks working together, and (2) because the opportunities to marvel at nature were simply rife. Like the juxtaposed images of Jesus crucified and Christ glorified, like croker sacks/white overseers/aching backs and sun/sky/singing voices/variegated insects/smells of earth, Mobley's and Walker's images of God present me with something fascinating to behold and ponder in the light of my black, womanist and Christian commitments. Perhaps in contemplating this mandala I can effect some relief from my sense of alienation, and find in it, as I did in the first and second mandalas, spiritual principles that bring meaning, purpose and direction to my life.

The appeal of the term *womanist* among black women scholars of religion cannot be gainsaid. One only has to note the growing number of book titles that convey a womanist perspective. Nevertheless, some scholars do not accept it. bell hooks, for example, fears that the designation detracts from feminist unity and power.[8] Other black women accept the womanist label in a limited way; not all components of the term Walker coined are embraced by all the black women who use it to describe themselves. Womanist ethicist Katie Cannon has argued that one cannot make the claim of being a womanist or of advocating womanism without embracing its whole meaning. Unfortunately, racism and classism, the profundity of unexplored misogynistic, heterosexist, self-abnegating tendencies, and the fear of vulnerability and transformation militate against the cultivation of womanist principles that enhance black women's ability to survive, be free and creatively express themselves. Sometimes black women stumble under the weight of so much domination.

The proper naming of things or persons calls them into existence or brings them to light so they may be seen in their proper relationship to other things or persons. White feminists for example, term male domination of women *patriarchy*. Black women do not deny the bonds of oppression that unite women. Williams, however, identifies a "substantial difference between [white women's] patriarchally-derived-privileged-oppression" and black women's "demonically-derived-annihilistic-oppression"–which she termed *demonarchy*.[9] In recent writings Williams has backed away from this usage, perhaps because it is essentialist, characterizes relations between black people and whites as always adversarial (which belies the courage of conviction shown by some white abolitionists and co-workers in the Civil Rights movement) and undercuts white accountability for racist thought and actions. Nonetheless, naming black women's oppression "demonarchy" sheds light on the differences between the womanist and feminist experiences and mandates.

In light of these difficulties, I offer some reflections on what it means to be a womanist theologian, with reference to each of the four instances of the definition articulated by Walker, and with the view in mind that each can become a source for helping African American women articulate critical perspectives on their own experiences of the crosses of racism, sexism, heterosexism/homophobia and classism.

TO BE A WOMANIST

Womanist theology is being developed by black women, who are *feminists of color*. Walker proffered the term "womanist" as an alternative to "feminist" because feminism is usually associated with white women's critique of sexism or patriarchy. Key issues in feminist theologies such as rape and domestic violence, women's work, female bonding, inclusive language and the gender of God, economic autonomy for women and heterosexism affect all women.[10] Still, most black women agree that white feminists do not adequately address the issues of black women.

To be black in America is to have suffered a collective history of chattel slavery and to have that history purportedly justified by divine sanction. White catechists told the slaves that they must endure servitude and its attendant miseries as a result of the "Hamitic curse" (Gn 9:18-29), deploying the hermeneutics of sacrifice. While it is true that white women were similarly circumscribed on the basis of their sex, they do not share in the exponentially charged experience of interstructured[11] oppression with black women, and in fact, are signal contributories, along with white children and men, in the oppression of black children, women and men. Although sexism is a constant in the oppression of all women and poverty *may* be part of white women's experience, the cultural value of white femininity/white skin and white women's relative wealth inure them from the kind of totalistic ontological assault black women/black people face. Linda Burnham, a member of the National Council of the Alliance Against Women's Oppression, warns African Americans not to adopt uncritically the view that poverty is becoming a phenomenon that is based solely or primarily on gender. This view, which some feminists advocate,

> presents a highly distorted picture of the general dynamics that are at the source of poverty in the U.S. These distortions are the inevitable result of a point that abstracts women as a group out of the overall socioeconomic trends in U.S. capitalist development.[12]

Burnham has written that the "feminization of poverty" theory obscures factors relevant to the impoverishment of black women, overstates white women's vulnerability to impoverishment, ignores or underestimates the impoverishment of black men and does not deal effectively with working-class exploitation as a constitutive element of late capitalism. As Burnham pointedly states, "The emiseration of black women has not been accompanied by a rise to affluence of black men."[13]

Despite hegemonic interpretations of the Bible that continue to relegate their lives to subservience and contentment therewith, African Americans in and since slavery counted their own experience as that through which the truth of the Bible was to be mediated. Reflecting on biblical ties that bound black families together in their suffering and that make collective, and in some ways, *exclusionary* reflection an ongoing, necessary condition of their theological project, Cannon states that, in slavery:

> Ideas and practices that favored equal rights of all people were classified as invalid and sinful because they conflicted with the divinely ordained structure that posited inequality between Whites and Blacks. The doctrine of biblical infallibility reinforced and was reinforced by the need for social legitimization of slavery. Thus, racial slavery was accepted as the necessary fulfillment of the curse of Ham. This had the effect of placing the truthfulness of God's self-revelation on the same level of Black slavery and white supremacy. The institutional framework that required Black men, women and children to be treated as chattel, as possessions rather than as human beings, was understood as being consistent with the spirit, genius and precepts of the Christian faith.[14]

Because of this eurocentric history of interpretation, womanist theological reflection is not wed to notions of biblical authority that support black peoples' and women's subservience. Womanist biblical scholar Clarice Martin agrees with feminist theologians on the need to use inclusive language, for example, in order to project alternative feminine images of God and paradigms for humankind.[15] She proposes that womanist theologians increasingly adopt and promote the use of inclu-

sive language in ways that go beyond the concerns of feminists to include the particularities of race and that demonstrate how biblical language is used to reinforce racial oppression. Martin postulates that faithfully rendering biblical terminology in appropriate English can yield a
"quadruocentric" hermeneutics that addresses issues of gender, class,
language and race. She denounces the way in which the Greek terms
for slave/slavery (*doulos/douleia*) have been euphemistically rendered in
English translations of the Bible in the rhetoric of servant/servanthood,
as does womanist theologian Jacquelyn Grant. In the American context
the effect of this has been to preclude substantive dialogue about slavery in theological, ethical, political and social discourse.

Although womanists have criticized eurocentric biblical interpretation, most have not rejected Christianity or the Bible wholesale but accept them as valid expressions of African Americans' striving toward an
understanding of both God and the moral and ethical obligations of the
community. Womanist ethicist Cheryl Sanders cites the liberation of
women and valuing *families* (namely, *heterosexual* families) as primary
obligations of black people.[16] Notwithstanding her emphasis, most
womanists resist making the family the central paradigm of oppression,
since doing so can obscure the interrelatedness of structural sins and
lead to further privatization of the meaning of oppression by (1) ob-
structing meaningful class analysis and (2) obfuscating the need for white
people to address (a) the presumption of privilege that upper- and middle-
class whites hold on the basis of whiteness, (b) the tenacity with which
they defend the privileges accorded themselves and (c) the rapacity with
which they deny the same to poor and non-white persons. The Personal
Responsibility Act of 1995, for example, debated in the U.S. Congress
on March 23 and 24, concerned the issue of "entitlements." Opposing
extensions in welfare benefits and the continuation of federally funded
meals for Head Start programs, the representative from Florida held up
a sign that read, "Do not feed the alligators." Several African American
members of Congress objected strenuously to the bestialization of poor
and working-class people, and to the inhumane implications of taking
meals from the mouths of their children, many of whom are black and
who benefit tremendously from the Head Start program. Williams implicates the genocidal intent of whites in the need of African Americans
to stand together against "white racial narcissism":

> White racial narcissism indicates a malfunction in the American
> national psyche that can ultimately lead the culture to self-destruct
> or can lead the powerful racially narcissistic group to genocide
> members of a less powerful racial group. One way of dealing with
> white racial narcissism in the culture is for the victimized group to

stand against the powerful, racially narcissistic group in a permanent posture of self-defense.[17]

Sanders identified the priority issues of black women that arose in consequence of slavery and that seek to thwart the genocidal intent of white supremacists. They include physical survival and spiritual salvation of the family (with equality between males and females); the redistribution of goods and services; encountering God as family; and ending white, gender and class supremacy.[18]

Despite the communal nature and locus of black oppression and black responses thereto, womanists are compelled to articulate their own understandings of their faith. Although black men are singularly targeted, censured and victimized by the American criminal justice system and constitute the majority of homeless people—significant factors in feminists' minimization of black impoverishment—many of them are still enslaved to the ideology of male superiority characteristic of patriarchy from primordial times. Black men, as well as white men, commit personal violence against black women; black men, as well as white men and white women, dehumanize black women, exploiting them in the work place and in the home.

Celie's and my mother's stories testify to the stranglehold of sexism in the African American community in each of its incarnations. Her image of God and my mandala also reveal one mechanism by which black people internalize racism and sexism: by imbibing cultural projections of whiteness and maleness as the standard of the holy. Influenced by the cultural revolution engendered in early nationalist sentiment and reprised in the Black Power movement underway in the late 1960s, black theologians reacted enthusiastically to the hypocrisy of white culture and of white theologians, who basically ignored the plight of African Americans as if it were a matter of no consequence in the theological enterprise. Dovetailing Bishop Turner's bold declaration that "God is a *Negro*," they posited the liberating intent of the "Black Christ,"[19] consistent with the christocentrism of the Black Church, radicalizing the black creative imagination concerning the Divine. Nonetheless, black theologians did not pose a self-critique concerning sexism within their ranks until summarily challenged by womanist theologians.[20] Jacqueline Grant's seminal essay "Black Theology and the Black Woman" incriminated the African American community's historical "focus on manhood" in the silencing of black women in the emergent discipline of black theology:

> By self-appointment, or by the sinecure of a male-dominated society, Black men have deemed it proper to speak for the entire Black

community, male and female. In a sense, Black men's acceptance of the patriarchal model is logical and to be expected. Black male slaves were unable to reap the benefits of patriarchy. Before emancipation they were not given the opportunity to serve as protector and provider for Black women and children, as White men were able to do for their women and children. Much of what was considered "manhood" had to do with how well one could perform these functions. It seems only natural that the post-emancipation black men would view as primary importance the reclaiming of their property—their women and children. Moreover, it is natural that Black men would claim their "natural" right to the "man's world." But it should be emphasized that this is logical and natural only if one has accepted without question the terms and values of patriarchy—the concept of male control and supremacy.[21]

To be a womanist is to be *outrageous, audacious, courageous, willful, responsible, in charge, serious—and curious* (that is, wanting to know more and in greater depth than is considered good for one). These qualities comport with black women's historic roles. Proto-womanists Phillis Wheatley, Sojourner Truth and Harriet Tubman evinced these qualities, which helped them endure, survive and resist forced breeding, separation from their children and spouses, and death. Accordingly, early womanists Grant, Williams, Cannon and others gave evidence of these qualities and proved themselves capable of developing their own theological perspectives and adjudicating their own moral responses to sexism, racism and classism.

Williams has stated that womanist theological methodology utilizes black women's history, literature, religious experience and other elements of African American culture in a diagnostic capacity and is informed by a multi-dialogical, liturgical and didactic intent.[22] Thus, womanist theology resists meta-narrative views of *his*tory, insisting upon a dialogical approach and emphasizing the importance of sharing *her*stories in order to provide context to theological speculations. For some black women, womanism means coming to voice, finding their voice, growing up. For these women, it is not so much a case of duplicity that impedes their total embrace of womanism but the need to discover themselves. In my case I entered the womanist enterprise with much trepidation. This was, in part, because I was accustomed to being silent and invisible; in part, because of my captivity to the Bible *vis-à-vis* the hermeneutics of sacrifice. I had to learn to watch, fight and pray and to tell my stories in order to find healing. Becoming an advocate of womanism and empowering others to do so is a task for the audacious, courageous and forbearing.

To be a womanist is to love *women and individual men, sexually and/or nonsexually.* Sanders challenged warrants for the use of womanist nomenclature on this point, expressing concern to make clear the distinction between what is consistent "Christian" doctrine (and therefore the proper task of the Christian theologian or ethicist) and what is not. In this instance of the definition of womanism Walker raises the issue of sexual preference by affirming lesbian and bisexual relationships, lifestyles the practice of which Sanders questioned as liberative praxes for the physical survival of the African American community and for which she questioned the endorsement of Christianity.[23] Walker evinces here a didactic and multi-dialogical intent. In a society that devalues blackness *and* femaleness and that exploits and denigrates women's bodies, that a womanist "loves women" and "*individual* men" is instructive. Womanist grounding enables black women to assert the worth of their lives apart from those men who engage with black women in ways that mimic dominant power dynamics. Moreover, it enables women who love women sexually to counter monolithic conceptions of the African American community by building on the same claims to freedom that black liberationists and heterosexual womanists make for themselves. Renee Hill, a self-identified lesbian, challenges womanist and black theologians to make the issues of heterosexism and homophobia within the African American community integral to their work:

> The lesbian voice is silenced in Christian womanist theology. Heterosexism and homophobia are nonissues in the Christian womanist paradigm for liberation. There is no widespread discussion of sexuality in African-American Christian theology in general. Christian womanists, like their male counterparts, focus for the most part on the impact of racism on the Black community. The Christian womanist focus on gender is to a great degree a focus on the retrieval of black women's stories, words and perspectives. There is no great emphasis on the impact of sexism on the Black community. This may be a key to the lack of discourse on sexuality.[24]

By acknowledging same-sex relationships womanism also counters antiquated biological and axiological assumptions concerning human sexuality that help maintain all women in subordinate positions. Through its open embrace this womanist principle has the power to bring the silenced voices and experiences of lesbians, gay men and bisexuals to conversations about the shape and means of black redemption. As Hill states:

> Sexuality is an issue for Christian womanist theologians. It is not any less or any more important than community or survival. It

simply is a part of community and survival. Sexuality (and male dominance) must be discussed in the Black community. Only then will we be able to address subjects like rape, the AIDS epidemic, as well as sexual orientation in the Black community.[25]

The freedom to love whomever one wills is a cherished tenet in liberal thinking. Still, the whims of love are not above critique. In the womanist view the affirmation provided in love relationships should be met in accordance with a praxis that enhances prospects for survival, liberation and creative self-expression. For me, the critical principle is self-love, irrespective of one's mate, as part of one's responsibility to oneself and God. For women to "love women," whether sexually or nonsexually, is to reject the misogynistic and heterosexist norms of patriarchy and demonstrate the inviolability of self-acceptance and self-love that are reflected in acceptance and love of one's own kind. It is to affirm the beauty of women and to celebrate the fecundity of women's gifts. To be a womanist is to be, traditionally, *capable.*

Womanists agree that black men and women can ill afford sectarianism in the struggle against the common experience of race oppression, but they rigorously advocate/agitate for the end of sexist oppression, not as a subordinate but as a concomitant ethical and moral necessity for the survival and liberation of the entire African American community. Dominant ideologies tend to portray power as a zero-sum game in which more power for some means less for others, thus dividing oppressed communities into factions competing for the crumbs of empowerment. Nevertheless, because womanists are linked to black men by familial ties and the common experience of race oppression, they are committed to the survival and wholeness of entire people, male and female. To be a womanist is to be, traditionally, *universalist.* Hence, womanists are *non-separatist.* (Except in matters of health. Because matters of health matter most, womanists refrain from emotionally or physically abusive relationships.) The womanist paradigm challenges those in the lived-world to model healthy intimate relations between women and women, and women and men, and remain true to its multi-dialogical and, I think, *sacramental,* intent.

To be a womanist is to love *music, dance, the moon, the Spirit, love, food, roundness, struggle, the folk, herself. Regardless.* It is to be both creation-affirming and God-affirming. It is to celebrate who black women are and who they can be in community and in God. In the religious experience of African Americans the ability to transcend and endure, while enjoying life, has proven essential for maintaining spiritual and emotional health in a context of oppression. The freedom to love *what* one loves (that is, to have *fun*) and to love *whom* one *is,* is fundamental to the worship of God in Walker's paradigm. Williams identifies self-love (*re-*

gardless) as the sine qua non of womanist thought,[26] evincing, again, a didactic intent. If self-love is the critical principle in effecting liberation, a proper exegesis of the nature of love is required. Consistent with the biblical injunction to love the neighbor as one loves oneself, black women need to love themselves so they can genuinely love others. Nevertheless, their historical roles as sustainers of their communities implicate them in their refusal to embrace fully their own liberation as women. Frequently black women do not assert their right to mutuality and respect in relationships. Yet without these basic elements a relationship cannot thrive.

Womanist is to feminist as purple is to lavender. This suggests heightened experience of the many possible negative ramifications of sexism. For example, black women are three times as likely to be raped as white women. By analogy the color purple evokes the impact of multiple oppressions together on their bodies and psyches. The analogy also recognizes that language developed at cost to black people and women. Womanist methodology thus is committed "both to reason and to the validity of female imagery and metaphorical language in the construction of theological statements."[27]

TRANSFORMING THE LANGUAGE OF SACRIFICE

As I have tried to indicate, I am aware of the problematical nature of the language of sacrifice, the potential and actual abuses thereof; nevertheless, I have cited from my mother's story in order to posit a transformed, *sacramental* notion of sacrifice that has saving significance for the African American community and for black women in particular. Hence, I agree with other womanists that I have the right and responsibility to challenge Christian language and tradition.

As a womanist liberationist I do not believe that oppressed people are obliged to love their oppressors categorically. Although I do not preclude this motivation as a response of a true devotee, my position is at odds with the hermeneutics of sacrifice, which exhorts enemy-love[28] and is recapitulated in the popular but unbiblical proposition to "love everybody." Although I wish to dispute neither the scriptural warrants nor the psychological benefit to be derived from this position, I take cues from the Johannine communities' stress on loving "one another"[29] and the biblical command to "love the neighbor" (Mt 22:39 and parallels)[30] whomever one is obliged to respond with the milk of human kindness, whoever needs you. Mobley, for example, channeled the pain of her son's death into community service, lecturing for the NAACP, eventually becoming a schoolteacher. When asked, she professed not to harbor bitterness toward Roy Bryant and Big Jim, W. J. Milam (the men who killed Emmett), or toward whites generally:

It certainly would be unnatural not to, yet I'd have to say I'm unnatural. From the very beginning that's the question that has always been raised: "What would you do to Milam and Bryant if you had the opportunity?" I came to the realization that I would do nothing. What they had done was not for me to punish and it was not for me to go around hugging hate to myself, because hate would destroy me. It wouldn't hurt them.[31]

While Mobley did not *profess* love for Milam and Bryant, she *confessed* that her son's death did not nullify the biblical command to love the neighbor and testified that it was God's empowerment that enabled her to keep it:

> The Lord gave me a shield, I don't know how to describe it myself. It was as if he put me in a neutral zone where I had no feeling whatsoever toward Milam and Bryant. I did not wish them dead. I did not wish them in jail. If I had to, I could take their four little children—they each had two—and I could raise those children as if they were my own and I could have loved them.[32]

Although Mobley grounds her love ethic in her evangelical faith,[33] she *struggles* to affirm God and the Spirit assists her efforts. Moreover, she does not make her claims uncritically, without a recognition of white brutality. Everyday she lives with the fact of her loss. It carries with it the kind of pain that the passing of time does not diminish. In my view Mobley is under no moral compulsion to love the men who murdered her son nor their children, yet she does not allow them to circumvent her freedom to love mercy and work for justice in the venues where she was called. This is what I think it means to witness *sacramentally* to the character of God: loving one's own, *not* loving others uncritically and, most important, *not* being defined by one's victimization but by one's commitments.[34]

In developing a *sacramental* understanding of sacrifice as a dimension of holistic spirituality I also take cues from the slave community, which proposed in song, "Lord, I *want* to love everybody [be a Christian] in my heart." I will to love all of creation, in accordance with the womanist sensibilities Walker describes in her image of God. Although I situate myself within the radical tradition of black theology, my personal praxis is pacifist activist, not merely because I believe it is sound strategy enhancing my prospects for survival, liberation and creative self-expression, but because I believe that there are some things that are worse than dying—namely, *killing*—for one's cause. Worse yet is killing without cause, a most horrible transgression of the Oneness in which I delight.

Nevertheless, I cannot in good conscience proscribe the liberative options of any people engaged in protracted struggle because I believe in self-defense as a human right that in no way reflects on the capacity to love another. In the imposition of sacrifice, protracted struggle is not seen under the rubric of self-defense but as a violation of the ethical codes of Vedic religion and Christianity. Despite the way the hermeneutics of sacrifice functions in Christian moral theory to misconstrue self-defense as violence, my interpretive model[35] in conversation with my particularities informs me that, since God is love, love cannot be prescribed, circumscribed or even defined. It can, however, be mediated through human instrumentality, a means by which God can do whatever God wills, whether God wills to forgive or "smite" the wicked. In my *sacramental* model the aim is to foster human freedom and to garner holistic spirituality from whatever sources are revealed. Thus, I do not seek to enjoin one image of God. Rather, God is, as revealed in Christ, loving and challenging, humane and sovereign, culturally engaged yet countercultural, personal, a healer and a mystic, a co-sufferer and a liberator. *Sacramentally* witnessing to the character of God as a black person, as a woman and as a Christian, I maintain, abrogates none of my duties or any of my human rights. The *Bhagavad Gita* also ascribes to this *sacramental* understanding of human agency on the part of its devotees.[36]

This has dramatic implications for women who are embroiled in abusive relationships, who remain in them for economic reasons and/or because their own self-concept is debased by the misogynistic norms of the church and the culture; who are themselves vulnerable to the murderous impulses of patriarchally driven persons; and who may be conflicted about defending themselves physically and/or emotionally.[37] Yet, in the imposition of sacrifice, the first word of Jesus (in the gospel of Mark), *repent*, is appropriated privatistically, so that the sinfulness of oppressors is never construed as a major issue.[38] I would argue that this is another conveniently missed exegetical consideration, along with Jesus' own profound militancy in his oppressive context. Nonetheless, I agree with the wisdom of this ancient testimony:

> Weapons are tools of bad omen,
> By gentlemen not to be used;
> But when it cannot be avoided,
> They use them with calm and restraint.
> Even in victory's hour
> These tools are unlovely to see;
> For those who admire them truly
> Are men who in murder delight.[39]

In the early church's appropriation of the language of sacrifice, Jesus' death on the cross was said to have been the pouring out of God's own life, ending sanction for sacred violence, *once for all.* This claim could only be made in the light of the whole story about Jesus, including the incarnation, ministry, suffering and death, resurrection and continuous intercession of the Holy Spirit. However, the martyrdom ethos in which Christianity was baptized virtually guaranteed that its central image would become the cross. This reality lent ultimacy to their claims concerning sacrifice. In truth, the martyrs evinced a *sacramental witness*; they sought to demonstrate bodily the utter feasibility of life in love and honor, as their association with Jesus had taught them.

Perhaps the cross is central to black Christian identity because black Christians suffer, like Jesus and the martyrs, unjustly. The cross in the African American experience *is* theodicy. Moreover, the death it points to is the way of all flesh. As theologians, it is tempting to forget that religious persons are concerned with what is beyond the grave and have constructed comforting myths that we will overcome its terror. Hence, some are "empty cross" Christians. I do not think that the problem is with the imagery per se; the cross, in its original sense, embodied a *scandal*, that something, anything, good could come out of such an event. Seen in this light, Jesus' sacrificial act was not the objective. Rather, it was the tragic, if foreseeable, result of his confrontation with evil. This bespeaks a view of Jesus and the martyrs as empowered, *sacramental*, witnesses, not as victims who passively acquiesced to evil.

As I stated before, anyone's death has saving significance inasmuch as we learn continuously from the life that preceded it. My baptism into the ethos of sacrifice compels me to reflect on it as a vital component of my self-understanding as a religious person and as a person in community. Although I may never be required to give up my life for the sake of my ultimate claims, the peculiar efficacy of my mother's sacrifice as well as the Christian story prevent me from discarding the idea altogether, particularly the notion of sacrifice as the surrender or destruction of something prized or desirable for the sake of something with higher claim, a potentially salvific notion with communal dimensions that got lost in the rhetorical impetus of the language of surrogacy. Yet I believe that in the final hours of her life, I became a higher and more pressing claim to my mother—more important than her addiction, more important than her companion, more important, even, than her life, which he had threatened on more than one occasion. I speculate that this prevented her from challenging my abusive father-figure sooner.

I believe that continuous learning will be facilitated for oppressed Christians by always situating the call to sacrifice in historical context; by employing liberative hermeneutics, taking note of dissonances within the text, the experiences of the community, and the community's understandings of God. My mother's ultimate sacrifice and those of count-less other black women, who suffer abuse and die at the hands of patri-archal, violence-driven persons; whose deaths go unreported and un-der-reported, unprosecuted and under-prosecuted—are potentially liberating for women if we learn from their experiences, if we see how they exercised or did not exercise their moral and creative agency. This seems a much more relevant view of the atoning worth of women's blood. Although it is true, as some feminists assert, that women's bloodloss has been devalued in Christian sacrificial tradition, Jesus' own life and *sacramental* example of affirming the intrinsic worth of women enable humankind to see women's blood as sacred.

CONCLUSION

The distinction between demonarchy and patriarchy recalls again the mandala of my youth. Although I unequivocally rejected the first, suffering image, I was never quite comfortable with the second, triumphalist image, because this God was in the image of my oppres-sors. Although he was clean, the visceral impact of watching him was subtly oppressive, like the sensation of being gently smothered. It took me a long time to articulate my discomfort, but once I was able to dis-cern the wisdom of Williams's insight on patriarchy/demonarchy, I rec-ognized that shifting my focus from the view of the suffering God to the view of the triumphalist God can, and often does, result in merely ex-changing paradigms of oppression. The alternative, spiritualized image seemed to imply that I would find the complete relief I sought in the afterlife, which left my suffering mitigated but unremitted. Yet I cannot gainsay the value of the Christian story for understanding and ordering the early phases of my life and vesting me with power to withstand the storms therein. Although I despised the melodrama captured in the depiction of Jesus crucified, I could not avoid contemplating the suffer-ing God because here was a mirror to my world. Viewing his pathos, I saw my mother's and my own. Secretly I despised Jesus, my mother and myself because I resented what seemed to be needless suffering. And yet I loved us all because I willed it, and because somehow I knew I *was* loved. It was evident in the Providence I encountered in nature, whom I could not believe sanctioned the suffering brought on by evil human choices. As a child of six or seven, having very little to go on doctrinally but having had devastating experiences of physical and emotional abuse on which to reflect, I reformulated the classical theodical statement in this God-affirming way: *Since* God is so good, why are people so evil? When I was eight years old, I "baptized" myself in a solemn ceremony so God would know that I chose not to be evil.

Like Mamie Mobley, like the early church, as a teenager I sought to find meaning in the suffering I encountered in the violent death of someone I loved and still love (I *believe* in the communion of saints). When I entered Seminary in 1987, I brought the questions of my youth with me and learned that structures of oppression exist that generate not only a world of sin but also a worldview of sin that reflects on the moral characteristics of individuals or on the presumed shortcomings of God. I learned to reformulate the question, What wrong with my mammy? into, What were the social and economic factors that led to her alienation and ultimately to her demise? To the question, Why I'm not good enough?, that is, for those who rejected me personally; for the racists who refused me employment; for the Black Church that sought to delimit the expression of my gifts, I came back with questions like, What benefits accrue to men/whites/male hierarchy from the circumscription of women/blacks? What notions of power are operative? On whose authority? No longer stigmatized, I began then to discern, resent, implicate and name the hermeneutics of sacrifice in the suffering that has pervaded my experience as a poor, African American woman who has also been called into ministry. One does not get to be a womanist by virtue of her blackness and femininity. Nor does one become a womanist simply because one reads, understands and makes the appropriate adjustments in her life. The lived-world struggle to appropriate self-love as the operative principle is formidable. Black women entering the womanist enterprise commit to exploring further the contradictions that shape their collective and personal lives in the spirit of critical inquiry and in the spirit of hope. I have pursued this project in quest of holistic spirituality, which entails communion with God and all of my neighbors, and freedom ever more to work, to love and to enjoy life. I have tried to show, through an exploration of the etiological moorings of my faith, that the received story—while rife with difficulty—can bring value to black women's lives. As I have matured as a woman, as a scholar and as a Christian, it has become increasingly necessary for me to learn more, more about Jesus and the redemption he putatively brings about for us, for all the particular communities of which I am a part. Hence, this treatise on the cross in the African American experience.

Notes

INTRODUCTION

1. Atonement is the process of reconciling or making "at one" humans and God. Doctrine of the Atonement is really a misnomer. There is no official dogma in the Protestant churches on the *opera Christi* (works of Christ), of which Jesus' death on the cross is of singular significance. Cf. Carl E. Braaten and Robert W. Jenson, eds., *Christian Dogmatics*, vol. 2 (Philadelphia: Fortress Press, 1984), pp. 5-9. Here and throughout I use the term *doctrine* loosely to denote the collective teachings on the subject, when I am not discussing a specific formulation.

2. In Jungian psychoanalytic theory, a *mandala* is a symbol representing the goal of psychic wholeness, a process of centering or producing a new center of personality. A mandala is "represented by the circle, the square, or the quaternity, by symmetrical arrangements of the number four and its multiples" around a central figure. The term has its origin in Asian cosmologies and is rife with individual and collective religious significance concerning possibilities for transformation. See Aniela Jaffe, ed., *C. G. Jung: Memories, Dreams, Reflections* (New York: Vintage Books, 1989 [1961]), pp. 396-397.

3. This was simulated by the use of a translucent medium.

4. Alice Walker, *The Color Purple* (New York: Washington Square Press, 1982), p. 176.

5. My use of *melodrama* is not limited to any artistic medium. All responses are mediated by their contexts or life circumstances. The intensified sentiment and exaggerated emotions in the rhetoric of early Christians, for example, have a parallel in the liturgy of African Americans. *Melodrama* does not in any way imply falsity. To the contrary, *absurdity* is that which is "glaringly opposed to manifest truth or reason." Both these communities used melodrama as a way to respond artistically to absurd social and political circumstances. These definitions inform the heuristic framework of my thesis.

6. Croker sacks hold twenty-five to thirty pounds of cotton. They are filled and dumped three to four times a day. (The average adult worker can pick about a hundred pounds of cotton.) Some workers use discarded fertilizer sacks or citrus-pulp sacks up to nine feet long that hold as much as two hundred to five hundred pounds of cotton. Five-pound capacity flour sacks are used by very young children. When this part of my narrative takes place (the early 1960s), the rate of pay was approximately five dollars per two hundred to three hundred pounds of cotton picked, which took an ambitious adult worker from sunup to sundown to accomplish.

7. I use *proto-womanist* to describe proactive sentiment, thought and/or behavior that reflect womanist qualities but that do not derive from womanism or necessarily adhere to the theoretical underpinnings of the various womanist disciplines.

8. Cf. Joseph R. Washington Jr., *Black Religion: The Negro and Christianity in the United States* (Boston: Beacon Press, 1964); James H. Cone, *Black Theology and Black Power* (Minneapolis: Seabury Press, 1969) and *God of the Oppressed* (San Francisco: Harper & Row, 1975). See also J. Deotis Roberts Sr., *Liberation and Reconciliation* (Philadelphia: Westminster Press, 1971); and Gayraud S. Wilmore, *Black Religion and Black Radicalism* (Maryknoll, N.Y.: Orbis Books, 1983 [1973]).

9. Christian theological anthropologies ask these questions: What are the qualities of human existence requiring redemption? What is the effective means of redemption? Typically, they cite universal sin as the purpose of the Atonement (conceived as the defining event in human history) and prescribe "brotherly" love in imitation of Christ.

10. Cf. Albert B. Cleage Jr., *The Black Messiah* (New York: Sheed and Ward, 1968); Martin Luther King Jr., *Strength to Love* (Philadelphia: Fortress Press, 1981 [1963]). James H. Cone, *A Black Theology of Liberation* (Philadelphia: J. B. Lippincott, 1970; Maryknoll, N.Y.: Orbis Books, 1986).

11. Theodicy is the attempt to account for evil in light of belief in the absolute goodness and sovereignty of God. Cf. Anthony Pinn, *Why Lord? Suffering and Evil in Black Theology* (New York: Continuum Publishing Co., 1995). In *Is God a White Racist?* (New York: Anchor Books/Doubleday, 1973), William R. Jones posited a seminal critique of black theologians' reliance on theodicy, identifying it as a rhetorical prison that does not permit them to question seriously the idea of God's goodness. Both Jones and Pinn advocate some form of *humanism* as a way for black people to exercise an additional faith option.

12. See Valerie Saiving Goldstein, "The Human Situation: A Feminine View," *Journal of Religion*, vol. 40, 1960, pp. 100-112; Susan Nelson Dunfee, "The Sin of Hiding: A Feminist Critique of Reinhold Niebuhr's Account of the Sin of Pride," *Soundings: An Interdisciplinary Journal*, vol. 65, spring 1962, pp. 316-327. Cf. Judith Plaskow, *Sex, Sin and Grace: Women's Experience and the Theologies of Reinhold Niebuhr and Paul Tillich* (Lanham, Md.: University Press of America, 1980).

13. Cf. Mary Daly, *The Church and the Second Sex* (New York: Harper & Row, 1968); *Beyond God the Father: Toward a Philosophy of Women's Liberation* (Boston: Beacon Press, 1973). See also Rosemary Radford Ruether, ed., *Religion and Sexism: Images of Woman in the Jewish and Christian Traditions* (New York: Simon and Schuster, 1974); idem, "Crisis in Sex and Race: Black Theology vs. Feminist Theology," *Christianity and Crisis*, April 15, 1974, pp. 67-73; idem, "New Women, New Earth: Sexist Ideologies and Human Liberation," *Union Seminary Quarterly Review*, vol. 32, spring-summer 1977, pp. 192-194.

14. Vicki L. Crawford, Jacqueline A. Rouse and Barbara Woods, eds., *Women in the Civil Rights Movement: Trailblazers and Torchbearers* (Brooklyn: Carlson Publishing, 1990).

15. Unpublished essay (circa 1985); republished as "Subjectification as a Requirement for Christological Construction," in Susan Brooks Thistlethwaite

and Mary Potter Engels, eds., *Lift Every Voice: Constructing Christian Theologies from the Underside* (San Francisco: HarperCollins Books, 1990; rev. ed. Maryknoll, N.Y.: Orbis Books, 1998). See Jacquelyn Grant, "Black Theology and the Black Woman," in James H. Cone and Gayraud S. Wilmore, eds., *Black Theology: A Documentary History, Volume 1: 1966-1979* (Maryknoll, N.Y.: Orbis Books, 1993, [1979]), pp. 323-338.

16. Frances Beale, "Double Jeopardy: To Be Black and Female," in Cone and Wilmore, *Black Theology: A Documentary History, Volume 1: 1966-1979*, pp. 284-292.

17. Theressa Hoover, "Black Women and the Churches: Triple Jeopardy," in Cone and Wilmore, *Black Theology: A Documentary History, Volume 1: 1966-1979*, pp. 293-303.

18. Rosemary Radford Ruether, "Feminist Theology in the Academy: How Not to Reinvent the Wheel," *Christianity and Crisis*, March 4, 1985, pp. 57-62.

19. Delores S. Williams, "The Color of Feminism," *Christianity and Crisis*, April 29, 1985, pp. 164-165.

20. Rosemary Radford Ruether, "For Whom, With Whom Do We Speak Our New Stories?" *Christianity and Crisis*, May 13, 1985, pp. 184-186.

21. Susan Brooks Thistlethwaite, *Sex, Race and God: Christian Feminism in Black and White* (New York: Crossroad Publishing Co., 1991).

22. Katie Geneva Cannon, "The Emergence of Black Feminist Consciousness," in Letty Russell, ed., *Feminist Interpretation of the Bible* (Philadelphia: Westminster Press, 1985), p. 39.

23. Marcia Riggs, "The Logic of Interstructured Oppression: A Black Womanist Perspective," in Susan Davies and Eleanor Haney, eds., *Redefining Sexual Ethics* (Cleveland: The Pilgrim Press, 1991), pp. 97-102.

24. Delores Williams has identified the survival tradition in the Hagar texts (Gn 16; 17:20ff.; 21:1-21) as highly symbolic of black women's lived experience. See her *Sisters in the Wilderness* (Maryknoll, N.Y.: Orbis Books, 1993). Kelly Brown Douglas cites the Lukan gospel as important evidence of Jesus' liberating ministry to the poor and the oppressed, the outcast and downtrodden. See Kelly Brown (Douglas), "God Is as Christ Does: Toward a Womanist Theology," *Journal of Religious Thought*, vol. 46, no. 1, summer-fall 1989, pp. 7-16.

25. Cf. Rita Nakashima Brock, *Journeys by Heart: A Christology of Erotic Power* (New York: Crossroad Publishing Co., 1988); and Joanne Carlson Brown and Carole R. Bohn, eds., *Christianity, Patriarchy and Abuse: A Feminist Critique* (New York: The Pilgrim Press, 1989).

26. Williams, *Sisters in the Wilderness*; "Black Women's Surrogacy Experience and the Christian Notion of Redemption," in Paula M. Cooey et al., eds., *After Patriarchy: Feminist Transformations of the World Religions* (Maryknoll, N.Y.: Orbis Books, 1991), pp. 1-14; see also Jacquelyn Grant, "The Sin of Servanthood and the Deliverance of Discipleship," in Emily Townes, ed., *A Troubling in My Soul: Womanist Perspectives on Evil and Suffering* (Maryknoll, N.Y.: Orbis Books, 1993), pp. 199-218.

27. Postmodernity is that period of social, political and economic development in the West after World War II. Culturally, it is marked by the invention

of television, which signaled the beginning of the age of information. Advocates of postmodernism resist "meta-narratives" of history (usually advanced by dominant cultures) purporting a *telos* that mystifies power arrangements and generally supports the status quo. Postmodernism has given rise to the debate on multiculturalism as a viable alternative to "master narrative" theories of history that seek to control the content of knowledge and the dissemination of information. See Jean-Francois Lyotard, *The Postmodern Condition: A Report on Knowledge,* Theory and History of Literature, vol. 10 (Minneapolis: University of Minnesota Press, 1984).

28. Delores S. Williams, "Womanist Theology: Black Women's Voices," *Christianity and Crisis,* March 2, 1987, p. 69.

1   THE REFINERS' FIRE

1. Daniel P. Mannix (with Malcolm Cowley), *Black Cargoes: A History of the Atlantic Slave Trade* (New York: Viking Press, 1962), pp. 24-25.

2. See Chancellor Williams, *The Destruction of Black Civilization:Great Issues of a Race from 4500 B.C. to 2000 A.D.* (Chicago: Third World Press, 1987), pp. 250-257, 257-272; see also Mannix and Cowley, *Black Cargoes,* pp. xi-xiii.

3. Winthrop Jordan, *White over Black: American Attitudes toward the Negro, 1550-1812* (New York: W. W. Norton, 1977 [1968]), pp. 44-66.

4. The Gold Coast encompasses a large area of West Africa from the Gambia River to the Gabon estuary. It is so called because of legendary accounts of vast deposits of gold in sub-Saharan Africa, which were at first mined and exploited by North Africans and later by the Europeans, beginning with the Portuguese. African Caribbean historian Walter Rodney speculates that disappointment concerning mining prospects spurred the Portuguese to turn to the more lucrative enterprise of slavery (see Richard Jobson, *The Golden Trade or A Discovery of the River Gambra and the Golden Trade of the Aethiopians,* ed. with a new introduction by Walter Rodney [London: Wm. Dawson and Sons Ltd., 1968 {1623}]). Ultimately the Gold Coast became a British territory. Although the British took the large majority of its slaves from this area to America (see Mannix and Cowley, *Black Cargoes,* p. 5), slave-ship manifests cite numerous places from which the slaves were taken through sale or capture: Sierra Leone, Gambia, Madagascar, Angola, Congo, Benin, Guinea, Cape Verde, Senegambia, Calabar, Bonny, Bande. See Darlene Clark Hine, ed., *Black Women in America: An Historical Encyclopedia* (Brooklyn: Carlson Publishing, 1993), s.v. "Slavery."

5. See Article I, section 2 of the Constitution of the United States of America, which precluded representation and taxation for the native populace and ostensibly permitted the same for three-fifths of the male slave populace.

6. Denying white women the right to vote, the patriarchal political establishment did not deny them rights as citizens, as they did the slaves, whose humanity they denied.

7. Evangelicalism coincided with the rise of pietistic movements in England, which instigated a series of "Great Awakenings" in the American religious con-

sciousness. The locus of the first of these was the northern colonies (c.1730-1760). The second coincided with westward and southward expansion (c.1800-1830) and bore even more directly on the admission of slaves into ecclesial communion with whites. A third, sprung from American soil, reprised in the Revivalism of late-nineteenth-century and early-twentieth-century social-gospel movements; a fourth extends from the early twentieth century to the present. Evangelicalism is informed by an interesting admixture of denominational traditions in the founding of Virginia, the first and largest of the colonies; at base Anglican, it was institutionalized in the Baptist, Methodist, Presbyterian, Disciples of Christ and Protestant Episcopal denominations. See Donald Mathews, *Religion in the Old South* (Chicago: University of Chicago Press, 1977); and William G. McLoughlin, *Revivals, Awakenings and Reform: An Essay on Religious and Social Change in America, 1607-1977* (Chicago: University of Chicago Press, 1978).

8. Mathews, *Religion in the Old South,* p. 17.

9. See Allan Kulikoff, *Tobacco and Slaves: The Development of Southern Cultures in the Chesapeake, 1680-1800* (Chapel Hill: University of North Carolina Press, 1986).

10. James Oakes, *The Ruling Race: A History of American Slaveholders* (New York: Alfred A. Knopf, 1982), p. 123. Oakes cites a letter from John Mills to Gilbert Jackson dated May 19, 1807.

11. *Cliometrics* is the application of mathematical and statistical methods to the reconstruction of economic development for a particular nation or region. Another way to describe those engaged in this enterprise is by use of the term *economic historian.* Arguing that the "main features of the actual operation of the slave economy are now clear," Fogel and Engerman claim that the central aim of their work is to discover "what really happened" in slavery. Robert William Fogel and Stanley L. Engerman, *Time on the Cross,* vol. 1: *The Economics of American Negro Slavery;* vol. 2: *Evidence and Methods—A Supplement* (New York: W. W. Norton, 1989 [1974]), p. 8.

12. Ibid., p. 3.

13. Ibid., pp. 109-126.

14. See John W. Blasingame, ed., *Slave Testimony: Two Centuries of Letters, Speeches, Interviews, and Autobiographies* (Baton Rouge: Louisiana State University Press, 1977); B. A. Botkin, ed., *Lay My Burden Down: A Folk History of Slavery* (Athens, Ga.: University of Georgia Press, 1945—Brown Thrasher Edition, 1989); James Mellon, ed., *Bullwhip Days: The Slaves Remember—An Oral History* (New York: Avon Books, 1988).

15. Mellon, *Bullwhip Days,* p. 244.

16. Ibid.

17. G.E.M. de Ste. Croix, *The Class Struggle in the Ancient Greek World* (London: Gerald Duckworth and Co., 1981), p. 227.

18. Gavin Wright, "Prosperity, Progress, and American Slaves, " in Paul David et al., eds., *Reckoning with Slavery: A Critical Study in the Quantitative History of American Negro Slavery* (New York: Oxford University Press, 1976), pp. 302-336.

19. Walter Rodney, *How Europe Underdeveloped Africa* (London: Bogle-L'Ouverture Publications, 1972). European and American dependence on the resources of Africa and other places in the Third World that are struggling to

develop and to obtain economic and political leverage is compounded by the debt structure and lending policies of the World Bank, International Monetary Fund and the influence of multinational corporations.

20. Ibid., p. 87.

21. See Jamie Hart and Elsa Barkley Brown, "Black Women in the United States: A Chronology," in Hine, *Black Women in America*, pp. 1309-1313.

22. Lerone Bennett Jr., *Before the Mayflower: A History of Black America* (Chicago: Johnson Publishing Co., 1987 [1962]), p. 468.

23. Thornton Stringfellow, "The Bible Argument: Or, Slavery in the Light of Divine Revelation," in *Cotton Is King, and Proslavery Arguments*, ed. E. N. Elliott, L.L.D. (Augusta, Ga.: Pritchard Abbott, 1860, pp. 461-546), p. 521.

24. Cited in Sterling Stuckey, *Slave Culture: Nationalist Theory and the Foundations of Black America* (New York: Oxford University Press, 1987), p. 195.

25. Frances Young, *The Use of Sacrificial Ideas in Greek Christian Writers from the New Testament to John Chrysostom* (Philadelphia: The Philadelphia Patristic Foundation, 1979), pp. 42-43, emphases mine.

26. Cf. Robert Warrior, "Canaanites, Cowboys and Indians: Deliverance, Conquest and Liberation Theology Today," *Christianity and Crisis*, vol. 49, September 12, 1989, pp. 261-265.

27. Cf. Lk 19:10; 20:9-18; Jn 3:17; 12:49; 13:16; Rom 5:8ff.; 8:32; Eph 2:16; Heb 2:17; 1 Jn 4:9-10. Also cf. Rom 6:10; 2 Cor 5:14-15, 21; Heb 7:27; 9:28; 10:12; 1 Ti 2:6; 1 Pt 3:18.

28. Cf. Rom 5:6ff.; 8:32ff.; 1 Cor 10:30; 15:3; Gal 1:4; Eph 5:2; 1 Thes 5:10; Ti 2:14. Extrabiblical sources emphasizing the *once for all* nature of Jesus' sacrifice *for our sins* include the *Didache* 9:3-5; *Epistle of Barnabas* 2:4ff.; 5:1-2; 12:1-2; Polycarp, *Epistle to the Philippians* 1:2; 8:1-2. In *Ancient Christian Writers*, vol. 6, ed. Johannes Quasten and Joseph C. Plumpe, trans. James A. Kleist (New York: Paulist Press, 1948).

29. Rudolf Bultmann, *Theology of the New Testament* (New York: Charles Scribner's Sons, 1951 [vol. 1], 1955 [vol. 2]), p. 42.

30. See George Smeaton, *The Doctrine of the Atonement According to the Apostles* (Peabody, Mass.: Hendrickson Publishers, 1988 [1870]).

31. See Bultmann, *Theology of the New Testament*, pp. 42-46.

32. After the destruction of the Temple, corporate sacrificial worship was rendered nearly impossible, although it certainly continued in local synagogues. By the time of the Council of Jamnia (c. 90), prayer was deemed a suitable substitute for animal sacrifice in corporate worship. Although always integral to the Jewish devotional aspect, with the council's stipulation prayer became a more prominent feature of the liturgy, eventually supplanting animal sacrifice in most Jewish liturgies. See Samuel Sandmel, *Judaism and Christian Beginnings* (New York: Oxford University Press, 1978), pp. 147-150. Cf. Allan F. Segal, *The Other Judaisms of Late Antiquity*, Brown Judaic Studies, no. 127, ed. Jacob Neusner et al. (Atlanta: Scholars Press, 1987).

33. Robert G. Hamerton-Kelly, *Sacred Violence: Paul's Hermeneutic of the Cross* (Minneapolis: Fortress Press, 1992), p. 70. A student of René Girard, postmodern bard and theorist of sacred violence, Hamerton-Kelly makes these claims in light of Paul's zeal for attacking the Law upon which the sacrificial system depended for its raison d'etre.

34. Roman policy allowed the peoples of occupied territories to practice their own religions as long as tributes were paid and sacrifices made to the Roman gods and the emperor, and as long as the requirements of a particular people's own gods were met. The administration of religions was thus a way to unify the Empire socially, politically and economically. A particular religion was regarded as *licita*–legal–or not, depending on whether it comported with these Roman religious and civic sensibilities. Judaism was *licita*; nonetheless, the Jewish people were exempted from the state sacrificial rites primarily owing to Roman respect for the antiquity of Judaism but also reflective of Rome's efforts to manage risks posed by Jewish resistance, the most obvious expression of which lay in the Jews' steadfast adherence to monotheism in a polytheistic culture. Otherwise, Paul's (*nee*, Saul) prior zealous collusion with Roman authorities to search out and destroy the schismatics is difficult to explain. As a politically conservative Jew, he would have wanted to protect this privilege afforded the Jewish people.

35. W.H.C. Frend, "The Persecutions: Some Links Between Judaism and the Early Church," in *Religion Popular and Unpopular in the Early Christian Centuries* (London: Variorum Reprints, 1976), pp. 148-149.

36. Herbert B. Workman, *Persecution in the Early Church* (Oxford: Oxford University Press, 1980 [1906]), pp. 56-61.

37. Allen Callahan, "A Note on 1 Corinthians 7:21," *Journal of the Interdenominational Theological Center*, vol. 17, fall 1989/spring 1990, nos. 1 and 2, pp. 110-114. See especially verses 21-23: "Were you a slave when called? Never mind. But if you can gain your freedom, avail yourself of the opportunity. For he who was called in the Lord as a slave is a freedman of the Lord. Likewise he who was free when called is a slave of Christ. You were bought with a price; do not become the slaves of men." See also the second-century document of Ignatius, *Ad Polycarp* 4:3, which describes procedure for what Callahan calls "ecclesial manumission." Callahan's retrospective methodology is questioned by J. Albert Harrill in *The Manumission of Slaves in Early Christianity* (Tubingen: J.C.B. Mohr/Paul Siebeck, 1995), pp. 106-107.

38. Vincent L. Wimbush, *Paul, The Worldly Ascetic* (Macon: Mercer University Press, 1987), p. 16.

39. Mathews, *Religion in the Old South*, pp. xvi-xvii.

40. I am grateful to James M. Washington, a leading African American church historian, for pointing out this resource for understanding the ideological underpinnings of slavery. See his *Frustrated Fellowship: The Black Baptist Quest for Social Power* (Macon: Mercer University Press, 1986).

41. In J. Stevenson, ed., *A New Eusebius* (Nashville: Abingdon Press, 1957), p. 18.

42. Cf. Jordan, *White over Black.*

43. William Byron Forbush, ed., *Fox's Book of Martyrs: A History of the Lives, Sufferings and Deaths of the Early Christian and the Protestant Martyrs* (Grand Rapids: Zondervan Press, 1967 [c.1563]), p. 6. See also Stevenson, *A New Eusebius*, p. 2.

44. The prodigious efforts of activist and proto-womanist Ida B. Wells-Barnett to document the horrors of lynching and catalogue the number of its victims in the late nineteenth and early twentieth centuries are recounted in numerous

books and articles by the author, selected essays of which may be found in Mildred I. Thompson, *Ida B. Wells-Barnett: An Exploratory Study of an American Black Woman, 1893-1930*, Black Women in United States History, vol. 15 (Brooklyn: Carlson Publishing, 1990). Cf. Ralph Ginzburg, *100 Years of Lynching: A Shocking Documentary of Race Violence in America* (New York: Lancer Books, 1962); Michael and Judy Ann Newton, *Racial and Religious Violence in America: A Chronology* (New York: Garland Publishing, 1991).

45. Arthur Frederick Ide, *Martyrdom of Women: A Study of Death Psychology in the Early Christian Church to 301 C.E.* (Garland, Tex.: Tanglewuld Press, 1985), pp. 38-44.

46. The proscription of sexual relations between black males and white females legalized the rape of black slave women by white men. The legal stipulation of *partus sequiter ventrem*, "the child follows the condition of the mother" regardless of the race of the father, enabled white males to sell their own children begotten of female slaves. See Linda Brent, *Incidents in the Life of a Slave Girl*, ed. L. Maria Child (New York: Harcourt Brace Jovanovich, 1973 [1861]); and Katie Geneva Cannon, *Black Womanist Ethics* (Atlanta: Scholars Press, 1988), pp. 34-38.

47. Forbush, *Fox's Book of Martyrs*, p. 6.

48. See Albert J. Raboteau, *Slave Religion: The "Invisible Institution" in the Antebellum South* (New York: Oxford University Press, 1978).

49. *To the Romans*, cited in Stevenson, *A New Eusebius*, p. 12.

50. Ibid., pp. 5-6.

51. See Gary A. Bisbee, *Pre-Decian Acts of Martyrs and Commentarii* (Philadelphia: Fortress Press, 1988). See also Herbert Musurillo, *The Acts of the Christian Martyrs* (Oxford: Clarendon Press, 1972).

52. See Herbert Aptheker, *American Negro Slave Revolts*, 5th ed. (New York: International Publishers, 1987); see also Eugene Genovese, *From Rebellion to Revolution: Afro-American Slave Revolts in the Making of the Modern World* (Baton Rouge: Louisiana State University Press, 1979); Gayraud S. Wilmore, *Black Religion and Black Radicalism: An Interpretation of the Religious History of Afro-American People* (Maryknoll, N.Y.: Orbis Books, 1986 [1973]; rev. ed. 1998); and C. W. Larison, M.D., *Sylvia DuBois: A Biografy of the Slav Who Whipt Her Mistress and Gand Her Fredom*, ed. Jared C. Lobdell (New York: Oxford University Press, 1988).

53. Herbert Aptheker, ed., *One Continual Cry: David Walker's Appeal to the Colored Citizens of the World* (New York: Humanities Press, 1965), p. 139. Henry Highland Garnet, a protégé of Walker, reported that some racist whites made a pact among themselves to pursue Walker to the extent of losing their own lives and were ultimately successful in poisoning him.

54. Forbush, *Fox's Book of Martyrs*, p. 8.

55. Cited in Dwight N. Hopkins, *Shoes That Fit Our Feet: Sources for a Constructive Black Theology* (Maryknoll, N.Y.: Orbis Books, 1993), p. vii.

56. Furthermore, class distinctions in the early church made the elite among them subject to less severe forms of punishment and torture. Occasionally an execution was delayed or a reprieve granted, reflecting the influence of wealthy Christians on the local political landscape. But whenever political misfortunes

arose, Christians were scapegoated and outright extirpation became the renewed focus of the state. See de Ste. Croix, *The Class Struggle in the Ancient Greek World.*

57. Patricia Cox Miller, "Dreaming the Body: An Aesthetics of Asceticism," in Vincent L. Wimbush and Richard Valantasis, eds., *Asceticism* (New York: Oxford University Press, 1995), pp. 281-300, quotation at p. 282. See also Peter Brown, *The Body and Society: Men, Women and Sexual Renunciation in Early Christianity* (New York: Columbia University Press, 1988), p. 31.

58. Vincent L. Wimbush, ed., *Ascetic Behavior in Greco-Roman Antiquity* (Minneapolis: Fortress Press, 1990), p. xiii.

59. *Webster's Encyclopedic Unabridged Dictionary of the English Language* (1989), s.v. "sacrifice."

60. Mt 5–7. The Sermon is also found in Luke, with some minor differences in details. Throughout, the Lukan text posits a decidedly economic criterion for blessedness. Specifically, Luke's text reads "Blessed are the poor," to which Matthew adds "in spirit," modifying Luke's critique of class relations, a theme which pervades that gospel. See Lk 6:17ff.

61. Reinhold Niebuhr, *Moral Man and Immoral Society* (New York: Charles Scribner's Sons, 1932), pp. 263-64.

62. Walter Wink, *Violence and Nonviolence in South Africa: Jesus' Third Way* (Philadelphia: New Society Publishers, 1987), pp. 19, 48-72.

63. René Girard, *Violence and the Sacred* (Baltimore: Johns Hopkins University Press, 1977); idem, *The Scapegoat* (Baltimore: Johns Hopkins University Press, 1986).

64. Mt 5–7. See especially 5:38-39: "You have heard that it was said, 'An eye for an eye and a tooth for a tooth.' But I say to you, Do not resist one who is evil. But if any one strikes you on the right cheek, turn to him the other also." According to Wink, to offer one's cheek hastily would prompt a backhand slap from the Roman soldier giving it. Because a backhand slap was something done in familial relations, to the Jewish person receiving it, such a blow would confer a parity of sorts. Not only would a tense situation be defused, but the last laugh would be that of the victim's.

65. Wink applied a comedic hermeneutics to the Sermon on the Mount in order to arm blacks fighting for political autonomy in South Africa with a humorous edge over their white oppressors and to demonstrate the power of enemy-love. But his assessment of power dynamics failed to understand that victims of oppression have no rights that oppressors are bound to respect. Where laws exist ostensibly to protect the oppressed, as they do in America, they are often subverted by the disingenuous use of social codes restricting and denying their participation in social, economic, political and cultural life. Where concord is presumed to exist, oppressors yet have privilege they can exercise at any time.

66. Girard, *Violence and the Sacred*, p. 4.

67. See the epigraph for this chapter. Phillis Wheatley, *On Being Brought from Africa to America*, in John C. Shields, ed., *The Collected Works of Phillis Wheatley* (New York: Oxford University Press, 1988), p. 18.

68. Ibid., p. 61.

69. In Herbert Aptheker, ed., *One Continual Cry: David Walker's Appeal to the Colored Citizens of the World* (New York: Humanities Press, 1965), pp. 126-127.

70. W.E.B. Du Bois, "A Litany of Atlanta," cited in James M. Washington, ed., *Conversations with God: Two Centuries of Prayers by African Americans* (New York: Harper Collins Publishers, 1994), pp. 102-104.

71. Jeremiah A. Wright Jr., *Africans Who Shaped Our Faith* (Chicago: Urban Ministries, 1995), p. 10.

72. Wheatley, *To the University of Cambridge, in New England,* cited in Shields, *The Collected Works of Phillis Wheatley*, pp. 15-16.

73. Wheatley, *On the Death of the Rev. Dr. Sewell,* cited in Shields, *The Collected Works of Phillis Wheatley*, p. 19.

74. In chapter 2 I discuss some of the historical matrices in which black theology was shaped, and in chapter 3 I delineate the views of black theologians on this love ethic, signifying the relationship between sacrifice and sacrament for each.

75. Olive Gilbert, *Sojourner Truth: Narrative and Book of Life* (New York: Arno Press, 1968 [1850, 1878]), p. 67.

76. Ibid., pp. 158-159. Cited also in Jacquelyn Grant, *White Women's Christ and Black Women's Jesus* (Atlanta: Scholar's Press, 1989), p. 214.

77. See Aptheker, *American Negro Slave Revolts*; Genovese, *From Rebellion to Revolution*; and Wilmore, *Black Religion and Black Radicalism.*

78. Reinhold Niebuhr, *Moral Man and Immoral Society* (New York: Charles Scribner's Sons, 1932), p. 268.

79. June Jordan, "The Difficult Miracle of Black Poetry in America or Something Like a Sonnet for Phillis Wheatley," in Joanne M. Braxton and Andree Nicola McLaughlin, eds., *Wild Women in the Whirlwind: Afra-American Culture and the Contemporary Literary Renaissance* (New Brunswick, N.J.: Rutgers University Press, 1990), pp. 22-34, quotation at p. 26.

80. Williston Walker, Richard A. Norris, David W. Lotz and Robert T. Handy, *A History of the Christian Church,* 4th ed. (New York: Charles Scribner's Sons, 1985), p. 8.

81. The Jewish people's historical belief in the inviolable nature of religious and political interests was demonstrated in the Deuteronomist's lament for the loss of theocratic rule; in the Maccabean Wars (180-161 B.C.E.; recounted in 1 and 2 Maccabees); and in the fervor of nationalist movements in Palestine during and since the time of Jesus.

82. The *Pax Romana* was instituted by Augustus/Octavian (31 B.C.E.–14 C.E.), the first emperor of the Julio-Claudian dynasty, and lasted through the time of Marcus Aurelius (161-180 C.E.). It must be regarded as a period of *relative* peace throughout the Roman Empire in light of Jewish resistance.

83. Some Christians were put to death by Jews as well as Romans—Stephen (Acts 7:58-60); James, son of Zebedee (Acts 12:2-3); and James, the "brother of the Lord" (Josephus, *Antiquities* XX ix 1, no. 200). Jesus' own death was a capitulation to the violent authority of Rome by Jewish leaders. Justin Martyr (c.100-163?) reports that during the Barcochba revolt (132-135), the leader "gave orders that Christians alone should be led to cruel punishments, unless they would deny Christ and utter blasphemy" (Justin Martyr, *Apology*, I. 31, cited in

Stevenson, *A New Eusebius*, p. 22). Apart from these deaths stemming from mob violence, *"Jewish complicity in Christian persecution was most often not a direct action but by way of denunciation to the Romans . . . Indirect participation through expulsions from the synagogues may have been part of the background for John's charges against 'the Jews.'"* Raymond Brown, *The Community of the Beloved Disciple* (New York: Paulist Press, 1979), p. 42.

2 THERE IS A FOUNTAIN

1. Cited in Paul Cartledge, "Rebels and Sambos in Classical Greece," in P. A. Cartledge and F. D. Harvey, eds., *Crux: Essays in Greek History* (London: Duckworth and Co., 1985), pp. 16-46, quotation at p. 21.

2. Legal historian Mary Frances Berry reports that "in times of crisis, such as slave revolts, local militia were supplemented by British regulars." According to Berry, this federal policy allowing local authorities to deal with civil unrest in the African American community and providing federal protection only when whites were threatened became entrenched in historical fact and enabled the rise of white vigilante groups, such as the Ku Klux Klan, which is yet constituted of a curious theological hybridization of evangelical tenets, white supremacy and American militarism. See Mary Frances Berry, *Black Resistance/White Law: Constitutional History in America* (New York: Penguin Books, 1995 [1971]), p. 2.

3. Established in 1607, Virginia was the first of all the colonies and the largest of the southern colonies. See Mathews, *Religion in the Old South* (Chicago: University of Chicago Press, 1977), p. 17.

4. Some whites opposed the Africans' religious autonomy because they feared the liberating effects of religion. This made the "paternalistic compromise" between slaves and slaveholders necessary. On the face of it, paternalistic compromise gave to slaveholders a tacit promise of loyalty and submission, in exchange for which the slaves received a modicum of agency and protection against total dehumanization. Although paternalism highlighted the slaveholders' moral authority, the slaves' ability to make a little spiritual agency go a long way made it possible for them to develop the only institution wholly controlled by African Americans, the Black Church, which is, to date, evangelical in its orientation. See Eugene D. Genovese, *Roll, Jordan, Roll: The World the Slaves Made* (New York: Random House, 1974), p. 148.

5. To summarize significant facts about the hermeneutics of sacrifice: the context of persecution and martyrdom gave to Christian claims about Jesus the distinctive flavor of ultimacy, some of which was codified over the first and second centuries into scripture. See Mt 8:19; 10:38ff., 16:24ff. and parallels (Mk 8:34ff.; 10:28; Lk 9:23ff.; 14:27; 17:33ff.; 18:28). See also Jn 8:12; 10:4ff.; 10:27; 12:23ff. The main root word used in the Pauline corpus is *mimetes* (imitate): 1 Cor 4:16; Phil 3:17; 1 Thes 1:6; 2:14; 2 Thes 3:7ff.). Other Pauline uses include the root *dioko* (pursue): 1 Cor 14:1; and *'akoloutheo* (follow): 1 Cor 10:4. The pastoral epistles use *peripateo* (Eph 2:2); *mimetes* (Eph 5:1); and *'akoloutheo* (1 Pt 2:21; 2 Pt 1:16; 2:2). Other NT books use *mimetes* (Heb 6:12; 13:7; 3 Jn 1:11) and

'akoloutheo (Rv 14:4). Significantly, each of these texts exhorts believers to imitate Christ through personal sacrifice to the point of death, the ultimate sacrifice. Luke 24:46ff. and the Johannine corpus use *martyres* (witnesses), from which derives its present sacrificial denotation but which had primarily legal connotations in the NT. In the gospels the main root word used to urge believers to "follow" or "imitate" Christ is *'akoloutheo,* which suggests a path or Way *(imitatio Christi)* that the Christian is obliged to follow, at whatever cost to personal identity or life.

6. Mathews, *Religion in the Old South,* pp. 9-10.

7. William Jacob Walls, *The African Methodist Episcopal Zion Church: Reality of the Black Church* (Charlotte, N.C.: AME Zion Publishing House, 1974), p. 39.

8. Mathews, *Religion in the Old South.*

9. Walls, *The African Methodist Episcopal Zion Church,* p. 39.

10. Richard Allen, *The Life Experience and Gospel Labors of the Rt. Rev. Richard Allen* (Nashville: Abingdon Press, 1960 [1793]), p. 29.

11. Carol V. R. George, *Segregated Sabbaths: Richard Allen and the Rise of Independent Black Churches, 1760-1840* (New York: Oxford University Press, 1973), pp. 17-18.

12. Allen, *The Life Experience,* p. 17.

13. George, *Segregated Sabbaths,* pp. 44-45.

14. Methodist Episcopal Church and the Methodist Episcopal Church *South,* in 1844. The branches repaired relations in 1939, forming the United Methodist Church. See, "Abolitionists vs. Apologists: Institutional Schism," in Edwin S. Gaustad, ed., *A Documentary History of Religion in America to the Civil War* (Grand Rapids: Wm. B. Eerdmans, 1982), pp. 491-494, which cites Frederick A. Ross, *Slavery Ordained of God* (Philadelphia: J. B. Lippincott, 1857), pp. 94-102.

15. As recorded in the minutes of yearly conferences of the ME Church. Walls, *The African Methodist Episcopal Zion Church,* p. 29.

16. Walls, *The African Methodist Episcopal Zion Church,* pp. 26-27.

17. Cornel West places a positive valuation on black rage in producing "psychic conversion" in "Malcolm X and Black Rage," in *Race Matters* (Boston: Beacon Press, 1993), pp. 93-105. The emphasis on psychic conversion comports with the evangelical orientation of present-day black Christianity.

18. Allen, "An Address to Those Who Keep Slaves and Approve the Practices," in *The Life Experience,* p. 71, emphases mine.

19. To employ *literalist* hermeneutics is to interpret biblical passages in a literal way that intends or effects exclusionary policy or practices. It is to project as standard the belief that the Bible, as the Word of God, is authoritative for saying how the world—society, the church, the family—should be ordered. The authority of the Bible is ascribed in various degrees of objectification ranging from absolute to arbitrary in literalist hermeneutics. Fundamentalist theologies, for example, ascribe absolute authority to the Bible and try to derive from the Bible a basic or *fundamental* body of concepts about human life and culture, a way of human relating that conforms to the "objective" standards in the Bible. However, not all literalists are fundamentalists. As African American biblical scholar William Myers notes, source-critical approaches emphasize that a biblical text has only *one* legitimate meaning, usually conceived as *the* orthodox

meaning, which is emphasized to predetermine the way biblical texts can be interpreted and appropriated. This contributes to an acute "hermeneutical dilemma" among African American exegetes, whose collective history of interpretation/appropriation reflects as much emphasis on the experience of racial oppression as on the presumed objectivity of the Bible. See William H. Myers, "The Hermeneutical Dilemma of the African American Biblical Student," in Cain Hope Felder, ed., *Stony the Road We Trod: African American Biblical Interpretation* (Minneapolis: Fortress Press, 1991), pp. 40-56.

20. "Abolitionists vs. Apologists: Institutional Schism," in Gaustad, *A Documentary History of Religion in America to the Civil War*, pp. 500-502.

21. Kenneth M. Stampp, "Chattels Personal," in Richard D. Brown and Stephen G. Rabe, eds., *Slavery in American Society* (Lexington, Mass.: D. C. Heath and Co., 1976), pp. 90-107, quotation at p. 94. Stampp cites from Helen T. Catterall, ed., *Judicial Cases concerning American Slavery and the Negro*, vol. 2 (Washington, D.C.: Carnegie Institution of Washington, 1926ff.), p. 168.

22. Ibid., p. 97. Justices, sheriffs, police and constabulary levied heavy fines against whites for trading with, selling liquor or giving passes to slaves, and teaching them to read or write. Concealing runaways and inciting rebellion among the slaves were capital offenses. The history of the death penalty closely follows upon the institution of slavery. The enforcement of the death penalty has nearly always been applied relative to the threat or potential threat to white persons or property in a way that punished both black people and white with equal severity. See Berry, *Black Resistance/White Law*.

23. Katie Geneva Cannon, *Black Womanist Ethics* (Atlanta: Scholars Press, 1988), pp. 36-39.

24. See bell hooks, *Ain't I a Woman: Black Women and Feminism* (Boston: South End Press, 1981); and Dorothy Sterling, ed., *We Are Your Sisters: Black Women in the 19th Century* (New York: W. W. Norton, 1984), pp. 18-31.

25. Brent, *Incidents in the Life of a Slave Girl*, pp. 52-53.

26. Mary Helen Washington, ed., *Invented Lives: Narratives of Black Women (1860-1960* (New York: Anchor Books, 1987), p. 5. See also Sterling, *We Are Your Sisters*.

27. Isabella Lucy Bird Bishop, *The Aspects of Religion in the USA* (New York: Arno Press, 1972 [1859]), pp. 1-2, 156-160, cited in Gaustad, *A Documentary History of Religion in America*, pp. 407-408.

28. G.E.M. de Ste. Croix, *The Class Struggle in the Ancient Greek World* (London: Gerald Duckworth and Co., 1981), p. 421.

29. hooks, *Ain't I a Woman?*, pp. 30-31.

30. Jarena Lee, *The Religious Experiences and Journal of Mrs. Jarena Lee* (Philadelphia, 1849), p. 20.

31. The AME Church approved the licensing of women preachers in 1884. In 1885 a black ecclesiastical activist, Bishop Henry McNeal Turner of North Carolina, attempted to parlay the license of one Sarah A.H. into deacon's orders. Bishop Turner was reprimanded at the General Conference of 1888. Women would not be ordained in the AME Church until 1948. Having also been denied opportunity to serve in the AME Church, Julia A. J. Foote (1823-1900) received deacon's orders from the AME Zion Church on 20 May 1894.

She became the first black and first Methodist woman in America to receive deacon's orders unchallenged, and the second woman to receive elder's orders, from the AME Zion Church. See Hine, ed., *Black Women in America* (Brooklyn: Carlson Publishing, 1993), s.v., "African Methodist Episcopal Preaching Women of the 19th Century" and "Lee, Jarena" (Jualynne Dodson), pp. 12-14, 707; and "Foote, Julia A. J." (Lillie Johnson Edwards), p. 440. See also Jualynne Dodson, "Nineteenth Century AME Preaching Women," in H. F. Thomas and R. S. Keller, eds., *Women in New Worlds* (Nashville: Abingdon Press, 1981), pp. 276-289.

32. The Pauline/Augustinian tradition upholds the primacy of sin as pride as opposed to sin as sexuality/sensuality as the prima facie cause of the fall in most Western Christian anthropologies. Nevertheless, because Augustine placed so much emphasis on his sexual experience, because of the crucial place of sexuality in human spirituality, and because of the rapacity of the church's historical attempts to control human sexuality, it is difficult to separate this tradition from others that state that sexual intercourse was in fact the proximate cause of the fall.

33. From there it was a short step to being slaves of other human beings, since some were deemed more godly than others, that is, those in power, who historically (and cross-culturally) have defended the notion of the divine right of monarchs in varying ascriptions of authority and power. See James B. Pritchard, ed., *The Ancient Near East*, vol. 1: *An Anthology of Texts and Pictures* (Princeton: Princeton University Press, 1958 [1973]); and vol. 2: *A New Anthology of Texts and Pictures* (Princeton: Princeton University Press, 1975 [1992]). See especially Tablet VI of "The Creation Epic" (*Enuma Elish*), trans. E. A. Speiser, 1:31-39. In Genesis 1:1-2:4 the captive Jews transformed the elements of the Babylonian myth to assert a different reason for the creation of the world, thus asserting a different basis of the civil and political order.

34. Mathews, *Religion in the Old South.*

35. See Cornel West, "A Genealogy of Modern Racism," in *Prophesy Deliverance! An Afro-American Revolutionary Christianity* (Philadelphia: Westminster Press, 1982), pp. 47-65.

36. Immanuel Kant, *Observations on the Feeling of the Beautiful and the Sublime*, trans. John T. Goldthwait (Berkeley: University of California Press, 1960 [1763]), p. 93.

37. One of Jefferson's main influences was British empiricist, John Locke (1632-1704), a forerunner of the Enlightenment, who defended both reason and piety. As chief architect of the Declaration of Independence, Thomas Jefferson posited Locke's doctrine of equality of all humankind, which he subverted through his own slaveholding and defense of slavery in his treatise "*Notes on Virginia*."

38. Kant, *Observations*, pp. 110-111. Kant's arguments are reflected in Jefferson's pro-slavery sentiments, despite the universalist rhetoric of the Declaration of Independence and the Constitution, which captured white disdain for blackness in the ontological degradation of black males to the status of three-fifths human.

39. In Mathews, *Religion in the Old South*, p. 136.

40. Thornton Stringfellow, "The Bible Argument: Or, Slavery in the Light of Divine Revelation," in *Cotton Is King, and Proslavery Arguments*, ed. E. N. Elliott, L.L.D. (Augusta, Ga.: Pritchard Abbott, 1860, pp. 461-546), p. 486, 493.

41. David Hodge, "The Fugitive Slave Law," in Elliott, *Cotton Is King*, p. 819.

42. Ibid., p. 835.

43. See Melville Herskovits, *The Myth of the Negro Past* (Boston: Beacon Press, 1958 [1924]); and E. Franklin Frazier, *The Negro Church in America* (New York: Schocken Books, 1964). See also Genovese, *Roll, Jordan, Roll*; and Albert J. Raboteau, *Slave Religion: The "Invisible Institution" in the Antebellum South* (New York: Oxford University Press, 1978).

44. James H. Cone, "Sanctification, Liberation and Black Worship," in *Theology Today*, July 1978, pp. 139-152.

45. Zora Neale Hurston, *The Sanctified Church* (Berkeley: Turtle Island, 1981), p. 91.

46. Cf. Michel Sobel, *The World They Made Together: Black and White Values in Eighteenth-Century Virginia* (Princeton, N.J.: Princeton University Press, 1987).

47. Cone, "Sanctification, Liberation and Black Worship," pp. 145-146.

48. Hurston, *The Sanctified Church*, p. 83.

49. Cf. James H. Cone, *The Spirituals and the Blues* (Maryknoll, N.Y.: Orbis Books, 1991 [1972]).

50. See Stuckey, *Slave Culture: Nationalist Theory and the Foundations of Black America* (New York: Oxford University Press, 1987).

51. Engelbert Mveng, S.J., "Black African Art as Cosmic Liturgy and Religious Language," in Kofi Appiah-Kubi and Sergio Torres, eds., *African Theology En Route* (Maryknoll, N.Y.: Orbis Books, 1979), pp. 137-138.

52. Cf. Cornel West, "Subversive Joy and Revolutionary Patience," *Prophetic Fragments* (Grand Rapids/Trenton: Wm. B. Eerdmans/Africa World Press, 1988), pp. 161-165.

53. Cf. Engelbert Mveng, "Essai D'Anthropologie Negro-Africaine: La Personne Humaine," in *L'Afrique Dans L'Eglise: Paroles D'un Croyant* (Paris: Editions L'Harmattan, 1985), p. 16. Mveng states, "The human being appears, throughout African tradition, as an extremely complex reality. He or she is the recapitulation of the mystery of the world, the rendezvous of all the tides of life coursing through the universe. The human being is that moment when the cosmos develops life and personality. The whole material universe is the infinite extension of his or her corporeal wrapping. Humankind embodies the whole of time in the seed of history. Humans link the ancestors and future generations. They set the rhythm of times and of seasons—they make it rain! They implore moon and sun: lightning flashes; the wind howls; thunder peals. They lend their hearts to the beasts of the field and to lifeless beings. Humankind is the flowering of the spirit in the chaos of matter" (translation mine). See also Augustine Musopole, *Being Human in Africa: Toward an African Christian Anthropology* (New York: Peter Lang, 1994); and John S. Mbiti, *African Religions and Philosophy* (Garden City, N.Y.: Anchor Books, 1970 [1969]).

54. Jeremiah A. Wright Jr., *Africans Who Shaped Our Faith* (Chicago: Urban Ministries, 1995).

55. W.E.B. Du Bois, *The Souls of Black Folks* (Greenwich, Conn.: Fawcett Publications, 1961 [1903]), p. 141.

56. Joseph R. Washington Jr., *Black Religion: The Negro and Christianity in the United States* (Boston: Beacon Press, 1964), pp. 235-236.

57. See Josiah Young, *Black and African Theologies: Siblings or Distant Cousins* (Maryknoll, N.Y.: Orbis Books, 1986); Emmanuel Martey, *African Theology: Inculturation and Liberation* (Maryknoll, N.Y.: Orbis Books, 1993). For discussion of the significance of African retentions for nonreligious cultural expressions, see also Anthony Pinn, *Why Lord? Suffering and Evil in Black Theology* (New York: Continuum Publishing Co., 1995); and Lawrence W. Levine, *Black Culture and Black Consciousness: Afro-American Folk-Thought From Slavery to Freedom* (New York: Oxford University Press, 1977).

58. Hurston, "The Wounds of Jesus," in *The Sanctified Church*, pp. 95-102.

59. Katie Geneva Cannon, "The Wounds of Jesus: Justification of Goodness in the Face of Manifest Evil," in Emily Townes, ed., *A Troubling in My Soul: Womanist Perspectives on Evil and Suffering* (Maryknoll, N.Y.: Orbis Books, 1993), pp. 219-231, quotation at p. 226.

60. Mveng, "Black African Art as Cosmic Liturgy and Religious Language," p. 141.

61. Levine, *Black Culture and Black Consciousness*, p. 34.

62. William Grimes, *Life of William Grimes* (New Haven, 1855), cited in Raboteau, *Slave Religion*, pp. 301-302.

63. Raboteau, *Slave Religion*, pp. 301-302, emphases mine.

64. Cited in John W. Blassingame, *The Slave Community* (New York: Oxford University Press, 1979), pp. 205-206.

65. Gayraud S. Wilmore, *Black Religion and Black Radicalism* (Maryknoll, N.Y.: Orbis Books, 1983), p. 65.

66. Ibid., pp. 57-62.

67. Aptheker, ed., *One Continual Cry: David Walker's Appeal*, p. 74.

68. Ibid.

69. Ibid., p. 88.

70. Ibid., p. 89.

71. Although it was easy for white northerners to denounce the South morally because the institution of slavery persisted on its soil, Walker recognized the hypocrisy of Thomas Jefferson's (influential) proslavery position, which was based on pseudoscientific assessments disparaging of black intelligence, dignity and beauty in contradistinction to the proslavery position of white southerners, who, in Jefferson's words, were "actuated by sordid avarice only." Aptheker, *One Continual Cry*, p. 91.

72. Lerone Bennett Jr., *Before the Mayflower: A History of Black America* (Chicago: Johnson Publishing Co, 1987 [1962]), p. 148.

73. See Booker T. Washington, *Up from Slavery: An Autobiography* (Garden City, N.Y.: Doubleday, 1925).

74. Although the Nation of Islam espouses beliefs foreign to Christianity and orthodox Islam, its ministers freely use the scripture, language and concepts of Western Christianity. The myth of Yacub is one such example, putatively referring to the creation of the Adam of Christian scripture (Gn 2:7-8; 18-24).

75. Cf. Elijah Muhammad, *Message to the Blackman in America* (Newport News: United Brothers Communications Systems, 1965); C. Eric Lincoln, *The Black Muslims in America* (Grand Rapids/Trenton: Wm.B. Eerdmans Publishing Co./ Africa World Press, 1994 [1961]). See also Claude Andrew Clegg III, *An Original Man: The Life and Times of Elijah Muhammad* (New York: St. Martin's Press, 1997).

76. Since the March, Minister Farrakhan has indicated a desire to have African Americans become a "third political force."

77. During Supreme Court Justice Clarence Thomas's confirmation hearings, he invoked black male victimization in slavery and the heyday of lynching, asserting that he was a victim of myths of black male sexual superiority (this rallied significant support in the black community). The media, properly chastised, never raised the prospect that myths associated with black women's sexuality were operative.

78. Delores Williams, "Black Women's Surrogacy Experience and the Christian Notion of Redemption," in Paula M. Cooey et al., eds., *After Patriarchy: Feminist Transformations of the World Religions* (Maryknoll, N.Y.: Orbis Books, 1991), p. 1.

79. Cf. Philip S. Foner, ed., *Frederick Douglas on Women's Rights, Contributions in Afro-American and African Studies*, no. 25 (Westport, Conn.: Greenwood Press, 1976). The abolitionists conscientized the American women's movement with the idea that struggle for the full humanity of all people is a worthy vocation. At Seneca Falls, New York, in 1848, Stanton introduced a resolution connecting universal suffrage with abolitionism. See also Angela Y. Davis, *Women, Race and Class* (New York: Vintage Books, 1983).

80. Davis, *Women, Race and Class*, p. 70.

81. Ibid., pp. 83-84. See also Hine, *Black Women in America*, s.v. "Suffrage Movement" (Rosalyn Terborg-Penn), pp. 1124-1128.

82. Ibid.

83. Historian Nell Irvin Painter could find no authenticating evidence that these were the actual words of Truth but a product of liberal whites' (such as her friend and biographer, Olive Gilbert and author Harriet Beecher Stowe) attempts to *manage* Truth's public image. Douglass recorded the question in this way: "Is God *gone?*" Painter affirms the "symbolic meaning" of the encounter between Truth and Douglass as indicative of the "spiritualism" that characterized Truth's witness to the Christian faith, shaped in the evangelical ethos of America. See Nell Irvin Painter, *Sojourner Truth: A Life, a Symbol* (New York: W. W. Norton, 1996), pp. 161-162.

84. Bert James Loewenberg and Ruth Bogin, eds., *Black Women in Nineteenth Century American Life: Their Words, Their Thoughts, Their Feelings* (University Park: Pennsylvania State University Press, 1976), p. 234.

85. Peter J. Paris, *The Social Teaching of the Black Churches* (Philadelphia: Fortress Press, 1985).

86. C. Eric Lincoln and Lawrence H. Mamiya, *The Black Church in the African American Experience* (Durham, N.C.: Duke University Press, 1990). These include the African Methodist Episcopal Church (AME); the African Methodist Episcopal Zion Church (AMEZ); the Christian Methodist Episcopal Church (CME);

the National Baptist Convention, USA, Incorporated (NBC); the National Baptist Convention of America, Unincorporated (NBCA); the Progressive National Baptist Convention (PNBC); and the Church of God in Christ (COGIC).

87. See Benjamin Elijah Mays and Joseph William Nicholson, *The Negro's Church* (New York: Arno Press, 1969), in which the authors include the Baptist, AME, AMEZ, CME, ME, Presbyterian, Congregational and Protestant Episcopal denominations.

88. Although it is easier to trace African influences to slave religion on southern plantations and hence, to poorer blacks, the extent to which northern blacks–slave and free–indulged in them is less well known. Yet it cannot therefore be assumed that no African influences and practices existed in those communions that derived from white denominations or that remain in them. Slave religion manifested itself everywhere slavery existed; the invisible institution gave birth to the Black Church and provides a context for understanding its present manifestations. That is why today, despite the structural givens of a particular denomination, continuity exists from black communion to black communion, in, for example, confessional utterances commonly heard in the Black Church. This is not simply the result of migrational patterns. Although surely cross-fertilization occurred, many practices and significations were common, while northern blacks and former slaves could give assent to others because they gave voice to their struggles and impetus toward victory.

89. Delores Williams, *Sisters in the Wilderness* (Maryknoll, N.Y.: Orbis Books, 1993), pp. 204-206.

90. James H. Cone, *For My People: Black Theology and the Black Church* (Maryknoll, N.Y.: Orbis Books, 1984), pp. 7-8.

91. Wilmore, *Black Religion and Black Radicalism*, pp. 135-166.

92. Rayford W. Logan, *The Negro in American Life and Thought: The Nadir 1877-1901* (New York: Dial Press, 1954).

93. James H. Cone, *Speaking the Truth: Ecumenism, Liberation and Black Theology* (Grand Rapids: Wm. B. Eerdmans, 1986), p. 115.

94. Examples include: "They hung him high; they stretched him wide; he hung his head, for me he died–that's love." "In God's chemical laboratory of redemption, Jesus took my black soul, dipped it in red blood, and I came out white as snow."

95. See James H. Cone, "Black Theology and the Black Church: Where Do We Go from Here?" in James H. Cone and Gayraud S. Wilmore, eds., *Black Theology: A Documentary History, Volume 1: 1966-1979* (Maryknoll, N.Y.: Orbis Books, 1993, [1979]), pp. 266-275.

96. J. Deotis Roberts, *The Prophethood of Black Believers* (Louisville: John Knox/ Westminster Press), p. 16.

97. Gayraud S. Wilmore, "Black Theology: Review and Assessment," *Voices from the Third World*, vol. 5, no. 2, 1982, pp. 3-16, quotation at p. 5.

98. See Cecil Cone, *The Identity Crisis in Black Theology* (Nashville: African Methodist Episcopal Church, 1975).

99. See James H. Cone, *The Spirituals and the Blues.*

100. See Irene V. Jackson, *Afro-American Religious Music: A Bibliography and a Catalogue of Gospel Music* (Westport, Conn.: Greenwood Press, 1979); Wyatt Tee Walker, *"Somebody's Calling My Name": Black Sacred Music and Social Change* (Val-

ley Forge, Pa.: Judson Press, 1979); Jon Michael Spencer, *Black Hymnody: A Hymnological History of the African American Church* (Knoxville: University of Tennessee Press, 1992); and idem, *Black Sacred Music: A Journal of Theomusicology* (Durham: Duke University Press, 1993).

101. Myers, "The Hermeneutical Dilemma," pp. 40-56.

102. Dwight N. Hopkins, *Shoes That Fit Our Feet: Sources for a Constructive Black Theology* (Maryknoll, N.Y.: Orbis Books, 1993).

103. Of the seven historically black churches, one, the Church of God in Christ, explicitly prohibits the ordination of women. According to Lincoln and Mamiya, black Baptist communions have no written policy against women's ordination but generally have not been supportive of women as preachers and pastors of churches. They report that the Progressive National Baptist Convention tends "to be only slightly more progressive on this issue of women pastors" (Lincoln and Mamiya, *The Black Church in the African American Experience,* p. 291). Although black Methodists historically have been more progressive on the issue of women's ordination, women ministers still have to contend for viable pastorates and denominational support.

104. Cf. George Kelsey, *Racism and the Christian Understanding of Man* (New York: Charles Scribner's Sons, 1965), pp. 9-11; 25-28.

105. Roberts, *The Prophethood of Black Believers,* p. 11.

106. Ibid., p. 22.

3   THE SCANDAL OF THE CROSS

1. James H. Cone, *God of the Oppressed* (San Francisco: Harper & Row, 1975), p. 116.

2. Whites who had accommodated to perceptions about their superior morality had no moral compunction about cheating blacks out of their rightful pay. In the autobiographical *Coming through the Fire: Surviving Race and Place in America* (Durham: Duke University Press, 1996), pp. 21-25, C. Eric Lincoln recounts such a "lesson in racial etiquette" that demonstrates the violence with which whites secured their place in the top echelon of the stratified post-slavery society. His story, like mine, attests to the role of cotton as a symbol of black oppression in southern agrarian economies.

3. See Phyllis Trible, *Texts of Terror: Literary-Feminist Readings of Biblical Narratives* (Philadelphia: Fortress Press, 1984).

4. On 26 January 1923 a southern filibuster tactic defeated the Dyer Anti-Lynching Bill. See Charles Christian, *Black Saga: The African American Experience—A Chronology* (Boston: Houghton Mifflin, 1995), p. 331. Today, occasional lynchings are heard of and legislative lynching of black and poor people has found new impetus in the Congress and in the Senate.

5. Manning Marable, *How Capitalism Underdeveloped Black America* (Boston: South End Press, 1983), pp. 33-35. See also Vincent Harding, *There Is a River: The Black Struggle for Freedom in America* (New York: Vintage Books, 1983), pp. 283-285.

6. Gayraud S. Wilmore, *Black Religion and Black Radicalism* (Maryknoll, N.Y.: Orbis Books, 1983 [1973]), pp. 135-166.

7. And with it, the spinning of updated theories of race. Although theories of race during the post-Enlightenment period appear to be based on premises that support white racial supremacy, anthropologists nevertheless characterize it as "science" since theorists and theories reflect the scientific wisdom of the age. Cf. George W. Stocking Jr., *Race, Culture and Evolution: Essays in the History of Anthropology* (Chicago: University of Chicago Press, 1982 [1968]).

8. Wilmore defines mainline churches as those large, urban, social action–oriented, institutional churches that derived from black denominations.

9. Founders include my third cousin Elder Nathaniel Scippio and his mother, my great-great aunt Delia Wilburn Scippio, whom I greatly resemble. Another third cousin, Elder Aaron Matthews Sr., was the small denomination's first bishop, and his son, Elder Willie W. Matthews, is bishop emeritus after nearly forty years of service. My grandfather, Elder Donison Henry (1896-1975) was converted in 1914. He was a noted preacher, teacher and planter of churches. Today, the Churches of God by Faith, Inc. is headquartered in Jacksonville, Florida, and has a majority of its churches in the South. See Frank Spencer Mead, *Handbook of Denominations in the United States* (Nashville: Abingdon Press, 1995 [1985]).

10. Marable, *How Capitalism Underdeveloped Black America*, p. 33.

11. Ibid.

12. See Edwin S. Redkey, ed., *Respect Black: The Writings and Speeches of Henry McNeal Turner* (New York: Arno Press/New York Times, 1971), p. 63.

13. See "Booker T. Washington and the Adaptive Person," in Robert Michael Franklin, *Liberating Visions: Human Fulfillment and Social Justice in African-American Thought* (Minneapolis: Fortress Press, 1990), pp. 11-42.

14. James H. Cone, *Martin and Malcolm and America: A Dream or a Nightmare?* (Maryknoll, N.Y.: Orbis Books, 1991), p. 11.

15. Although he was a primogenitor of the black radical tradition, David Walker had opposed emigration to Africa, as that was advocated by the censured American Colonization Society. Walker discerned that its program to repatriate free blacks in Africa would result in the continued exploitation of Africa and in unbridled abuse toward the slaves remaining in the South.

16. Seeking to galvanize black churches toward social activism, The Revs. George Washington Woodbey (b. 1854) and George W. Slater Jr. applied a socialist hermeneutics to the Bible, lending ideological strength to arguments from moral suasion. Cf. Philip S. Foner, *American Socialism and Black Americans: From the Age of Jackson to World War II* (Westport, Conn.: Greenwood Press, 1977). See also Philip S. Foner, *Black Socialist Preacher* (San Francisco: Synthesis Publications, 1983).

17. *Civil Rights movement* is an umbrella term for organizations that advocated integration with whites: the National Association for the Advancement of Colored Peoples (NAACP, led by Roy Wilkins); the Urban League (UL, led by Whitney Young); the Congress of Racial Equality (CORE, led by James Farmer); and the Southern Christian Leadership Conference. Ministers, theology students, seminary dropouts and college students joined with the black masses around the country to comprise the King-led SCLC and its affiliates. See Wilmore, *Black Religion and Black Radicalism*, p. 178.

The term *black power* was a slogan of young radicals generated in response to the nonviolent philosophy of King and the Civil Rights movement. It embraces the concept of self-determination "by any means necessary," including self-defense, which Christians in the movement believed comported with the exercise of their religious beliefs.

18. Cf. Bishop Joseph Johnson, *The Soul of the Black Preacher* (Philadelphia: The Pilgrim Press, 1971).

19. Delores Williams, *Sisters in the Wilderness* (Maryknoll, N.Y.: Orbis Books, 1993), p. 205.

20. Martin Luther King Jr., *Stride toward Freedom: The Montgomery Story* (New York: Harper & Row, 1986 [1958]), p. 45.

21. Ibid., pp. 90-93.

22. Ibid., p. 99.

23. Cf. Larry Rasmussen, ed., *Reinhold Niebuhr: Theologian of Public Life* (Minneapolis: Fortress Press, 1991), p. 23.

24. King, *Stride toward Freedom*, p. 93.

25. Ibid.

26. Reinhold Niebuhr, *Moral Man and Immoral Society* (New York: Charles Scribner's Sons, 1932), pp. 263-264.

27. Church historian James Washington states that when King became the president of the MIA, he was unaware that he was using the philosophy of nonviolence until activists who were already in the peace movement pointed it out. They were Glenn Smiley, a white minister and national field secretary of the Fellowship of Reconciliation and Bayard Rustin, who was then executive secretary of the War Resisters League. In James Washington, ed., *A Testament of Hope: The Essential Writings of Martin Luther King, Jr.* (San Francisco: Harper & Row, 1986), p. 82. See also David J. Garrow, *Bearing the Cross: Martin Luther King, Jr. and the Southern Christian Leadership Conference* (New York: Vintage Books, 1986) and Taylor Branch, *Parting the Waters: America In the King Years, 1954-1963* (New York: Simon and Schuster, 1988).

28. Reinhold Niebuhr, *The Nature and Destiny of Man*, vol. 2 (New York: Charles Scribner's Sons, 1943), p. 88.

29. Kenneth B. Clark, *King, Malcolm and Baldwin: Three Interviews* (Middletown, Conn.: Wesleyan University Press, 1985 [1963]), p. 25.

30. Martin Luther King Jr., "Pilgrimage to Nonviolence," in Washington, *A Testament of Hope*, p. 38.

31. Martin Luther King Jr., "The Power of Nonviolence," in Washington, *A Testament of Hope*, p. 13.

32. King, *Stride toward Freedom*, p. 35.

33. Cf. Cone, *Martin and Malcolm and America*, p. 122, and Garrow, *Bearing the Cross*.

34. Lewis V. Baldwin, *There Is a Balm in Gilead: The Cultural Roots of Martin Luther King, Jr.* (Minneapolis: Fortress Press, 1991); and idem, *To Make the Wounded Whole: The Cultural Legacy of Martin Luther King, Jr.* (Minneapolis: Fortress Press, 1992).

35. Cf. James H. Cone, "Martin Luther King: The Source of His Courage to Face Death," *Concilium*, vol. 183, March 1983, pp. 74-79.

36. Clark, *King, Malcolm and Baldwin,* p. 29.

37. See Cone, *Martin and Malcolm and America,* pp. 128-129.

38. Julius Lester, "The Angry Children of Malcolm X," in August Meier, Elliott M. Rudwick and Francis L. Broderick, eds., *Black Protest Thought in the Twentieth Century* (New York: Macmillan, 1971), p. 482.

39. Martin Luther King Jr., *Playboy* interview, January 1965.

40. See "Black Power" Statement by the National Committee of Negro Churchmen, 31 July 1966, in James H. Cone and Gayraud S. Wilmore, eds., *Black Theology: A Documentary History, Volume 1 (1966-1979)* (Maryknoll, N.Y.: Orbis Books, 1993 [1979]), pp. 19-26. Cf. Mark L. Chapman, *Christianity on Trial: African-American Religious Thought before and after Black Power* (Maryknoll, N.Y.: Orbis Books, 1996).

41. Cf. Winthrop Hudson, *Religion in America,* 5th ed. (New York: Macmillan, 1992 [1965]), p. 254, note, on the origins of the United Church of Christ.

42. Chapman, *Christianity on Trial,* pp. 96-97.

43. Albert B. Cleage Jr., "A Black Man's View of Authority," in Clyde Manschreck, ed., *Erosion of Authority* (Nashville: Abingdon Press, 1971), pp. 59-91, quotation at p. 77.

44. Ibid., p. 62.

45. Chapman, *Christianity on Trial,* pp. 94-95.

46. Hiley H. Ward, *Prophet of the Black Nation: Albert B. Cleage, Jr.* (Philadelphia: The Pilgrim Press, 1969), p. 24.

47. Albert B. Cleage Jr., *The Black Messiah* (New York: Sheed and Ward, 1968), p. 8.

48. Chapman, *Christianity on Trial,* p. 96.

49. Cf. Randall F. Burkett, *Garveyism as a Religious Movement* (Metuchen, N.J.: The Scarecrow Press, 1978).

50. Riggins Earl, *Toward a Black Christian Ethic: A Study of Alexander Crummell and Albert Cleage,* Ph.D. dissertation (Nashville: Vanderbilt University, 1978), p. 216.

51. Cleage, *The Black Messiah,* p. 8.

52. Ibid., p. 3.

53. In James J. Gardiner, and J. Deotis Roberts Jr., eds., *Quest for a Black Theology* (Philadelphia: The Pilgrim Press, 1971), pp. ix-x.

54. Earl, *Toward a Black Christian Ethic,* p. 216.

55. Albert B. Cleage Jr., *Black Christian Nationalism* (New York: William Morrow, 1972), p. 32.

56. Cleage, "A Black Man's View of Authority," p. 85.

57. Ibid., pp. 6-7.

58. Cleage, *The Black Messiah,* p. 33.

59. James H. Cone, *My Soul Looks Back* (Maryknoll, N.Y.: Orbis Books, 1986), p. 22.

60. Recounting personal history is part and parcel of Cone's liberation methodology.

61. Cf. Rufus Burrows, *James H. Cone and Black Liberation Theology* (Jefferson, N.C.: McFarland and Co., 1994).

62. Cone, *God of the Oppressed,* pp. 2-3.

63. Ibid., p. 138

64. James H. Cone, "Christianity and Black Power," in *Is Anybody Listening to Black America?*, ed. C. Eric Lincoln (New York: Seabury Press, 1968).

65. Cf. J. Deotis Roberts, *Liberation and Reconciliation: A Black Theology* (Philadelphia: Westminster Press, 1971).

66. James H. Cone, *The Spirituals and the Blues* (Maryknoll, N.Y.: Orbis Books, 1991 [1972]), p. 29.

67. King used this phrase on many occasions to denounce the legal maneuvers of whites intended to deprive black people of their civil rights. See his "Letter from a Birmingham City Jail," in Washington, *A Testament of Hope*, pp. 289-302.

68. See Paula Giddings, *When and Where I Enter: The Impact of Black Women on Race and Sex in America* (New York: William Morrow, 1984), p. 314 ff. The historic emasculation of black men caused by slavery; their economic emasculation as non-principals in the post-slavery work force; and black men's need for affirmation have been cited as reasons for the paternalistic shift in the ways black men and women came to relate to each other. According to Giddings this led to the elevation of the familial functions of black women and their circumscription as principals in both the Civil Rights and Black Power movements.

69. Ibid.

70. This phenomenon may be seen, for example, in the witness of Father George Stallings (of Imani Temple) and Father Clarence Joseph Rivers, who has edited a hymnal of favorite black hymns for use in Catholic churches. Recently, in Chicago, I preached at the Catholic Community of Saint Sabina Church, where Fr. Michael Pfleger, a white priest, is pastor of a predominantly black congregation. Although the Catholic rites are maintained, the cultural forms are recognizable from the Black Church tradition.

4 RETHINKING SACRIFICE

1. Cf. Mircea Eliade, ed., *Encyclopedia of Religion*, vol. 8, s.v. "liturgy" (New York: Macmillan, 1987), p. 581. Cf. Robert W. Hovda, *Strong, Loving and Wise: Presiding in Liturgy* (Collegeville, Minn.: Liturgical Press, 1984).

2. Cf. Elizabeth Cady Stanton et al., *The Woman's Bible* (Seattle: Coalition Task Force on Women and Religion, 1990 [1875]).

3. Cf. Valerie Saiving Goldstein, "The Human Situation: A Feminine View," *Journal of Religion*, vol. 40, 1960.

4. Cf. Angela Y. Davis, *Women, Race and Class* (New York: Vintage Books, 1983); and Susan Brooks Thistlethwaite, *Sex, Race and God: Christian Feminism in Black and White* (New York: Crossroad Publishing Co., 1991).

5. Frances Beale, "Double Jeopardy: To Be Black and Female," in James H. Cone and Gayraud S. Wilmore, eds., *Black Theology: A Documentary History, Volume 1: 1966-1979* (Maryknoll, N.Y.: Orbis Books, 1993, [1979]), pp. 284-292.

6. Cf. Walker, *In Love and in Trouble: Stories of Black Women* (New York: Harcourt Brace Jovanovich, 1974); *Meridian* (New York: Pocket Books, 1989 [1976]); *The Third Life of Grange Copeland* (New York: Pocket Books, 1991 [1970].

See also Walker, *Revolutionary Petunias and Other Poems* (Orlando: Harcourt Brace and Co., 1973).

7. Carl E. Braaten and Robert W. Jenson, eds., *Christian Dogmatics*, vol. 2 (Philadelphia: Fortress Press, 1984), pp. 14-15.

8. Cf. Gustaf Aulen, *Christus Victor: An Historical Study of the Three Main Types of the Idea of the Atonement* (New York: Macmillan, 1969).

9. This argument demonstrates the entrenched authority of the hermeneutics of sacrifice in the Middle Ages.

10. Peter Abelard, *Exposition of the Epistle to the Romans*, book 2, part 2, in Eugene Fairweather, ed., *A Scholastic Miscellany: Anselm to Ockham* (Philadelphia: Westminster Press, 1956), p. 281.

11. Abelard, *Exposition of the Epistle to the Romans*, pp. 283-284.

12. Steven E. Ozment, *The Reformation in the Cities: The Appeal of Protestantism to Sixteenth-Century Germany and Switzerland* (New Haven: Yale University Press, 1975), p. 134.

13. Williams, *Sisters in the Wilderness* (Maryknoll, N.Y.: Orbis Books, 1993), pp. 199-200.

14. Rita Nakashima Brock, *Journeys by Heart: A Christology of Erotic Power* (New York: Crossroad Publishing Co., 1988). See also idem, "And a Little Child Will Lead Us: Christology and Child Abuse," in Joanne Carlson Brown and Carole R. Bohn, eds., *Christianity, Patriarchy and Abuse: A Feminist Critique* (New York: The Pilgrim Press, 1989).

15. Jacquelyn Grant, *White Women's Christ and Black Women's Jesus* (Atlanta: Scholar's Press, 1989), p. 212.

16. Ibid., p. 209.

17. Ibid., p. 216.

18. Kelly Brown Douglas, *The Black Christ* (Maryknoll, N.Y.: Orbis Books, 1994), p. 86.

19. Grant, *White Women's Christ and Black Women's Jesus*, p. 219. Grant cites her forerunner, Jarena Lee, a nineteenth-century proto-womanist and preacher in the AME Church.

20. Patricia Hill Collins, *Black Feminist Thought: Knowledge, Consciousness, and the Politics of Empowerment* (New York: Routledge, 1991).

21. Kelly Brown Douglas, "God Is As Christ Does: Toward a Womanist Theology," in *Journal of Religious Thought*, vol. 46, no. 1, summer-fall 1989, p. 16.

22. Cf. Geoffrey Wainwright, *The Ecumenical Moment: Crisis and Opportunity for the Church* (Grand Rapids: Wm. B. Eerdmans, 1983).

23. Douglas, *The Black Christ*, p. 31.

24. Ibid., p. 19.

25. Ibid., p. 22.

26. See James H. Cone, *Black Theology and Black Power* (Minneapolis: Seabury Press, 1969); and idem, *A Black Theology of Liberation* (Philadelphia: J. B. Lippincott, 1970; Maryknoll, N.Y.: Orbis Books, 1986).

27. Delores Williams, "Black Women's Surrogacy Experience and the Christian Notion of Redemption," in Paula M. Cooey et al., eds., *After Patriarchy: Feminist Transformations of the World Religions* (Maryknoll, N.Y.: Orbis Books, 1991), pp. 1-14.

28. See Patricia Hill Collins, "Mammies, Matriarchs and Other Controlling Images" in *Black Feminist Thought*, pp. 67-90.

29. Cf. Gayraud S. Wilmore, ed., *Black Men in Prison: The Response of the African American Church* (Atlanta: The ITC Press, 1990).

30. Williams, "Black Women's Surrogacy Experience," p. 11.

31. Ibid.

32. The "Re-Imagining Conference" (4-7 November 1993) was held in Minneapolis, Minnesota. It was an international gathering of women participating in the World Council of Churches' Ecumenical Decade in Solidarity with Women and consisted of, among other things, audiotaped lecture/discussion series. The following quotations cite Williams's lecture and the question-and-answer session that came after it in the session titled, "Re-Imagining Jesus," taped on 5 November 1993. Other participants included Korean feminist theologian Kwok Pui-lan and Lutheran feminist theologian and preacher Barbara Lundblad.

33. Williams, "Re-Imagining Truth," *The Other Side*, May-June 1994, pp. 53-54.

34. Although black theologians' attempts at reimaging God/Christ are consistent with the Judeo-Christian tradition of anthropomorphizing God, in light of the redirected impetus of the love ethic in nationalist thought it can be argued that the opposite, *theomorphizing* blacks in their own eyes, was a serendipitous effect, which moreover portends specific warrants for the development of womanist Christology.

35. Delores S. Williams, "The Color of Feminism," *Christianity and Crisis*, April 29, 1985, pp. 164-165.

36. Cf. United States Department of Labor, Office of Policy, Planning and Research, *The Negro Family: The Case for National Action* (commonly known as *The Moynihan Report*), 1965; and Daryl C. Dance, "Black Eve or Madonna? A Study of the Antithetical Views of the Mother in Black American Literature," in Roseann P. Bell, Bettye J. Parker and Beverly Guy-Sheftall, eds., *Sturdy Black Bridges: Visions of Black Women in Literature* (Garden City, N.Y.: Anchor Books/ Doubleday, 1979), pp. 123-132.

37. Grant, *White Women's Christ and Black Women's Jesus*, pp. 135-136.

38. Brown (Douglas), "God Is As Christ Does," p. 16.

39. Ibid., p. 14.

40. C. Eric Lincoln and Lawrence H. Mamiya, *The Black Church in the African American Experience* (Durham, N.C.: Duke University Press, 1990), p. 287.

41. Jacquelyn Grant, "The Sin of Servanthood and the Deliverance of Discipleship," in Emily Townes, ed., *A Troubling in My Soul: Womanist Perspectives on Evil and Suffering* (Maryknoll, N.Y.: Orbis Books, 1993), pp. 199-218.

42. Cf. Genesis 9:25, the basis of the so-called Hamitic curse. See also Genesis 3:16, which putatively establishes the dominance of males.

43. Grant, "The Sin of Servanthood," p. 201.

44. Jacquelyn Grant, from the lecture/discussion series "Re-Imagining Language—Word," taped on 6 November 1993. Other participants included Johanna Bos and Rosario Battle. The citations refer to Grant's lecture, "The Power of Language/The Language of Empowerment."

45. Ibid.

46. John Kingsley Holton, "Remembering His Vision, Visualizing the Future: Dr. Martin Luther King Jr. and the African American Child," an address given at the Annual Martin Luther King Day celebration of the Joint Pan-African Ministries Program of the Hyde Park Cluster of Theological Schools, Chicago, Illinois, 15 January 1997.

47. Williams, "Re-Imagining Jesus."

48. See Mt 21:33-46 and synoptic parallels, Mk 12:1-12; Lk 20:9-19.

49. Aeschylus, *Prometheus Bound,* in *Ten Greek Plays in Contemporary Translation,* ed. L. R. Lind, trans. Rex Warner (Boston: Houghton Mifflin, 1957). Cf. Allen C. Myers, ed., *The Eerdmans Bible Dictionary,* s.v. "Zeus" (Grand Rapids: Wm. B. Eerdmans, 1987), p. 1089. In other versions of the mythology surrounding the play, Prometheus' punishment came as a result of his assistance, literally, to mankind (womankind was created later), giving evidence of the evolution/universalization of the God-principle in Greek thought, in which Zeus is seen in a more benevolent light. Cf. Edith Hamilton, *Mythology* (Boston: Little, Brown and Co., 1942).

50. Cf. Wendy Farley, *Tragic Vision and Divine Compassion: A Contemporary Theodicy* (Louisville: Westminster/John Knox Press, 1990).

51. James G. Williams, *The Bible, Violence and the Sacred* (San Francisco: Harper Collins Publishers, 1991), p. 30.

52. Delores Williams, "A Crucifixion Double-Cross?" in *The Other Side,* September-October 1993, pp. 25-27, quotation at p. 26.

53. Ibid., p. 27.

5   OUR MOTHERS' GARDENS

1. Cf. Jacquelyn Grant, "Womanist Theology: Black Women's Experience as a Source for Doing Theology, with Special Reference to Christology," *Journal of the Interdenominational Theological Center,* vol. 13, no. 2, spring 1986, pp. 195-212.

2. Alice Walker, *The Color Purple* (New York: Washington Square Press, 1982), pp. 175-179.

3. Ibid., p. 178.

4. *Bhagavad-Gita As It Is,* trans. His Divine Grace A. C. Bhaktivedanta Swami Prabhupada (New York: Collier Books, 1972 [1974]), p. 300. Cf. Barbara Stoler Miller, ed., trans., *Love Song of the Dark Lord: Jayadeva's Gitagovinda* (New York: Columbia University Press, 1977).

5. *Bahgavad-Gita As It Is,* p. 478.

6. Lecture, 28 April 1992.

7. Cf. James B. Pritchard, ed., *The Ancient Near East,* vol. 1: *An Anthology of Texts and Pictures* (Princeton: Princeton University Press, 1958 [1973]); and vol. 2: *A New Anthology of Texts and Pictures* (Princeton: Princeton University Press, 1975 [1992]).

8. bell hooks, *Feminist Theory from Margin to Center* (Boston: South End Press, 1984), p. 26. A cursory reading of hooks's writings reveals that she never employs the definite article when referring to *feminist movement* (*not* the feminist

movement). For hooks, this rhetorical technique refutes monolithic conceptions of the nature of women's involvement in feminism, which she describes as a "movement to end sexist oppression."

9. Delores S. Williams, "The Color of Feminism," *Christianity and Crisis,* April 29, 1985, pp. 164-165.

10. Karen Ludwig, "Womanist Theology/Feminist Theology: A Dialogue, *Daughters of Sarah,* vol. 15, no. 2, March/April 1989, pp. 6-7. The article reports on what several black women think is distinctive about womanist theology, citing a lecture on womanist and feminist theologies given by ethicist Cheryl Sanders.

11. See Marcia Riggs, "The Logic of Interstructured Oppression: A Black Womanist Perspective," in Susan Davies and Eleanor Haney, eds., *Redefining Sexual Ethics* (Cleveland: The Pilgrim Press, 1991).

12. Linda Burnham, "Has Poverty Been Feminized in Black America?" *The Black Scholar,* March/April 1985, pp. 14-24, quotation at p. 14.

13. Ibid., p. 17.

14. Katie Geneva Cannon, "Slave Ideology and Biblical Interpretation," in *Katie's Canon: Womanism and the Soul of the Black Community* (New York: Continuum Publishing Co., 1995), p. 41.

15. Clarice Martin, "Womanist Interpretations of the New Testament: The Quest for Holistic and Inclusive Translation and Interpretation," *Journal of Feminist Studies in Religion,* vol. 6, no. 2, 1990, pp. 41-61.

16. Cheryl Sanders, *Empowerment Ethics for a Liberated People: A Path to African American Social Transformation* (Minneapolis: Fortress Press, 1995).

17. Williams, *Sisters in the Wilderness* (Maryknoll, N.Y.: Orbis Books, 1993), p. 88.

18. Ludwig, "Womanist Theology/Feminist Theology: A Dialogue," p. 7.

19. Cf. Alex Poinsett, "The Quest for a Black Christ," *Ebony,* March 1969.

20. I applaud the work of Cone and other black theologians who have attempted to make the womanist critique integral to their work because I am challenged in turn to understand the peculiar plight of black men in the American context. See his preface to the revised edition of *A Black Theology of Liberation* (Maryknoll, N.Y.: Orbis Books, 1990 [1986, 1970]).

21. Jacquelyn Grant, "Black Theology and the Black Woman," in James H. Cone and Gayraud S. Wilmore, eds., *Black Theology: A Documentary History, Volume 1: 1966-1979* (Maryknoll, N.Y.: Orbis Books, 1993, [1979]), pp. 323-338, quotation at pp. 325-326.

22. Delores S. Williams, "Womanist Theology: Black Women's Voices," *Christianity and Crisis,* March 2, 1987, p. 69.

23. Cheryl Sanders et al., "Roundtable Discussion: Christian Ethics and Theology in Womanist Perspective," *Journal of Feminist Studies in Religion,* vol. 5, no. 2, fall 1989. Although almost no one disputes the apparent heterosexism and/or homophobia of Sanders's query, Sanders's criticisms are also methodological. A major question that arose from her inquiry is, Without clear Christian commitments, is Womanist Theology a proper discipline in which Christian scholars should engage? Although Walker's definition of womanism is not exclusive of Christianity, it is not particularly inclusive of it either, especially not concep-

tions of Christianity that derive from a literalist biblical perspective. Although this proclivity is apparent in Sanders's early essay, as of this writing she employs the womanist label and focuses on the development of Africentric ethics within the discipline.

24. Renee L. Hill, "Who Are We for Each Other? Sexism, Sexuality and Womanist Theology," in Cone and Wilmore, eds., *Black Theology: A Documentary History, Volume 2: 1980-1992* (Maryknoll, N.Y.: Orbis Books, 1993), pp. 345-351, quotation at p. 346.

25. Ibid., p. 347.

26. Delores S. Williams, "The Color Purple," *Christianity and Crisis*, July 14, 1986, pp. 230-232.

27. Ibid.

28. Cf. Walter Wink, *Violence and Nonviolence in South Africa: Jesus' Third Way* (Philadelphia: New Society Publishers, 1987).

29. See especially, 1 Jn 4:7-12: "Beloved, let us love one another; for love is of God, and he who loves is born of God and knows God. He who does not love does not know God; for God is love. In this the love of God was made manifest among us, that God sent his only Son into the world, so that we might live through him. In this is love, not that we loved God but that he loved us and sent his Son to be the expiation for our sins. Beloved, if God so loved us, we also ought to love one another. No man has ever seen God; if we love one another God abides in us and God's love is perfected in us." Cf. Jn 15:12-17.

30. See also Mt 5:43, 19:19; Rom 13:9; Ga 5:14; Jas 2:8.

31. Studs Terkel, *Race: How Blacks and Whites Think and Feel about the American Obsession* (New York: The New Press, 1992), p. 21.

32. Ibid.

33. Ibid., pp. 21-22. Mobley is a member of the Church of God in Christ, the largest Pentecostal denomination in the United States.

34. Thus, as a black liberation theologian, I would restate the womanist principle in this way: A black liberationist loves black people and *individual* whites. This affirms African Americans' worth apart from whites *and* their right to love whomever they will, or must.

35. In my interpretive model scripture *becomes* the word of God when it mediates a word that *witnesses* to the creativity, goodness, oneness and power of God in a person or a community. It is predicated upon my belief that the point of theology is in its *doing*, both in what it does to people and in what it makes people do. This makes theology, including scripture-making, a Divine and a human project.

36. Gandhi advocated the critical principle of *ahimsa* or *non-injury*, along with *satyagraha* or *truth-force* in Hinduism as the basis for his call to nonviolence. Many Western interpreters conveniently overlook the exegetical consideration that the *Bhagavad Gita*, from whence these principles derive, is an exhortation by the Lord Krishna to the warrior Arjuna to be the instrument of God and to fight, *literally*, in the cause of righteousness. Thus, a liberation impulse in Vedic scripture specifically enjoins humanity to be instruments of God's love and justice as warriors in the cause of righteousness, having, therefore, the authority of God to effect their liberation as exigencies arise.

In the purports of the *Gita, ahimsa* is described as "not arresting the progressive life of any living entity." A positive way of stating this might be that the principle seeks to further the spiritual happiness of the people in general, so that their full purpose might be realized. This Vedic witness is consistent with the principle, "There can be no reconciliation without liberation." The fact that many oppressed people have had to kill–and many more have died–for these congruent principles is mitigated by the fact that the non-realization of *ahimsa* carries with it the understanding that one kills with authority.

37. Cf. Angela Browne, *When Battered Women Kill* (New York: The Free Press, 1989).

38. Yet, in Israelite sacrifice, sin was regarded with such odiousness that the moral onus was placed on the subsequent actions of the one/ones for whom the sacrifice was performed.

39. Lao Tzu, *Tao Tĕ Ching (Way of Life)*, trans. R. B. Blakney (New York: Mentor Books, 1955), poem 31, p. 83.

Bibliography

Abelard, Peter. *Exposition of the Epistle to the Romans* (excerpt); *Ethics*, in Eugene R. Fairweather, ed. *A Scholastic Miscellany: Anselm to Ockham* (Philadelphia: Westminster Press, 1956), pp. 276-287, 288-297.

Aeschylus. *Prometheus Bound.* In *Ten Greek Plays in Contemporary Translation*, ed. L. R. Lind, trans. Rex Warner (Boston: Houghton Mifflin, 1957).

Allen, Richard. *The Life Experience and Gospel Labors of the Rt. Rev. Richard Allen* (Nashville: Abingdon Press, 1960 [1793]).

Andrews, William L., ed. "The Life and Religious Experience of Jarena Lee," *Sisters of the Spirit: Three Black Women's Autobiographies of the Nineteenth Century* (Bloomington: Indiana University Press, 1986), pp. 35-37.

Anselm of Canterbury. *Cur Deus Homo*, ed. and trans. Jasper Hopkins and Herbert Richardson (Toronto/New York: Edwin Mellen Press, 1975-76).

Appiah-Kubi, Kofi, and Sergio Torres, eds. *African Theology En Route* (Maryknoll, N.Y.: Orbis Books, 1979).

Aptheker, Herbert. *American Negro Slave Revolts* (New York: International Publishers, 1987).

———, ed. *One Continual Cry: David Walker's Appeal to the Colored Citizens of the World* (New York: Humanities Press, 1965).

Aulen, Gustaf. *Christus Victor: An Historical Study of the Three Main Types of the Idea of the Atonement*, trans. A. G. Herbert (New York: Macmillan, 1969).

Baillie, Donald M. *God Was in Christ*, "Why Atonement?"; "The Lamb of God" (New York: Charles Scribner's Sons, 1948), pp. 157-179; 180-202.

Baldwin, Lewis V. *To Make the Wounded Whole: The Cultural Legacy of Martin Luther King, Jr.* (Minneapolis: Fortress Press, 1992).

———. *There Is a Balm in Gilead: The Cultural Roots of Martin Luther King, Jr.* (Minneapolis: Fortress Press, 1991).

Beale, Frances. "The Black Church in America," in *Progressions*, a Lilly Endowment Occasional Report, vol. 4, no. 1, February 1992.

———. "Double Jeopardy: To Be Black and Female," in Cone and Wilmore, *Black Theology: A Documentary History, Volume 1: 1966-1979*, pp. 284-292.

Bell, Roseann P., Bettye J. Parker, and Beverly Guy-Sheftall, eds. *Sturdy Black Bridges: Visions of Black Women in Literature* (Garden City, N.Y.: Anchor Press/Doubleday Books, 1979).

Bennett, Lerone, Jr. *Before the Mayflower: A History of Black America* (Chicago: Johnson Publishing Co., 1987 [1962]).

Berry, Mary Frances. *Black Resistance/White Law: Constitutional History in America* (New York: Penguin Books, 1995 [1971]).

Bhagavad-Gita as It Is, trans. His Divine Grace A. C. Bhaktivedanta Swami Prabhupada (New York: Collier Books, 1972 [1974]).

Bisbee, Gary A. *Pre-Decian Acts of Martyrs and Commentarii* (Philadelphia: Fortress Press, 1988).

Bishop, Isabella Lucy Bird. *The Aspects of Religion in the USA* (New York: Arno Press, 1972 [1859]).

Blakney, R. B., trans. *Tao Te Ching* (New York: Mentor Books, 1955).

Blassingame, John W. *The Slave Community: Plantation Life in the Antebellum South* (New York: Oxford University Press, 1979).

————, ed. *Slave Testimony: Two Centuries of Letters, Speeches, Interviews, and Autobiographies* (Baton Rouge: Louisiana State University Press, 1977).

Botkin, B. A., ed. *Lay My Burden Down: A Folk History of Slavery* (Athens, Ga.: University of Georgia Press, 1945–Brown Thrasher edition, 1989).

Braaten, Carl E., and Robert W. Jenson, eds. *Christian Dogmatics*, vol. 2, "Reconciliation with God"; "Atonement as Actual Event" (Philadelphia: Fortress Press, 1984), pp. 65-78; 79-104.

Branch, Taylor. *Parting the Waters: America in the King Years, 1954-1963* (New York: Simon and Schuster, 1988).

Braxton, Joanne M., and Andree Nicola McLaughlin, eds. *Wild Women in the Whirlwind: Afra-American Culture and the Contemporary Literary Renaissance* (New Brunswick, N.J.: Rutgers University Press, 1990).

Brent, Linda. *Incidents in the Life of a Slave Girl,* ed. L. Maria Child (New York: Harcourt Brace Jovanovich, 1973 [1861]).

Brock, Rita Nakashima. *Journeys by Heart: A Christology of Erotic Power* (New York: Crossroad Publishing Co., 1988).

Brown, Joanne Carlson, and Carole R. Bohn, eds. *Christianity, Patriarchy and Abuse: A Feminist Critique* (New York: The Pilgrim Press, 1989).

Brown, Peter. *The Body and Society: Men, Women and Sexual Renunciation in Early Christianity* (New York: Columbia University Press, 1988).

Brown, Raymond. *The Community of the Beloved Disciple* (New York: Paulist Press, 1979).

Brown, Richard D., and Stephen G. Rabe, eds. *Slavery in American Society* (Lexington, Mass.: D. C. Heath and Co., 1976).

Browne, Angela. *When Battered Women Kill* (New York: The Free Press, 1989).

Bultmann, Rudolf. *Theology of the New Testament* (New York: Charles Scribner's Sons, 1951 [vol. 1], 1955 [vol. 2]).

Burkett, Randall F. *Garveyism as a Religious Movement* (Metuchen, N.J.: The Scarecrow Press, 1978).

Burnham, Linda. "Has Poverty Been Feminized in Black America?," *The Black Scholar,* March/April 1985, pp. 14-24.

Burrows, Rufus. *James H. Cone and Black Liberation Theology* (Jefferson, N.C.: McFarland and Co., 1994).

Bushnell, Horace. *The Vicarious Sacrifice* (Hicksville, N.Y.: The Regina Press, 1975 [1865]).

Cade (Bambara), Toni, ed. *The Black Woman: An Anthology* (New York: Signet Books, 1970).

Callahan, Allen. "A Note on 1 Corinthians 7:21," *Journal of the Interdenominational Theological Center*, vol. 17, fall 1989/spring 1990, nos. 1 and 2, pp. 110-114.

Calvin, John. "The Knowledge of God the Redeemer," book II, chaps. 15-17; "The Way We Receive the Grace of Christ," book III, chaps. 8-9, *Institutes of the Christian Religion*, ed. John T. McNeill et al. (Philadelphia: Westminster Press, 1960), pp. 494-534; 702-719.

Cannon, Katie G. *Black Womanist Ethics* (Atlanta: Scholars Press, 1988).

———. *Katie's Canon: Womanism and the Soul of the Black Community* (New York: Continuum Publishing Co., 1995).

———. "Moral Wisdom in Black Women's Literary Tradition," *Annual of the Society of Christian Ethics* (Vancouver, B.C.: Society of Christian Ethics, Vancouver School of Theology, 1984), pp. 171-192.

———. "The Sign of Hope in Three Centuries of Despair: Women in the Black Church Community," in *Human Rights and the Global Mission of the Church*, Boston Theological Institute Annual Series, vol. 1 (Cambridge, Mass., 1985).

Cartledge P. A., and F. D. Harvey, eds. *Crux: Essays in Greek History* (London: Duckworth and Co., 1985).

Chadwick, Henry. *The Early Church* (Middlesex, England: Penguin Books, 1986 [1967]), pp. 100-113.

Chapman, Mark L. *Christianity on Trial: African-American Religious Thought before and after Black Power* (Maryknoll, N.Y.: Orbis Books, 1996).

Christian, Charles. *Black Saga: The African American Experience: A Chronology* (Boston: Houghton Mifflin, 1995).

Clark, Elizabeth, and Herbert Richardson. *Women and Religion: A Feminist Sourcebook of Christian Thought* (San Francisco: Harper & Row, 1977).

Clark, Kenneth B. *King, Malcolm and Baldwin: Three Interviews* (Middletown, Conn.: Wesleyan University Press, 1985 [1963]).

Cleage, Albert B., Jr. *Black Christian Nationalism* (New York: William Morrow, 1972).

———. *The Black Messiah* (New York: Sheed and Ward, 1968).

Clegg, Claude Andrew, III. *An Original Man: The Life and Times of Elijah Muhammad* (New York: St. Martin's Press, 1997).

Coleman, Paulette. "Women in the Church, African Methodist Episcopal Women Moving into the Eighties," *The A.M.E. Church Review*, April-June 1991, pp. 12-18.

Collins, Patricia Hill. *Black Feminist Thought: Knowledge, Consciousness, and the Politics of Empowerment* (New York: Routledge, 1991).

Cone, Cecil W. *The Identity Crisis in Black Theology* (Nashville: African Methodist Episcopal Church, 1975).

Cone, James H. *For My People: Black Theology and the Black Church* (Maryknoll, N.Y.: Orbis Books, 1984).

———. "The Gospel of Jesus, Black People and Black Power," *Black Theology and Black Power* (Minneapolis: Seabury Press, 1969; rev. ed. Maryknoll, N.Y.: Orbis Books, 1997), pp. 31-61.

———. "Jesus Christ in Black Theology," *A Black Theology of Liberation* (Philadelphia: J. B. Lippincott, 1970; Maryknoll, N.Y.: Orbis Books, 1986, reprinted 1990), pp. 110-128.

————. *Martin and Malcolm and America: A Dream or a Nightmare?* (Maryknoll, N.Y.: Orbis Books, 1991).

————. "Martin Luther King: The Source of His Courage to Face Death," *Concilium*, vol. 183, March 1983, pp. 74-79.

————. *My Soul Looks Back* (Maryknoll, N.Y.: Orbis Books, 1986).

————. "Sanctification, Liberation and Black Worship," in *Theology Today*, July 1978, pp. 139-152.

————. *Speaking the Truth: Ecumenism, Liberation and Black Theology* (Grand Rapids: Wm. B. Eerdmans, 1986).

————. *The Spirituals and the Blues*, "The Meaning of God: Jesus Christ" (San Francisco: Harper & Row, 1972), pp. 47-57. Revised edition (Maryknoll, N.Y.: Orbis Books, 1991), pp. 43-52.

————. "Who Is Jesus Christ for Us Today?"; "Divine Liberation and Black Suffering," *God of the Oppressed* (San Francisco: Harper & Row, 1975), pp. 108-137, 163-194. Revised edition (Maryknoll, N.Y.: Orbis Books, 1997), pp. 99-126, 150-178.

————, and Gayraud S. Wilmore, eds. *Black Theology: A Documentary History, Volume 1: 1966-1979* and *Black Theology: A Documentary History, Volume 2: 1980-1992* (Maryknoll, N.Y.: Orbis Books, 1993 [original one-volume edition 1979]).

Cooey, Paula M. et al., eds. *After Patriarchy: Feminist Transformations of the World Religions* (Maryknoll, N.Y.: Orbis Books, 1991).

Crawford, Vicki L., Jacqueline Rouse, and Barbara Woods, eds. *Women in the Civil Rights Movement: Trailblazers and Torchbearers* (Brooklyn: Carlson Publishing, 1990).

Daly, Mary. *Beyond God the Father: Toward a Philosophy of Women's Liberation* (Boston: Beacon Press, 1973).

————. *The Church and the Second Sex* (New York: Harper & Row, 1968).

Dance, Daryl C. "Black Eve or Madonna? A Study of the Antithetical Views of the Mother in Black American Literature," in Roseann P. Bell et al., eds., *Sturdy Black Bridges: Visions of Black Women in Literature* (Garden City, N.Y.: Anchor Books, 1979), pp. 123-132.

David, Paul, et al., eds. *Reckoning with Slavery: A Critical Study in the Quantitative History of American Negro Slavery* (New York: Oxford University Press, 1976).

Davies, Susan, and Eleanor Haney, eds. *Redefining Sexual Ethics* (Cleveland: The Pilgrim Press, 1991).

Davis, Angela Y. *Violence against Women and the Ongoing Challenge to Racism* (Latham, N.Y.: Kitchen Table/Women of Color Press, 1985).

————. *Women, Race and Class* (New York: Vintage Books, 1983).

de Ste. Croix, G.E.M. *The Class Struggle in the Ancient Greek World* (London: Gerald Duckworth and Co., 1981).

Douglas, Kelly Brown. *The Black Christ* (Maryknoll, N.Y.: Orbis Books, 1994).

————. "God Is as Christ Does," *The Journal of Religious Thought*, vol. 46, no. 1, summer-fall 1989, pp. 7-16.

Du Bois, W.E.B. *The Souls of Black Folks* (Greenwich: Fawcett Publications, 1961 [1903]).

Dunfee, Susan Nelson. "The Sin of Hiding: A Feminist Critique of Reinhold Niebuhr's Account of the Sin of Pride," *Soundings: An Interdisciplinary Journal,* vol. 65, spring 1962, pp. 316-327.

Earl, Riggins. *Toward a Black Christian Ethic: A Study of Alexander Crummell and Albert Cleage,* Ph.D. dissertation (Nashville: Vanderbilt University, 1978).

Eliade, Mircea, ed. *Encyclopedia of Religion* (New York: Macmillan, 1987).

Elliott, E. N., L.L.D. ed. *Cotton Is King, and Proslavery Arguments* (Augusta, Ga.: Pritchard Abbott, 1860).

Erdey, Susan. "Womanist Theologian Inspires Students to Work for Justice," *The Witness,* vol. 73, June 1990, pp. 24-25.

Farley, Wendy. *Tragic Vision and Divine Compassion: A Contemporary Theodicy* (Louisville: Westminster/John Knox Press, 1990).

Felder, Cain Hope, ed. *Stony the Road We Trod: African American Biblical Interpretation* (Minneapolis: Fortress Press, 1991).

Fogel, Robert William, and Stanley L. Engerman. *Time on the Cross,* volume 1: *The Economics of American Negro Slavery;* vol. 2: *Evidence and Methods–A Supplement* (New York: W. W. Norton, 1989 [1974]).

Foner, Philip S. *American Socialism and Black Americans: From the Age of Jackson to World War II* (Westport, Conn.: Greenwood Press, 1977).

———. *Black Socialist Preacher* (San Francisco: Synthesis Publications, 1983).

———, ed. *Frederick Douglas on Women's Rights, Contributions in Afro-American and African Studies,* no. 25 (Westport, Conn.: Greenwood Press, 1976).

Forbush, William Byron, ed. *Fox's Book of Martyrs: A History of the Lives, Sufferings and Deaths of the Early Christian and the Protestant Martyrs* (Grand Rapids: Zondervan Press, 1967 [c.1563]).

Fortune, Marie M. *Violence in the Family* (Cleveland: The Pilgrim Press, 1991).

Franklin, Robert Michael. *Liberating Visions: Human Fulfillment and Social Justice in African-American Thought* (Minneapolis: Fortress Press, 1990).

Frazier, E. Franklin. *The Negro Church in America* (New York: Schocken Books, 1964).

Frend, W.H.C. *Religion Popular and Unpopular in the Early Christian Centuries* (London: Variorum Reprints, 1976).

Gardiner, James J., and J. Deotis Roberts Sr., eds. *Quest for a Black Theology* (Philadelphia: The Pilgrim Press, 1971).

Garrow, David J. *Bearing the Cross: Martin Luther King, Jr. and the Southern Christian Leadership Conference* (New York: Vintage Books, 1986).

Gaustad, Edwin S. ed. *A Documentary History of Religion in America to the Civil War* (Grand Rapids: Wm. B. Eerdmans, 1982).

Genovese, Eugene D. *From Rebellion to Revolution: Afro-American Slave Revolts in the Making of the Modern World* (Baton Rouge: Louisiana State University Press, 1979).

———. *Roll, Jordan, Roll: The World the Slaves Made* (New York: Random House, 1974).

George, Carol V. R. *Segregated Sabbaths: Richard Allen and the Rise of Independent Black Churches, 1760-1840* (New York: Oxford University Press, 1973).

Giddings, Paula. *When and Where I Enter: The Impact of Black Women on Race and Sex in America* (New York: William Morrow, 1984).

Gilbert, Olive. *Sojourner Truth: Narrative and Book of Life* (New York: Arno Press, 1968 [1850, 1878]), p. 67.

Gilkes, Cheryl Townsend. "The Role of Church and Community Mothers," *Journal of Feminist Studies in Religion*, vol. 2, no. 1, spring, 1986.

———. "The Role of Women in the Sanctified Church," *The Journal of Religious Thought*, vol. 32, no. 1, 1975.

Ginzburg, Ralph. *100 Years of Lynching: A Shocking Documentary of Race Violence in America* (New York: Lancer Books, 1962).

Girard, René. *The Scapegoat*, trans. Yvonne Freccero (Baltimore: Johns Hopkins University Press, 1986).

———. *Violence and the Sacred* (Baltimore: Johns Hopkins University Press, 1977).

Grant, Jacquelyn. *White Women's Christ and Black Women's Jesus: Feminist Christology and Womanist Response* (Atlanta: Scholar's Press, 1989).

Hamerton-Kelly, Robert G. *Sacred Violence: Paul's Hermeneutic of the Cross* (Minneapolis: Fortress Press, 1992), pp. 63-87.

Harding, Vincent. "Black Power and the American Christ," in Wilmore and Cone, *Black Theology: A Documentary History*, pp. 35-42.

———. "The Religion of Black Power," in Cone and Wilmore, *Black Theology: A Documentary History, Volume 1: 1966-1979.*

———. *There Is a River: The Black Struggle for Freedom in America* (New York: Vintage Books, 1983).

Harrill, J. Albert. *The Manumission of Slaves in Early Christianity* (Tubingen: J.C.B. Mohr/Paul Siebeck, 1995).

Harvey, Van A. *A Handbook of Theological Terms* (New York: Macmillan, 1964).

Herskovits, Melville. *The Myth of the Negro Past* (Boston: Beacon Press, 1958 [1924]).

Hine, Darlene Clark, ed. *Black Women in America: An Historical Encyclopedia* (Brooklyn: Carlson Publishing, 1993).

hooks, bell. *Ain't I a Woman? Black Women and Feminism* (Boston: South End Press, 1981).

———. *Feminist Theory from Margin to Center* (Boston: South End Press, 1984).

———. *Talking Back: Thinking Feminist, Thinking Black* (Boston: South End Press, 1988).

Hopkins, Dwight N. *Shoes That Fit Our Feet: Sources for a Constructive Black Theology* (Maryknoll, N.Y.: Orbis Books, 1993).

———, and George Cummings. "Slave Theology," *Cut Loose Your Stammering Tongue: Black Theology in the Slave Narratives* (Maryknoll, N.Y.: Orbis Books, 1991).

Hovda, Robert W. *Strong, Loving and Wise: Presiding in Liturgy* (Collegeville, Minn.: Liturgical Press, 1984).

Hoyt, Thomas, Jr. "The African American Worship Experience and the Bible," *The Journal of the Interdenominational Theological Center*, vol. 14, nos. 1 and 2, fall 1986/spring 1987, pp. 1-22.

Hubert, Henri, and Marcel Mauss. *Sacrifice: Its Nature and Functions* (London: Cohen and West, 1964 [trans. 1898]).

Hudson, Winthrop. *Religion in America*, 5th edition (New York: Macmillan, 1992 [1965]).

Hurston, Zora Neale. *The Sanctified Church* (Berkeley: Turtle Island, 1981), p. 91.

Ide, Arthur Frederick. *Martyrdom of Women: A Study of Death Psychology in the Early Christian Church to 301 C.E.* (Garland, Tex: Tanglewuld Press, 1985).

Jackson, Irene V. *Afro-American Religious Music: A Bibliography and a Catalogue of Gospel Music* (Westport, Conn.: Greenwood Press, 1979).

Jaffe, Aniela, ed. *C. G. Jung: Memories, Dreams, Reflections* (New York: Vintage Books, 1989 [1961]).

Jobson, Richard. *The Golden Trade or a Discovery of the River Gambra and the Golden Trade of the Aethiopians*, ed. Walter Rodney (London: Wm. Dawson and Sons Ltd., 1968 [1623]).

Johnson, Bishop Joseph. *The Soul of the Black Preacher* (Philadelphia: The Pilgrim Press, 1971).

Jones, Major J. *The Color of God: The Concept of God in Afro-American Thought* (Macon: Mercer University Press, 1987), pp. 75-100; 29-44.

Jones, William R. *Is God a White Racist?* (New York: Anchor Press/Doubleday, 1973).

———. "Theodicy: The Controlling Category for Black Theology," *The Journal of Religious Thought*, vol. 30, no. 1, spring-summer 1973, pp. 28-38.

Jordan, Winthrop. *White over Black: American Attitudes toward the Negro, 1550-1812* (New York: W. W. Norton, 1977 [1968]).

Josephus, Flavius. *The Life and Works of Flavius Josephus*, trans. William Whiston (New York: Holt, Rinehart and Winston, 1957).

Kant, Immanuel. *Observations on the Feeling of the Beautiful and the Sublime*, trans. John T. Goldthwait (Berkeley: University of California Press, 1960 [1763]).

Kelsey, George. *Racism and the Christian Understanding of Man* (New York: Charles Scribner's Sons, 1965).

King, Martin Luther, Jr. "Pilgrimage to Nonviolence," in Washington, *A Testament of Hope*.

———. *Strength to Love* (Philadelphia: Fortress Press, 1981 [1963]).

———. *Stride toward Freedom: The Montgomery Story* (New York: Harper & Row, 1986 [1958]).

Kulikoff, Allan. *Tobacco and Slaves: The Development of Southern Cultures in the Chesapeake, 1680-1800* (Chapel Hill: University of North Carolina Press, 1986).

Larison, C. W. *Sylvia DuBois: A Biografy of the Slav Who Whipt Her Mistres and Gand Her Fredom*, ed. Jared C. Lobdell (New York: Oxford University Press, 1988).

Lee, Jarena. *The Religious Experiences and Journal of Mrs. Jarena Lee* (Philadelphia, 1849). *See* William L. Andrews, *Sisters of the Spirit.*

Levine, Lawrence W. *Black Culture and Black Consciousness: Afro-American Folk Thought from Slavery to Freedom* (New York: Oxford University Press, 1977).

Lincoln, C. Eric. *The Black Muslims in America* (Grand Rapids/Trenton: Wm. B. Eerdmans/Africa World Press, 1994 [1961]).

————. *Coming through the Fire: Surviving Race and Place in America* (Durham: Duke University Press, 1996).

————, ed. *Is Anybody Listening to Black America?* (New York: Seabury Press, 1968).

————, and Lawrence H. Mamiya. "The Religious Dimension," *The Black Church in the African American Experience* (Durham: Duke University Press, 1990).

Loewenberg, Bert James, and Ruth Bogin, eds. *Black Women in Nineteenth Century American Life: Their Words, Their Thoughts, Their Feelings* (University Park: Pennsylvania State University Press, 1976).

Logan, Rayford W. *The Negro in American Life and Thought: The Nadir 1877-1901* (New York: Dial Press, 1954).

Ludwig, Karen. "Womanist Theology/Feminist Theology: A Dialogue, *Daughters of Sarah*, vol. 15, no. 2, March/April 1989, pp. 6-7.

Luther, Martin. "Admonition to Peace: A Reply to the Twelve Articles of the Peasants in Swabia," in *Luther's Works: The Christian in Society*, vol. 46, ed. Robert C. Schultz (Philadelphia: Fortress Press, 1967).

————. *Luther's Works: Lectures on Galatians—1535*, vol. 26, ed. Jaroslav Pelikan (St. Louis: Concordia Publishing House, 1963).

Lyotard, Jean-Francois. *The Postmodern Condition: A Report on Knowledge*, Theory and History of Literature, vol. 10 (Minneapolis: University of Minnesota Press, 1984).

Mannix, Daniel P. (with Malcolm Cowley). *Black Cargoes: A History of the Atlantic Slave Trade* (New York: The Viking Press, 1962).

Manschreck, Clyde, ed. *Erosion of Authority* (Nashville: Abingdon Press, 1971).

Marable, Manning. *How Capitalism Underdeveloped Black America* (Boston: South End Press, 1983).

Martey, Emmanuel. *African Theology: Inculturation and Liberation* (Maryknoll, N.Y.: Orbis Books, 1993).

Martin, Clarice. "Womanist Interpretations of the New Testament: The Quest for Holistic and Inclusive Translation and Interpretation," *Journal of Feminist Studies in Religion*, vol. 6, no. 2, 1990, pp. 41-61.

Mathews, Donald. *Religion in the Old South* (Chicago: University of Chicago Press, 1977).

Mays, Benjamin Elijah, and Joseph William Nicholson. *The Negro's Church* (New York: Arno Press, 1969).

Mbiti, John S. *African Religions and Philosophy* (Garden City, N.Y.: Anchor Books, 1970 [1969]).

McLoughlin, William G. *Revivals, Awakenings and Reform: An Essay on Religious and Social Change in America, 1607-1977* (Chicago: University of Chicago Press, 1978).

Mead, Frank Spencer. *Handbook of Denominations in the United States* (Nashville: Abingdon Press, 1995 [1985]).

Meier, August, Elliott M. Rudwick, and Francis L. Broderick, eds. *Black Protest Thought in the Twentieth Century* (New York: Macmillan, 1971).

Mellon, James, ed. *Bullwhip Days: The Slaves Remember—An Oral History* (New York: Avon Books, 1988).

Miller, Barbara Stoler, ed. and trans. *Love Song of the Dark Lord: Jayadeva's Gitagovinda* (New York: Columbia University Press, 1977).

Mitchell, Henry H. *Black Belief: Folk Beliefs of Blacks in America and West Africa* (New York: Harper & Row, 1975).

Mofokeng, Takatso A. *The Crucified among the Crossbearers* (Kampen, South Africa: Uitgeversmaatschappij J.H. Kok, 1983).

Moltmann, Jürgen. *The Crucified God*, trans. R. A. Wilson and John Bowden (New York: Harper & Row, 1974).

Morrison, Roy D., II. "The Emergence of Black Theology in America," *The A.M.E. Zion Quarterly Review*, vol. 94, no. 3, October 1982, pp. 2-17.

Moyd, Olin P. *Redemption in Black Theology* (Valley Forge: Judson Press, 1979).

Muhammad, Elijah. *Message to the Blackman in America* (Newport News: United Brothers Communications Systems, 1965).

Musopole, Augustine. *Being Human in Africa: Toward an African Christian Anthropology* (New York: Peter Lang, 1994).

Musurillo, Herbert. *The Acts of the Christian Martyrs* (Oxford: Clarendon Press, 1972).

Mveng, Engelbert. *L'Afrique dans l'Eglise: Paroles d'un Croyant* (Paris: L'Harmattan, 1985).

Newton, Michael and Judy Ann. *Racial and Religious Violence in America: A Chronology* (New York: Garland Publishing, 1991).

Niebuhr, Reinhold. *Moral Man and Immoral Society* (New York: Charles Scribner's Sons, 1932).

———. *The Nature and Destiny of Man* (New York: Charles Scribner's Sons, 1943).

———. *Why the Christian Church is Not Pacifist* (London: Student Christian Movement Press, 1940).

Oakes, James. *The Ruling Race: A History of American Slaveholders* (New York: Alfred A. Knopf, 1982).

Ozment, Steven E. *The Reformation in the Cities: The Appeal of Protestantism to Sixteenth-Century Germany and Switzerland* (New Haven: Yale University Press, 1975).

Painter, Nell Irvin. *Sojourner Truth: A Life, A Symbol* (New York: W. W. Norton, 1996).

Paris, Peter J. *The Social Teaching of the Black Churches* (Philadelphia: Fortress Press, 1985).

Patton, Gwen. "Black People and the Victorian Ethos," in Toni Cade, ed., *The Black Woman: An Anthology* (New York: Signet Books, 1970), pp. 143-148.

Pinn, Anthony. *Why Lord? Suffering and Evil in Black Theology* (New York: Continuum Publishing Co., 1995).

Plaskow, Judith. *Sex, Sin and Grace: Women's Experience and the Theologies of Reinhold Niebuhr and Paul Tillich* (Lanham, Md.: University Press of America, 1980).

Poinsett, Alex. "The Quest for a Black Christ," *Ebony*, March 1969.

Pritchard, James B., ed. *The Ancient Near East*, vol. 1: *An Anthology of Texts and Pictures* (Princeton: Princeton University Press, 1958 [1973]); and vol.

2: *A New Anthology of Texts and Pictures* (Princeton: Princeton University Press, 1975 [1992]).

Quasten, Johannes, and Joseph C. Plumpe, eds. *Ancient Christian Writers*, vol. 6, trans. James A. Kleist (New York: Paulist Press, 1948).

Raboteau, Albert J. *Slave Religion: The "Invisible Institution" in the Antebellum South* (New York: Oxford University Press, 1978).

Rasmussen, Larry, ed. *Reinhold Niebuhr: Theologian of Public Life* (Minneapolis: Fortress Press, 1991).

Redkey, Edwin S., ed. *Respect Black: The Writings and Speeches of Henry McNeal Turner* (New York: Arno Press/New York Times, 1971).

Roberts, J. Deotis, Sr. "The Black Caucus and the Failure of Christian Theology," *The Journal of Religious Thought* (Washington, D.C.: Howard University Press, 1969), Summer Supplement, p. 15.

————. *Black Theology in Dialogue* (Philadelphia: Westminster Press, 1987).

————. *Liberation and Reconciliation* (Philadelphia: Westminster Press, 1971; rev. ed. Maryknoll, N.Y.: Orbis Books, 1994).

————. *Opening Closed Doors: Redemption and Reconciliation* (St. Louis: O. W. Wake, Christian Board of Publication, 1973).

————. *The Prophethood of Black Believers* (Louisville: John Knox/Westminster Press, 1994).

————, and James J. Gardiner, eds. "Black Consciousness in Theological Perspective," in *Quest for a Black Theology* (Philadelphia: United Church Press, 1971).

Rodney, Walter. *How Europe Underdeveloped Africa* (London: Bogle-L'Ouverture Publications, 1972).

Ruether, Rosemary Radford. "Crisis in Sex and Race: Black Theology vs. Feminist Theology," *Christianity and Crisis*, April 15, 1974, pp. 67-73.

————. "Feminist Theology in the Academy: How Not to Reinvent the Wheel," *Christianity and Crisis*, March 4, 1985, pp. 57-62.

————. "For Whom, with Whom Do We Speak Our New Stories?" *Christianity and Crisis*, May 13, 1985, pp. 184-186.

————. "New Women, New Earth: Sexist Ideologies and Human Liberation," *Union Seminary Quarterly Review*, vol. 32, spring-summer 1977, pp. 192-194.

————, ed. *Religion and Sexism: Images of Woman in the Jewish and Christian Traditions* (New York: Simon and Schuster, 1974).

Russell, Letty, ed. *Feminist Interpretation of the Bible* (Philadelphia: Westminster Press, 1985).

Saiving (Goldstein), Valerie. "The Human Situation: A Feminine View," *Journal of Religion*, vol. 40, 1960, pp. 100-112.

Sanders, Cheryl. *Empowerment Ethics for a Liberated People: A Path to African American Social Transformation* (Minneapolis: Fortress Press, 1995).

————. "Roundtable Discussion: Christian Ethics and Theology in Womanist Perspective," *Journal of Feminist Studies in Religion*, vol. 5, no. 2, fall 1989.

Sandmel, Samuel. *Judaism and Christian Beginnings* (New York: Oxford University Press, 1978), pp. 147-150.

Segal, Allan F., *The Other Judaisms of Late Antiquity*, Brown Judaic Studies, no. 127, ed. Jacob Neusner et al. (Atlanta: Scholars Press, 1987).

Shields, John C., ed. *The Collected Works of Phillis Wheatley* (New York: Oxford University Press, 1988).

Smeaton, George. *The Doctrine of the Atonement According to the Apostles* (Peabody, Mass.: Hendrickson Publishers, 1988 [1870]).

Sobel, Michel. *The World They Made Together: Black and White Values in Eighteenth-Century Virginia* (Princeton, N.J.: Princeton University Press, 1987).

Spencer, Jon Michael. *Black Hymnody: A Hymnological History of the African American Church* (Knoxville: University of Tennessee Press, 1992).

————. *Black Sacred Music: A Journal of Theomusicology* (Durham: Duke University Press, 1993).

Stanton, Elizabeth Cady, et al. *The Woman's Bible* (Seattle: Coalition Task Force on Women and Religion, 1990 [1875]).

Sterling, Dorothy, ed. *We Are Your Sisters: Black Women in the 19th Century* (New York: W. W. Norton, 1984).

Stevenson, J., ed. *A New Eusebius* (Nashville: Abingdon Press, 1957).

Stocking, George W., Jr. *Race, Culture and Evolution: Essays in the History of Anthropology* (Chicago: University of Chicago Press, 1982 [1968]).

Stuckey, Sterling. *Slave Culture: Nationalist Theory and the Foundations of Black America* (New York: Oxford University Press, 1987).

Terkel, Studs. *Race: How Blacks and Whites Think and Feel about the American Obsession* (New York: The New Press, 1992).

Thistlethwaite, Susan Brooks. *Sex, Race and God: Christian Feminism in Black and White* (New York: Crossroad Publishing Co., 1991).

————, and Mary Potter Engels, eds. *Lift Every Voice: Constructing Christian Theologies from the Underside* (San Francisco: HarperCollins Books, 1990; rev. ed. Maryknoll, N.Y.: Orbis Books, 1998).

Thomas, H. F. and R. S. Keller, eds. *Women in New Worlds* (Nashville: Abingdon Press, 1981).

Thomas, Kathy. "Creating a Womanist Theology: Why Feminist Theology Is Not Enough for the African American Woman," *A.M.E. Zion Quarterly Review*, 1989, pp. 26-34.

Thompson, Mildred I. *Ida B. Wells-Barnett: An Exploratory Study of an American Black Woman, 1893-1930*, Black Women in United States History, vol. 15 (Brooklyn: Carlson Publishing, 1990).

Townes, Emily, ed. *A Troubling in My Soul: Womanist Perspectives on Evil and Suffering* (Maryknoll, N.Y.: Orbis Books, 1993).

Trible, Phyllis. *Texts of Terror: Literary-Feminist Readings of Biblical Narratives* (Philadelphia: Fortress Press, 1984).

United States Department of Labor, Office of Policy, Planning and Research, *The Negro Family: The Case for National Action* (commonly known as *The Moynihan Report*), 1965.

Wainwright, Geoffrey. *The Ecumenical Moment: Crisis and Opportunity for the Church* (Grand Rapids: Wm. B. Eerdmans, 1983).

Walker, Alice. *The Color Purple* (New York: Washington Square Press, 1983).

————. *In Love and in Trouble: Stories of Black Women* (New York: Harcourt Brace Jovanovich, 1974).

————. *In Search of Our Mothers' Gardens: Womanist Prose* (Orlando: Harcourt Brace Jovanovich, 1983).

————. *Meridian* (New York: Pocket Books, 1989 [1976]).

————. *Revolutionary Petunias and Other Poems* (Orlando: Harcourt Brace and Co., 1973).

————. *The Third Life of Grange Copeland* (New York: Pocket Books, 1991 [1970]).

Walker, Williston, Richard A. Norris, David W. Lotz, and Robert T. Handy. *A History of the Christian Church*, 4th ed. (New York: Charles Scribner's Sons, 1985).

Walker, Wyatt Tee. *"Somebody's Calling My Name": Black Sacred Music and Social Change* (Valley Forge, Pa.: Judson Press, 1979).

Walls, William Jacob. *The African Methodist Episcopal Zion Church: Reality of the Black Church* (Charlotte, N.C.: AME Zion Publishing House, 1974).

Ward, Hiley H. *Prophet of the Black Nation: Albert B. Cleage, Jr.* (Philadelphia: The Pilgrim Press, 1969).

Warrior, Robert. "Canaanites, Cowboys and Indians: Deliverance, Conquest and Liberation Theology Today," *Christianity and Crisis*, vol. 49, September 12, 1989, pp. 261-265.

Washington, Booker T. *Up from Slavery: An Autobiography* (Garden City, N.Y.: Doubleday, 1925).

Washington, James M. *Frustrated Fellowship: The Black Baptist Quest for Social Power* (Macon: Mercer University Press, 1986).

————, ed. *Conversations with God: Two Centuries of Prayers by African Americans* (New York: HarperCollins Books, 1994).

————, ed. *A Testament of Hope: The Essential Writings and Speeches of Martin Luther King, Jr.* (San Francisco: HarperCollins Books, 1986).

Washington, Joseph R., Jr. *Black Religion: The Negro and Christianity in the United States* (Boston: Beacon Press, 1964).

Washington, Mary Helen, ed. *Invented Lives: Narratives of Black Women, 1860-1960* (New York: Anchor Press, 1987).

West, Cornel. *Prophesy Deliverance! An Afro-American Revolutionary Christianity* (Philadelphia: Westminster Press, 1982).

————. *Prophetic Fragments* (Grand Rapids/Trenton: Wm. B. Eerdmans/Africa World Press, 1988).

————. *Race Matters* (Boston: Beacon Press, 1993).

Williams, Chancellor. *The Destruction of Black Civilization: Great Issues of a Race from 4500 B.C. to 2000 A.D.* (Chicago: Third World Press, 1987).

Williams, Delores S. "The Color of Feminism," *Christianity and Crisis*, April 29, 1985, pp. 164-165.

————. "The Color Purple," *Christianity and Crisis*, July 14, 1986, pp. 230-232.

————. "A Crucifixion Double-Cross?," *The Other Side*, September-October 1993.

————. "Reimagining Truth," *The Other Side*, May-June, 1994.

————. *Sisters in the Wilderness: The Challenge of Womanist God-Talk* (Maryknoll, N.Y.: Orbis Books, 1993).

————. "A Womanist Perspective on Sin," in Emily Townes, ed., *A Troubling in My Soul: Womanist Perspectives on Evil and Suffering* (Maryknoll, N.Y.: Orbis Books, 1993).

————. "Womanist Theology: Black Women's Voices," *Christianity and Crisis*, March 2, 1987, p. 69.

————. "Women's Oppression and Life-line Politics in Black Women's Religious Narratives," *Journal of Feminist Studies in Religion* vol. 1, no. 2, fall 1985.

Williams, James G. *The Bible, Violence and the Sacred* (San Francisco: HarperCollins Books, 1991).

Wilmore, Gayraud S. *Black Religion and Black Radicalism: An Interpretation of the Religious History of Afro-American People* (Maryknoll, N.Y.: Orbis Books, 1983 [1973]; rev. ed. 1998).

————. "Black Theology: Review and Assessment," *Voices from the Third World*, vol. 5, no. 2, 1982, pp. 3-16.

————, ed. *Black Men in Prison: The Response of the African American Church* (Atlanta: The ITC Press, 1990).

————, and James H. Cone, eds. *Black Theology: A Documentary History, 1966-1979* (Maryknoll, N.Y.: Orbis Books, 1979; rev. ed. 1993 [2 vols.]).

Wimbush, Vincent L. *Paul, the Worldly Ascetic* (Macon: Mercer University Press, 1987).

————, ed. *Ascetic Behavior in Greco-Roman Antiquity* (Minneapolis: Fortress Press, 1990).

————, and Valantasis, Richard, eds. *Asceticism* (New York: Oxford University Press, 1995).

Wink, Walter. *Violence and Nonviolence in South Africa: Jesus' Third Way* (Philadelphia: New Society Publishers, 1987).

Witvliet, Theo. "In Search of a Black Christology," *Cross Currents*, spring 1987, 17-32.

————. *The Way of the Black Messiah*, trans. John Bowden (Oak Park, Ill.: Meyer Stone Books, 1987).

Workman, Herbert B. *Persecution in the Early Church* (Oxford: Oxford University Press, 1980 [1906]).

World Council of Churches. "Violence, Nonviolence and the Struggle for Social Justice," statement commended by the Central Committee, August 1973, reprinted in *The Ecumenical Review*, vol. 25, no. 4, October 1973.

Wright, Jeremiah A., Jr. *Africans Who Shaped Our Faith* (Chicago: Urban Ministries, 1995).

Young, Frances. *The Use of Sacrificial Ideas in Greek Christian Writers from the New Testament to John Chrysostom* (Philadelphia: Philadelphia Patristic Foundation, 1979).

Young, Josiah. *Black and African Theologies: Siblings or Distant Cousins* (Maryknoll, N.Y.: Orbis Books, 1986).